The Stress of
My Life

Hans Selye

The Stress of My Life

A Scientist's Memoirs

with a 32-page section
of photographs

Second Edition

VNR VAN NOSTRAND REINHOLD COMPANY
NEW YORK   CINCINNATI   ATLANTA   DALLAS   SAN FRANCISCO
LONDON   TORONTO   MELBORNE

A 32-page section of photographs appears after page 119.
These are from the author's own collection.

Portions of the text in this book originally appeared in **From Dream to Discovery** by
Hans Selye, M.D. Copyright ©1964, 1975 by Hans Selye, M.D. Reprinted with permission
of McGraw-Hill and Arno Press.
The excerpt on pages 35–46 previously appeared under the title "What Makes Basic Research
Basic?" in **Adventures of the Mind** (Vintage Books, 1962). Reprinted with permission of
The Saturday Evening Post, ©1959, The Curtis Publishing Company.
Excerpt on page 69, "Science and Poetry" by David Landsborough Thomson, reprinted
with permission of the **Aberdeen University Review.**
Excerpt on pages 198–199 from **Stress Without Distress** by Hans Selye, M.D. Copyright
©1974 by Hans Selye, M.D. Reprinted with permission of J.B. Lippincott Company.

Van Nostrand Reinhold Company Regional Offices:
New York Cincinnati Chicago Millbrae Dallas

Van Nostrand Reinhold Company International Offices:
London Toronto Melbourne

Copyright ©1979 by Litton Educational Publishing, Inc.

Library of Congress Catalog Card Number: 78-21278
ISBN: 0-442-27659-1

Manufactured in the United States of America

Published by Van Nostrand Reinhold Company
135 West 50th Street, New York, N.Y. 10020

Published simultaneously in Canada by Van Nostrand Reinhold Ltd.

15 14 13 12 11 10 9 8 7 6 5 4 3 2 1

Library of Congress Cataloging in Publication Data

Selye, Hans, 1907-
    The Stress of my life.

    Includes index.
    1. Selye, Hans, 1907-   2. Medical
scientists—Québec (Province)—Montréal—Biography.
3. Stress (Physiology) I. Title.
R464.S4A3   1979   610'.92'4   78-21278
ISBN 0-442-27659-1

To
Louise Selye
née Drevet

All the good writers of confessions,
from Augustine onwards, are still a
little in love with their sins —

Anatole France

Other Books by Hans Selye
(A selected list for the general reader)

The Story of the Adaptation Syndrome
Montreal: Acta Inc., Med. Pub., 1952

The Stress of Life
New York: McGraw-Hill, 1956
Revised ed., 1976
Paperback ed., 1978

From Dream to Discovery
New York: McGraw-Hill, 1964
Paperback ed., New York: Arno Press, 1975

In Vivo. The Case for Supramolecular Biology
New York: Liveright, 1967

Stress Without Distress
New York: J. B. Lippincott Co., 1974
Paperback ed., New York: Signet Books, 1975

The Stress of *My Life*
Toronto: McClelland and Stewart, 1977

Stress in Health and Disease
Reading (Mass.): Butterworths, 1976

Selye's Guide to Stress Research, Vol. I
New York: Van Nostrand Reinhold (in press)

ACKNOWLEDGMENTS FOR THE PRESENT REVISED EDITION

This is a considerably updated version of the previous Canadian edition, because even at the age of seventy-one, a great deal can happen in a single year, both in one's private and professional life.

Although the changes in the early part of this American edition are not extensive, they are extremely important, because they bring my life up to date, and by now I mustered sufficient courage to describe, or at least hint at, all the most personal matters which were kept out of the original version.

Of course, my expression of gratitude to all those who have helped me with the first edition remains unchanged, but I would again like to extend special thanks to my friend and long-standing collaborator in all editorial matters, Ovid Da Silva, as well as to my present editors, Rodney Rawlings and Olga Leshkevich. Among the many American editors who gave me valuable advice, I am particularly grateful to Mr. Ashak M. Rawji of Van Nostrand Reinhold for deciding to bring out the book in the form in which you can read it now.

Preface

This book is not a loose collection of reminiscences, a diary or even an autobiography in the true sense of the word, but perhaps a mixture of all these. I wrote a French version at the urging of my Quebec publisher, Alain Stanké, a long-time exponent of my ideas through the media. Because of the many questions addressed to him and to me about my work and myself, he felt that such a book would be desirable.

My hope is that this book will give the reader a general idea of what makes one scientist tick — and tick happily — even after many personal tragedies and fifty years of research in laboratories and clinics. These pages summarize my most important scientific and private concerns. If this book helps others discover the elements of a philosophy of life — a new code of behavior that keeps them as happy throughout their lives as I am at seventy-one — I will feel that my purpose has been accomplished.

It is hard to describe the personal satisfaction I have derived from my many years of research on stress and the insight it gave me to reach my chosen port of destination and to help others reach theirs. For many readers, the more technical aspects of my research may be difficult to comprehend. I have tried to avoid the complex scientific notions inherent in the stress concept, yet if my life is to be understood, my work must also be clear. My primary aim is to illustrate what can be learned from the story of a scientist entirely devoted to understanding and coping with the stress of life.

It is humiliating for one who has spent so much effort trying to provide a sound code of behavior for humanity to admit that he has made a mess of two marriages, despite all his intense efforts to succeed. I never was a typical "family man," but I have a fatherly feeling for my scientific and office associates, all of whom seem related to me and to one another by the common bond of serving what we think is a worthwhile cause.

My oldest co-worker, Louise Drevet (to whom I have dedicated the first version of this book) has been with me in one capacity or another for over eighteen years. She progressed from technician to chief of the institute's pharmacy at the University of Montreal. Now she is my wife and occupies the place of *chatelaine*, looking after everyone's well-being, acting as receptionist, chauffeur, hostess, office girl, bookkeeper and personal confidante. But most important, she is a stabilizer and supporter of her very difficult boss — who just a few weeks ago became her husband.

In my younger days, I studied and held minor academic positions in Czechoslovakia, France and Italy, as well as the United States, where I also did post-doctoral work at Johns Hopkins University. In 1932 I started my more systematic medical research at McGill University in Montreal, and it was there that the stress concept was originally formulated.

In 1945 I became director of the *Institut de médecine et de chirurgie expérimentales* (the Institute of Experimental Medicine and Surgery) at the University of Montreal, the world's second-largest French-language university. At present, I still maintain an office at the University of Montreal. A branch of the International Institute of Stress, which has been incorporated as a separate nonprofit organization, is still functioning here for the time being. However, we have also established a Downtown Center. My stress library has been transferred to this new location, together with the key personnel necessary for the maintenance of our international documentation service. The center was previously my private home; now I retain only one bedroom and a study, and the rest of the house is at the disposal of our institute. It is subdivided into fourteen offices, many of which house the largest stress library and documentation service in existence. Our large living room, with its open fireplace, provides a warm atmosphere for holding board meetings, receptions and scientific conferences to groups which gather here to discuss the complex topic of stress as applied to every aspect of daily life or medicine.

It gratifies me to see that my home has gradually become the world center for stress research.

Hans Selye

Contents

The Stress of
My Life

CHAPTER ONE

First Warning

In writing this book, *I promise to tell the truth and nothing but the truth – but not all the truth.* If I went any further, it might become a public confession and would be embarrassing to me and to many of those with whom I have been associated.

Perhaps I might mention as a mitigating circumstance, to those who still consider my ways objectionable, that I can hardly serve as an example of the average citizen because of the singular characteristics of my personal history and especially of my unusual motivation with regard to the aims I set for myself.

I never really had a "private life" because what one usually considers a private life is separate from one's occupation and work, while in my case the two have always been intermixed.

I have had two previous wives, both of them stunningly beautiful. The first, Frances, came from the "high society" of Pittsburgh's coal industry, and with her I had a daughter, Catherine.

With my second wife, Gabrielle, who is from Quebec and used to be my secretary, I had four children—Michel, Jean, Marie and André. I lived for twenty-eight years with this second family, and my relationship with them was just as profoundly affected by my work, especially by its psychological and sociological implications, as my work was influenced by the pleasures and disappointments I experienced at home.

Despite my almost abnormal reluctance to deviate from the generally approved, conventional ethics of a university professor, and especially one who professes to be able to teach people how to adapt their lives, I succeeded—after twenty-eight years—in declaring my independence of my second wife also. Fortunately, the marriage turned out to be invalid in Quebec and I did not even

1

have to get a divorce. I stayed with her only to give my children a home until they were old enough to leave. I am ashamed only of the fact that it took me twenty-eight years to reach this stage of independence without doing any harm to the children, all of whom are adults now.

I have always felt that in most other respects my personal background is not especially noteworthy. I lived through World War I in Europe and my father was away from home for five years. The food was terrible and scarce, but I certainly did not suffer from severe starvation. I survived the great flu epidemic of 1918; although relatives, friends and acquaintances died all around me, I myself did not catch it. During World War II, I was sheltered here in Canada though I was not able to get much news about my few relatives in Europe; in effect, the drama always occurred around me without my active participation.

Of course, one cannot help being affected by all of life's turmoil. But these events were experienced by so many people that, in retrospect, the only characteristic feature I can single out is that I managed to emerge unscarred, whereas most others probably would have become bitter. Perhaps this reveals something of my personality, especially my tendency to disregard or quickly forget unpleasant things. In doing so I follow an old Austrian peasant saying:

Mach es wie die Sonnenuhr,
zähl die heiter'n Stunden nur!

(Imitate the sundial's ways,
count only the pleasant days!)

CHAPTER TWO

The Way It All Started

The first problem I met and the cause of all others was my birth. It happened in Vienna on January 26, 1907, at the time when that beautiful city was still the capital of the mighty Austro-Hungarian Empire. My first enterprise upon entering this vale of tears was no obvious fountainhead for my subsequent career, but it must have made a great impression because I was told of it so often. I emptied my bladder with the force of a fire hose, upon which the assembled members of the family all exclaimed with great satisfaction, "It's a boy!"

This event took place on the eve of St. John Chrisostomos and, in keeping with the custom of the time, I was baptized Hans (the German equivalent of John). Chrisostomos means "golden-mouthed," as my venerable patron saint was allegedly a good orator. Whenever this point is raised, one of my assistants unfailingly remarks that my success undoubtedly owes a lot to clever oratory. But who could know to what extent the name of the patron saint can influence a man's ability to express scientific thoughts?

My father, Hugo Selye, was a surgeon. He served in the Austro-Hungarian Imperial Army and later founded a private surgical clinic, which was administered by my mother, Maria Felicitas.

My earliest recollection is of an event that took place on the seashore of the then-fashionable Adriatic resort of Abbazia. I was three years old, and my father took me out to the beach on a sunny summer day. Having perched me on his shoulders, he walked slowly into the ocean. Even though I was comfortably seated on his back, I was terrified by the immense mass of water that surrounded us. Yet I did not ask my father to take me back to the shore. Even at the age of three, I refused to accept defeat. This sense of challenge was later reinforced during my "equestrian period," when riding unmanageable horses became my greatest fascination. My early fear of the ocean must have left some scars on my personality, for I remember the event today, sixty-eight years later. However, my relations with aquatic surroundings were not permanently damaged, as swimming became my favorite sport, and as a student I won several trophies in competitions on the Danube.

Other pictures of my early childhood also remain vivid. I can see myself again in Abbazia at the more mature age of five. My hair was shoulder-length and I was dressed in a sailor suit. Upon my return to Vienna I was asked innumerable questions (already!) about my holidays. With great pride, I answered, "Everyone told Mommy I was the most elegant gentleman in Abbazia." This inclination to boast, as well as the yearning to always be first, are traits of my personality which – alas – I have not yet been able to overcome.

I never really had any nationality of my own. Or I could say I had so many! Although in later years I was accepted as a "local boy" by many nations, in the early part of my life I never felt quite at home anywhere because of my multinationalism. My father was Hungarian and inordinately proud of it. My mother was Austrian like myself, in that both of us first saw the light of day in Vienna. I was educated in Komárom, a small town about midway between Vienna and Budapest, divided by the Danube. The two parts were connected by bridges, but we lived in the Hungarian part of the Empire. The intense Magyar nationalism of my teachers there, combined with my father's strong patriotic feelings, left a profound impression on me. Besides, while my first name is Austrian, my surname is Hungarian.

As though I did not have enough complications with my dual nationality – being despised as an Austrian in Hungary and as a Hungarian in Austria – I suddenly became a Czechoslovakian without even moving out of my house. The Czechs and Slovaks had many disagreements with each other, but they were unanimous in detesting both Austrians and Hungarians. So you can imagine where that left me when, in 1918, with the collapse of the Empire, half of Komárom was given to the newly-founded state. Had we lived on the other side of the Danube, we would have remained Hungarian, but at eleven years of age I found myself with a second binational country.

This led to a curious situation some years later. I arrived at the Canadian border from the United States (where I worked as a post-doctoral student at Johns Hopkins University) and showed my Czechoslovak passport to the immigration officer.

"Are you Czech or Slovak?" he asked.

"Neither." I explained that in 1918 I had acquired a new nationality quite unintentionally.

"So you were born in Austro-Hungary?" the officer continued the inquisition. "Now, are you Austrian or Hungarian?"

"Both! I'm Austrian by virtue of my birth in Vienna and my mother's nationality, but Hungarian on my father's side."

Eventually he became tired of this game and allowed me into Canada without further questions.

However, the same difficulty reappeared in exaggerated form after I had acquired – this time by choice – my Canadian citizenship. Whenever I went to the United States with my Canadian passport, I was asked, probably because of my accent, "Are you French- or English-Canadian?" As I had to cross the border often, this game became monotonous and frustrating; it invariably ended with the exhaustion of the still-unconvinced immigration officers. As I had a Canadian passport and evidence of residence in Montreal, they must have decided that I couldn't be very dangerous.

I can brag of having six native tongues: German, Hungarian, Czech, Slovak, French and English. As all of them were my national languages at one time or another, I learned to speak each fluently. For this I claim no special credit – obviously, you ought to be able to speak your own language.

My mother told me that even at the age of four I spoke four languages equally well, although I perhaps had a better accent in one and a greater vocabulary in the other, depending on the frequency with which I used them. I owe this early linguistic advantage to my mother, who insisted on a polyglot instruction. My father was interested only in Hungarian, although he spoke both German and French very well. Like many Hungarians, he was not too fond of German and refused to speak it except with my mother. Even after thirty-five years of marriage she could not express herself well in Hungarian (a rather complicated language) and they had to communicate somehow.

My mother was a highly-cultured woman. She read first-rate literature in a number of languages and always insisted I should have the same advantage.

Today, in addition to French and English, my present national languages, I still speak German and Hungarian without accents and use these four languages virtually every day, at home or with members of my staff. At one time or another I was also able to lecture on stress (without a manuscript, although not without grammatical errors) in Russian, Czech, Slovak, Spanish, Italian and Portuguese.

If I have to give a series of lectures in Spanish, my Italian becames contaminated and I can get into it again only by practice. I similarly mix up any languages that are closely related, if I have not used them for a while. But I never confuse totally unrelated languages – for example, Russian with Spanish. In preparation for a lecture tour to foreign countries, I can get into even the most rarely used among my nine languages within a few weeks by playing records of language courses. Relearning is even more rapid if I stay in the country for a while and am forced to speak its language daily.

Even though many psychologists don't agree with me on this point, I am convinced that the human brain has only a limited "storage space" for memory – a space which is rapidly over-crowded – at least with regard to prompt retrieval of memories. When the front space is filled up, each time you enter a new fact another one is pushed farther back out of reach into the darkness of the subconscious; and only repeated, intense practice brings it forward again to make it readily accessible. That is how things appear to present themselves in my case, not only with regard to languages but also for virtually any fact (anatomical details, chemical formulas, surgical techniques, etc.).

In addition to the ease of communication with colleagues throughout the world, my knowledge of languages has given me the intense pleasure of being able to read the original versions of books of my choice. Few things give me as much emotional and intellectual contact with foreign cultures as the ability to communicate with people in their own tongues. Very often I have the impression of belonging intimately to a foreign nation merely by reading an anecdote, a descriptive, colorful popular expression or a joke that is characteristic of a given people and culture.

When I was a child, I had two governesses: Madame Totier, who spoke only French, and Miss Johnson, who spoke English (British, I should say). Instead of kindergarten I went on long walks with Madame Totier in the morning and with Miss Johnson in the afternoon. My French governess came from Avignon and taught me French with a southern (Provençal) accent but by now I have lost my British and Provençal accents to a nondescript American-Québecois. Although I spent an equal amount of time with both of them, I recall curiously little about Miss Johnson. She seems to have been an efficient teacher but a desiccated old maid, devoid of personality and feelings. In my childish eyes she could never compare with my beloved French governess, who became an important part of my emotional life and whom I considered as my second mother. In fact, Miss Johnson left us after a while, and then I spent more time with Madame Totier than with my own mother. I do not remember having suffered from the fact that I had a mother substitute, perhaps because of Madame Totier's warm personality.

She had settled in Vienna after the death of her husband, at which time my mother hired her on a permanent basis. During World War I many people criticized our family for employing a French-woman, thereby permitting the enemy to put foreign ideas into my head. But I remember only one incident where I was exposed to her "seditious attitudes."

In addition to her normal task of giving me a French education, Madame Totier was responsible for my daily physical grooming. She placed me on a little stool every morning, bringing me up to her great height of five-foot-one, so that she might wash my ears and curl my long hair with a hot iron, in the fashion of the time.

I intensely disliked this procedure for good reason, I believe, because it was not unusual for her to accidentally burn my cheeks.

One day, after placing me on my little stool following the morning ablutions, Madame Totier asked me, "Do you know that Emperor Francis Joseph has died?" She announced this national catastrophe with such nonchalance, as if she might have been saying, "Do you know that it's raining?" Suddenly I experienced a profound hatred for this woman because, for me, Francis Joseph represented a divine being, a personality of capital importance to the entire world.

The imperial mentality is difficult to grasp. One might compare it to the feelings of loyalty that the Mikado used to inspire. For a Kamikaze pilot to crash his bomb-carrying plane into an American battleship and die for his Mikado was not a sacrifice. In my childish heart I felt that to die for Francis Joseph would have been a great honor. For me he was not a man but a god, and I could not understand how Madame Totier could speak of his death with so little emotion and respect. After the initial shock of her indifference to His Majesty, I once again became intensely attached to her.

In retrospect, I am baffled by the feeling that it was my teacher who played the traditional maternal role, while my real mother was undoubtedly my greatest teacher. Madame Totier cuddled me and consoled me when I was confused by life's complexities. It was she, and not my mother, who nursed me when I was sick and, whatever the day's trauma happened to be, always managed to comfort me with her warm, maternal attitude.

On the other hand, I don't remember my mother ever hugging me, although she must have, especially when I was a baby. Instead, I think of her in terms of education and culture, affairs of the mind but not of the heart. She never cried, as Madame Totier occasionally did, and she could not tolerate little boys with tears in their eyes. But children can't help crying once in a while, and as a result I spent more time in the company of my governess than with my mother.

Madame Totier died at the age of eighty, back in her native France. By that time I was in Canada but had maintained the closest relations with the old lady, visiting her several times on trips to Europe. I am still in correspondence with her son René, who was my playmate on our summer vacations in Vienna and went to Hungarian schools when we were in Komárom. Eventually he spoke German and Hungarian without an accent and gradually forgot his French, for he did not live in our house and had more contact with the local people in boarding school than with his mother, who lived with us and was occupied with me all the time. As far as I could see, no conflict was created for René by this situation. We accepted each other as pals and spent a good deal of time together in the company of our Austrian and Hungarian friends. Nevertheless, he always seemed conscious of the social difference between us, and he treated me with friendly respect just because his mother was in the service of mine.

However, occasionally we beat each other up, as boys of that age do. Usually when we had these competitions I would manage to win at wrestling but, much to my dismay and humiliation at the time, he almost always trounced me at chess. He continued to do so throughout our years together, and recently he sent me a newspaper clipping in which his photograph appears as President of the Chess Champions of Provence, France.

Had I tried, however, I might have defeated my great uncle Leopold, who never won at chess, no matter whom he challenged. My maternal grandfather's brother, Leopold was a mild old bachelor who lived as a sort of appendage to Grandpa's family. He had his own little room both in their city house and in their summer residence in suburban Dornbach. I don't remember what his occupation was, but he had no special talents and the family considered his job inferior. After forty years of service he was given the traditional engraved gold watch, which he displayed very proudly whenever anyone would pay attention.

Leopold was a passionate chess player and, as he had no other outlets in his free time, he used to go every night to the corner coffeehouse to challenge his cronies. After a few years I noticed that he was no longer making his nightly trip, and I asked him why he'd given up the game. "I really can't say," he replied. "They always used to beat me, but even so they just don't like to play with me anymore."

How many times I've met this attitude! So many people are content to carry out orders and give in to others, never making any bid for independent recognition, never attempting to take on a dominant role or any kind of responsibility. Yet they fail to understand that doing menial jobs for others without striving to become indispensable will not earn them respect or gratitude.

As the offspring of a well-respected family, I was brought up to believe, on the contrary, that to earn the respect of my peers and be a leader rather than a follower was the way to live. In this, my father served as a good example. I was seven years old when World War I broke out, and I clearly recall my father leaving for the Russian front at the head of the staff of the Imperial and Royal *(Kaiserlich und Königlich)* Military Hospital Number 5/5 *(Fünf/Fünf)*, which was garrisoned in Komárom. On horseback, his sword unsheathed, he proudly led his men to what was supposed to be a "war to end all wars," of course only through the inevitable defeat of the "despicable" enemy. I can still see him on the day after the declaration of war, riding to the accompaniment of martial music past the balcony of our house, where Mother and I waved farewell. She wore a black-and-yellow shoulder sash, representing the imperial colors of Austria. My father sported a similar one in the red, white and green of Hungary; and I had two very thin shoulder sashes, one black and yellow and one red, white and green. It was symbolic of the beginning of my multinational make-up, representing the two nations of my origin.

As soon as my father left for the Russian front, my mother took me to her parents' home in Vienna. I had to leave my Hungarian school and, in order not to mix up my education too much, I was provided with a Hungarian private tutor who continued to give me instruction in the language of the college where I had started my studies with the Benedictine Fathers of Komárom. As I had a teacher all to myself, I managed to do two years in one during the war, merely going back to Komárom for examinations. I do not recollect much about this tutor, except that he gave me a course in the cimbalom (the Hungarian gypsy dulcimer) with very little success, because I really had no gift for music. However, as my father was such an ardent patriot, he insisted upon my learning to play this typically Hungarian instrument.

During the war I did not see my father for five years because he was at the front, and even after the war ended it took a long time for him to get home. Once, however, while he was stationed at a hospital a few miles behind the battle lines, I was allowed to visit him briefly with my mother. I will never forget this trip, on which we traveled by train through occupied Poland, in the summer of 1915 or 1916. I was deeply stirred by the picture of complete devastation. All we could see were shell holes and ruins of villages.

Upon our arrival, Father bought me a beautiful jet-black Arab pony to cheer me up. I loved this horse dearly, but she had one curious habit: from time to time, for no apparent reason, she would jump into the air on all four feet simultaneously and neigh "Kweech." Accordingly, she was christened "Kweechka."

Her performance was very amusing to watch but not to experience. I fell off every time she kweeched, and one day I broke my arm on hitting the ground. Father watched this occurrence with seeming equanimity, then quietly took me to surgery and put my arm in plaster. But as soon as he had finished, he ordered me right back on Kweechka "because," he said, "if you don't mount her now you will always be afraid of horses." Suffering from acute pain and shivering with fear, I followed my father's orders as he quietly added, "In case of defeat, don't be a loser. It becomes a habit in life to give in, and you must be prepared to overcome many defeats before you become a man." I am still grateful to my father for his behavior at this critical point. Because of him, I do not quickly get discouraged by failure—I still don't give in easily!

This reminds me of a visit to our institute by a very modest scientist who subsequently became a Nobel Prize laureate. He came to our house for dinner and an informal chat with my assistants and graduate students. Someone asked him why he chose research as a career. He replied that, having been the son of very poor parents, he had great difficulty in earning money for his studies. After much effort he landed a job as a laboratory technician with a great biochemist. However, his work was judged unsatisfactory and finally his chief told him he was considering firing him.

"That's why I became a scientist. When I learned that the chief didn't think I was good enough, I told myself *I simply won't get fired!* I decided I should leave when *I* wanted to."

It seems that, beginning at this moment, the young man had started to work with such fanatic motivation that a year later, when he wanted to accept another position, his chief went to infinite pains and gave him several promotions to retain him on the staff.

So many great scientists who have made invaluable contributions to the intellectual life or well-being of man were originally motivated, not by curiosity or a great desire to serve humanity, but because of an emotional reluctance to accept defeat by anybody or anything, not even by the complexities of Nature.

Perhaps because of incidents like the Kweechka episode, I am very self-disciplined. One day I decided I should give up smoking, and I never smoked again, although I had become attached to the habit over a period of about thirty-five years. I also tend to be stubborn in continuing with things that I think have value, no matter what others may think.

I do not know to what extent I inherited this streak of persistence and to what extent it was learned. Science is constantly striving to distinguish between what is innate (genetically determined) and what is due to our environment. I do not believe it is possible scientifically to clearly separate these elements in any particular case, as it is the interaction between our genetic heritage and our environment that makes us what we are.

The same external event can encourage one individual and discourage another. It is useless to persist in trying to find any single cause responsible for our personalities or the diseases we acquire. All of these are "pluricausal" – they depend as much upon what happens to us as upon the way we react to our fate.

Ever since my earliest childhood, the occasions when I have had to assume positive attitudes in the face of adversity have had a great formative influence upon me and, Lord knows, there were plenty of such opportunities. World War I and its aftermath undoubtedly left an imprint upon my future life – perhaps not an entirely unfavorable one.

One character who made an outstanding impression on me in those days was Márton, a young Hungarian hussar who lived with us for some time. He was one of two orderlies assigned to my father. When he went to the front, Father took one of the orderlies with him, leaving Márton home with us to take care of the household, which consisted of Mother, Madame Totier, two maids and myself. In civilian life Márton had been a handyman, but once in the service he became very attached to the army, his elegant uniform and particularly my father. Consequently, he took his job as "the man of the house" very seriously.

As the war progressed it became increasingly difficult to find decent food, yet whenever Mother sent him to the weekly market, Márton managed to return not only with the necessities but also with a variety of delicacies. We wondered how he accomplished such a feat when nobody else could get to the peasant women fast enough to obtain some of the choicer farm products they would bring to sell in the main square.

At that time Mother considered it her duty as the commanding officer's wife to entertain the wives of the other officers on Father's staff. She held rather formal weekly tea parties where the women would congregate to exchange news of the front and, at the same time, cheer each other up. The conversation always revolved around their worries about the war and about the difficulties of obtaining food. While Mother shared the first preoccupation, whenever the subject of food came up she proudly announced that her Márton always managed to find chickens, eggs and rare treats. The other ladies would smile, exchanging meaningful glances.

Finally, one of the guests had the gumption to respond, "Well, do you know how Márton gets all those things?"

"No," Mother replied naïvely. "But he's such a charming young man that I suppose he can talk the women into doing almost anything. He seems to obtain favors from all the servant girls in town. I guess he's just irresistible!"

The ladies exchanged embarrassed smiles, and some of them giggled. The brave woman who had raised the question volunteered the answer: "You see, Márton goes out to the market and literally kneels down, crying to the peasant women, 'For God's sake, please sell me that chicken! If I come home without food Mrs. Selye beats me with a horsewhip till I ache all over for a week!' He can always find some kindhearted peasant who wants to save him from such a cruel fate. But he's such a talented actor that half the town believes his story!"

It took Mother some time to convince Márton that his exaggerated devotion was not, in truth, helping her much.

I once overheard a conversation between Márton and the orderly of the officer whose family lived next door to ours. Márton was speaking of his devotion to my father, praising him as an able surgeon and noble officer. "Not only that," he added, "my boss is so friendly that half of the time we're on a first-name basis."

"What do you mean by 'half the time'?" inquired the orderly.

"Well, he calls me 'Márton' and I call him 'Sir.' "

Having spent almost two years at the front before his domestic assignment, Márton was not very well adapted to civilian life. The first time he came home with a live chicken he presented it to my mother as if it were the spoils of military victory. Never having dealt with such distasteful things as slaughtering a chicken for a meal, neither Mother nor Madame Totier nor the servant girls had the heart to kill the bird. Mother called Márton back, informed him that this was a man's job and told him to carry out the execution.

Márton snapped his heels together in his disciplined military way, saying "I have never done this before, but I shall do my very best." He carried the chicken off to the courtyard while the rest of us gazed after him. A few moments later we heard three shots. Márton lumbered back toward the house, his bounty in tow. He had used the only means of killing he knew, executing his victim with his large-caliber army revolver. He was obviously not very good at it, however, because it took so many shots to finish off the poor bird, whose mangled, bleeding cadaver was hardly an elevating sight – let alone an appetizing one.

I spent a lot of time with Márton and he was fond of bragging about his wartime exploits. I must have been a rapt audience – a young boy, fascinated by the glory of war and the heroism of soldiers. But Márton's tales exposed me to the horror of battle as well as the excitement. He was a peculiar fellow, full of life and fun, and he would unfold his dramatic stories with a strange air of complete detachment, as if he were speaking about a weekend in the countryside.

Being assigned to a cavalry regiment, he usually fought on horseback, but occasionally he had been commanded to take part in bayonet charges on the Russian front. "The Cossacks are terrific soldiers, I have to admit that," he would say. "They don't know what fear is so they're difficult to fight and, like our hussars, they're cavalrymen. I got used to meeting them on horseback, but when I had to face them on foot I didn't know how to go about it, and neither did they. But they were brave all right.

"You could stick a bayonet into a Cossack and even while he was bleeding to death he would shoot at you. Finally I found one method to kill off a Cossack quickly: you run straight at him with your bayonet, stick it into his belly, then take your gun with both your hands and lift it up with a strong jerk. Then all his guts tumble out and he collapses so fast that he can't get back at you, so there's no more danger. As far as I know, it's the only way to kill a Cossack."

When Márton would go into these descriptive tales I would be sick for weeks afterwards, but I was too fascinated to make him stop. Despite my revulsion I admired the hussar for his equanimity because I saw in him the same bravery that I so respected in my father. Even though just a child, I could appreciate the mental strength it took to face the horrors of war and adapt to the inevitable. I was awed at his ability to put all this behind him and come back to the civilian world with such smiling, boyish charm.

If Márton hinted at the tragic nature of the battleground, my father's return confirmed the terrible consequences of war. We all celebrated when we heard that World War I had finally ended, and although we had lost, I was overjoyed because my father would be coming home at last. I had looked forward impatiently to having him around again after so many years, but he came home totally demoralized with one of the straggling groups of our beaten army. Like so many of the Imperial officers, he had been physically ill-treated by the discontented leftist elements among the troops, who tore off the insignia and medals from his uniforms. In addition, he suffered from infectious jaundice, a disease that was prevalent among the survivors of the army, and it took him quite some time to recover completely. Looking back, I would have to say that for some time after his return the lifestyle of our family was worse and not better than during his absence. I particularly remember a pathetic scene soon after he arrived home. Not having noticed my entrance, he stood in our large drawing room, inspecting himself in one of the floor-to-ceiling mirrors, his mutilated, shabby uniform hanging loosely from his emaciated body. I watched silently from the other end of the room in the open doorway, and I shall never forget the dejected expression on his jaundiced face that said so clearly, "Well, this is what I have come to."

During Father's recuperation, Komárom was first shelled by communist remnants of the army and then invaded by the victorious Czechoslovak forces who annexed it to their newly-formed republic. This had been agreed upon as part of the Versailles treaty, which cut off large chunks of Hungary and gave them to adjacent nations.

I was about eleven years old during this turmoil, and we lived through a period of almost continuous machine-gun and cannon fire. Air raids were common and there was always fighting in the streets, which were littered with dead people and horses. My father recovered sufficiently to open an emergency surgical service in our cellar, and the dirty storeroom became a first-aid station where he looked after the wounded as best he could. During the long weeks of fighting it served at the same time as our permanent home and air-raid shelter, where we were relatively safe from aerial bombardment and cannon shells. In the occasional quiet periods, I went out with the other boys, collecting spent shells and pieces of fresh meat from the fallen horses.

Sometimes we even dared to go up and sleep in our bedrooms on the first floor, but this was dangerous, as shooting often began unexpectedly. My parents' bedroom was sprayed with machine-gun fire and my mother insisted on leaving the furniture unrepaired for years afterwards. The bullet holes provided our home with a unique and macabre reminder of the times we managed to survive.

This sounds more horrible in retrospect than it seemed at the time, either because I did not then fully grasp the terror of the situation, or because even then I had already acquired the ability to erase any unpleasant episodes from my mind, "imitating the sundial's ways."

Life's uncertainty and the insignificance of personal property were engraved on my character as a result of our experiences. During the war we constantly had to change residences and, when the Austro-Hungarian Empire collapsed, my parents lost nearly their entire fortune.   Since the Empire had survived so many calamities over a thousand years, including the occupation by the Turks and the invasion by Napoleon's armies, my father had invested all his savings in what were considered to be the safest possessions, Austrian crown bonds, which now became totally worthless.

Even more painfully, he lost his rather high rank in the Imperial Army with the collapse of the Hapsburg monarchy. He told me then, "The only thing that is really yours is what you can learn. Nobody can take it away from you without also taking your life, and if that happens the rest does not matter."

That lesson has served me well. In fact, it is one of the basic principles of my code of behavior that knowledge and skills, rather than wordly assets, make you useful to others. Being useful is a strength that can never be devaluated. The essence of this code is summarized in the phrase, "*Earn* thy neighbor's love through altruistic egoism," a guideline I shall discuss in more detail later.

Curiously, one of my greatest sources of feelings of inferiority is the fact that my family was well-to-do, at least until the collapse of the Empire. Having had such a sheltered youth and having received so much help during my formative years, I can never convince myself that I could have accomplished anything worthwhile unaided. I continue to look with envy at every self-made man, and shudder to think what would have become of me had I been the son of poor, uneducated parents.

Although he lost all his money with the total devaluation of the Austrian crown bonds, my father managed to establish a flourishing private surgical clinic, using funds realized from the sale of my mother's valuable collection of jewels. Because I was an only child and wanted to become a physician, my father cherished the idea that I would eventually take over the Selye Surgical Clinic. However, I was certainly not the kind of young man who would follow the beaten path just because it was expected of him. Besides, I must admit that I was a pretty bad student at the college of the good Benedictine Fathers in Komárom. I barely passed my exams, and I suspect that my success was mainly due to the fact that, as a sideline, my father acted as house physician for the Benedictine monastery in Komárom, and my teachers didn't have the heart to disappoint him by making it obvious that I was just no good. I was simply not motivated by the bookish teaching I received at college. All the subjects seemed devoid of practical value. Ironically, I felt this most intensely about biology, which I hated. We had practically no laboratory work and the professor himself did not seem interested in his subject. For him, to be a good student meant to memorize a prescribed number of textbook pages every day.

Even if they brought me no favor at home, my poor scholastic record and often unruly behavior earned me some marginal advantages during my first year with the Benedictines. It so happened that the girl I liked best in the class was also a badly behaved student, and one of the fringe benefits of our academic career was that we always managed to get punished together by being kept at school after hours. Our saintly Benedictine Fathers apparently never considered how very enjoyable it might be for two twelve-year-olds to be locked up together, entirely safe from any external interferences for two blissful hours. She was a very pretty and affectionate little girl, the ideal partner for incarceration! We made as good a use of this punishment as possible at age twelve and, in fact, these few hours always seemed the shortest ones of the day.

As a student, I also reaped good dividends from the fact that my name starts with an "S," because we were usually called upon in alphabetical order to answer questions. Being toward the end of the list gave me a lot of time to profit by what others said to build up my own strategy.

The only two areas in which I led my class were philosophy and athletics. My parents were very disappointed about my scholastic accomplishments (or rather the lack of them); but in my defense, I pointed out with some arrogance that, after all, mine was the Roman ideal of accomplishment – *mens sana in corpore sano* (a healthy mind in a healthy body) – and what could be better proof of it than to be the first in philosophy and athletics? To tell the truth, I took to philosophy only because our teacher, Father Bognár, was an admirable man. He was the only one of the Fathers who, in addition to his college teaching, was also visiting professor at the University of Budapest. He knew his subject and loved it. His enthusiasm was contagious.

Just as Madame Totier had become my substitute mother, Father Bognár became a second father to me, especially during the years when my father was still away in the army. I was between the ages of seven and eleven, just the time when a boy really needs a male influence, and Father Bognár was there to fill the gap left by my father's absence. We used to take long walks along the shores of the Danube, during which he spoke to me as if I were an adult. He was the one who first asked me a question which is essential for all human beings: "What do you want to do with your life?" He was responsible for whetting my appetite for philosophical studies (logical, morals, metaphysics) and psychology.

I dearly loved both Professor Bognár and Madame Totier, though admittedly I sometimes referred to them in conversations with schoolmates as grumpy old fools. Had they heard me, I'm sure they would not have minded, because they also liked and understood me. Owing to the political upheavals in Europe, both of them spent their old age in abject poverty, and it warmed my heart that it was to me they turned for assistance in their need, although we hadn't seen each other for decades.

My indifference to scientific subjects and particularly to biology continued until I arrived at the University of Prague Medical School. There I immediately became first in my class, because the professors managed to present Nature as she was, not as described in texts. As for athletics, I excelled here by necessity. As a child I was fat and flabby. All the kids in the class delighted in ridiculing me for it, beating me up for fun whenever the occasion presented itself. This provoked me into getting my body into shape so as to lick every one of the tough guys at school. My room was turned into a gymnasium with a trapeze hanging down from the ceiling, parallel bars and weights. My determination helped me eventually to develop my muscles to a noteworthy

degree.   Always this strong motivation, the urge to make sure
that nobody could beat me! There is perhaps some animal instinct
at the root of all this; in any case, being able to beat up all the
tough guys gave me infinite delight.   I used this talent at the
slighest provocation.

I still feel the need for physical exercise, although this diminishes more rapidly with age than does the desire for mental activity.
Usually the body ages before the mind. But if we do not find any
outlet for our energy we lose control over it, and as a result of
boredom it turns against us through processes causing pathological
self-destruction.

Inactivity, due to laziness or any other cause, induces a feeling
of insecurity and depression often accompanied by an excessive
hypochondriac preoccupation with the body and mind.   Highly
active people have no time to waste on their worries; inactive
people tend to think of their troubles to while away the time.
Creative people have an insatiable appetite for the utilization
of their intellectual energy; after they have developed a strong
taste for the adventures of the mind, all the rest seems unimportant to them.

The atmosphere during my youth was certainly one that encouraged creativity and achievement.   This was true both in my
home life and, it seems to me, throughout the general Hungarian
culture.   The great biochemist Albert Szent-Györgyi once explained this to me by the following story, which he subsequently
published in the journal *Leonardo* under the title "On Scientific
and Artistic Creativity."

I am often asked why so many of my fellow Hungarian immi-
grants to American have achieved excellence in the arts and
sciences but not in business, finance or politics. I think it was
because of the social environment in Hungary, certainly not a
racial matter, for there were many Jews among us. I can give
some enlightenment on this with an anecdote from my own
life. First, it must be understood that traffic police in Budapest
consisted mostly of very simple, unsophisticated peasant boys.
One day while driving my car I violated a traffic regulation. A
policeman stopped me and asked my name. When I told

it to him he looked up and said 'but not the Nobel Prize scientist?' Upon my affirmative answer, he tore up the ticket and held up the traffic so I could drive away more easily. Had I been a millionaire or a leading industrialist, he would have fined me double!

Throughout my life, I retained the motivation needed to accomplish something meaningful in the face of difficulties and to muster the self-discipline and enforce the scientific exactness which is so necessary to do anything in my field. I was considerably helped by association with various people who passionately admired greatness.

I admire excellence for its own sake, and I feel that the achievement of greatness is a worthwhile aim in virtually any field. Whether or not I consider the achievement to be moral is a distinct issue; even if I know that someone's goals are not morally correct, I can appreciate his persistence in reaching them. I strongly disapprove of Al Capone's actions, and such people must be destroyed to protect society, but I cannot deny that he accomplished what he set out to do, and in doing so had a profound influence on many people. Of course, I would prefer it if he had directed his energy toward more noble goals, but still, within his field, Capone proved himself to be strong and purposeful.

I know that my admiration of such unsavory characters may bring me criticism. Perhaps "admiration" is not the best word for my feelings, but I can think of none better. A beautiful tropical flower in full bloom represents some of the most aesthetic aspects of Nature, and can give us pleasure merely by existing and allowing us to behold its beauty; a devastating earthquake reveals one of the most horrifying features. One force is positive, the other negative, yet both contain elements of astonishing power, and both intrigue me.

The character of the Mafia leader portrayed in *The Godfather* is abominable but also somehow fascinating. Hitler displayed every trait that I despise, but he was a genius at moving the masses. I marvel at such evil accomplishments, but I also admire the brilliant achievements of Picasso, Goethe, Einstein and Michelangelo. Even among such very different personalities, one trait is outstanding – greatness. Greatness is a quality devoid of moral connotations. The Grand Canyon, the eruption of Mount Vesuvius, the St. Lawrence River, Notre Dame Cathedral – all have the common bond of greatness. They are not necessarily useful, beautiful or desirable, but all are undeniably great.

My mother always stood in speechless admiration before anything truly unique and great. She probably influenced me at a very early age more than anyone else, much as Konrad Lorenz imprinted his geese by looking after them immediately upon hatching and being accepted and followed everywhere as their natural mother. This feeling has become the most intimate characteristic of my nature. As soon as someone has accomplished something great – whatever his field of action – I can only disapprove of the direction of his activity but I must admire the genius of the act, the intrinsic value of greatness needed to accomplish it.

Personally, I don't think that Napoleon did much good for humanity or even for his own people, but I admire him because there are few men who could do what he did. It is perhaps the singularity of the thing, a sort of uniqueness exceptional among men, that impresses me. You need several qualities in order to arrive at such summits; among others, you must have perseverance in the face of attacks on your work and even personal abuse. Few people possess these qualities. A Napoleon must know how to lose lives of soldiers or even entire battles in order to win wars. It is the same for Al Capone or Louis Pasteur. When I was young, I received valuable advice from my parents in this respect: to persevere when you can (or at least might) achieve something really great, but not to waste effort on hopeless or trivial causes. I later taught my students not to split up or fritter away their talents; not to undertake hundreds of minor things; not to build many little unconnected houses if they have the chance to construct one great cathedral. No number of stereotyped bungalows will ever equal the majesty of a great cathedral.

In my life I shall have accomplished only one thing: a better understanding of stress. I have written thirty-eight books and approximately 1,600 technical articles, but in some manner all were related to the same subject; and as long as I live, whether I have to use chemical, microscopic, pharmacological or psychological methods, I shall work on stress. Stress will have been my cathedral and I shall polish and perfect it by adding new data, weeding out the errors which constantly contaminate it, and maintaining its harmony.   That will require understanding and coordination of research from all over the world on this one subject, a task I shall continue as long as I can.   Although I know my "child" will outlive me, I feel that by now it has reached the critical degree of maturity and independence (physicists would speak of "the critical mass") that will assure its ability to survive and grow without my help.

CHAPTER THREE

Becoming a Scientist

I have often wondered why and when I decided to become a scientist, and what the first factors were that oriented me in this direction. Undoubtedly the cultural atmosphere of Austro-Hungarian life, so well depicted in Szent-Györgyi's anecdote, had a profound influence, but after so many years it is difficult to reconstruct a chain of events. We all tend to forget what really happened at the beginning of our lives and usually remember only the images of our early experiences. In other words, we only remember the recollections of our recollections. So many things have happened since the first event that they have tended to cover and blot out the true, original picture.

Nevertheless, as far as I can remember, the factors that most decisively influenced me were the principles that guided our family: the remarks made, the opinions expressed around the family's dinner table. The disdain for mediocrity of any sort, the admiration for anything that was outstanding in science, art or literature continually impressed me when listening to conversations between my parents.

My decision to become a physician was as much due to the influence of my family as to my natural instinct. For me, the desire to heal seems to be an innate and irresistible drive. I was "programmed" in this direction ever since my birth. On my father's side, I represent the fourth generation of physicians. I cannot say whether, and to what extent, my choice of a career depended upon genetic factors or upon the tendency to follow in the footsteps of my predecessors due to constant exposure to the values they cherished. For the Selye boys, to become adults meant to become doctors as much as it meant that their voices would change and they would have to start shaving.

When I was still very formally religious, ministering to the soul seemed comparable to the profession I had chosen; both religion and medicine contained the element of assisting those who needed help for their weaknesses and suffering. (At the age of 10, I even briefly considered entering the clergy. Since I knew that nothing would satisfy me unless I could become a pope—and that seemed rather unlikely—I soon gave up the idea.) I had a great tendency to look down upon other occupations. On my mother's side almost everybody was in law or finance, but for me these were not careers I could have chosen with equal pride and satisfaction. To relieve suffering and prevent premature death – these impressed me as the most noble occupations one could select. I was still a very young boy when my father first took me along on his visits to patients. At that time, even well-known physicians and surgeons used to make house calls under emergency conditions. I remember accompanying him in a horse-drawn carriage, sometimes on rides of several hours during the middle of the night, because medical help was urgently needed in some village around Komárom.

Very often these nocturnal trips to poor peasant homes brought in no money. In fact, sometimes my father left some cash to help out his patients during the difficult period after the birth of a child; this was done out of *noblesse oblige*, a feeling that such sacrifices are part of a physician's vocation. For in those days it was a vocation, not just a job. The physician became part of the family, a father figure similar to a priest, minister, rabbi or foster parent, someone who came in times of trouble and brought relief and reassurance by merely entering the house. Often it was the same physician who delivered the baby, looked after all of his childhood diseases and eventually delivered the children of the next generation. The doctor was there even when medicine could do no more for grandpa at his deathbed, but his presence and reassuring words brought as much comfort as the last rites administered by the priest. On the other hand, at Christmas time and whenever the farm products were plentiful, these peasants came in from the surrounding villages for the weekly market in Komárom, and they never forgot to visit my parents to present live chickens, eggs, homemade sausages, cheese and other goodies. I particularly remember the enormous, fattened goose livers, a delicacy of which I am still inordinately fond.

Physicians valued this direct contact with the people. They did not base their behavior upon any scientifically legitimized code of "altruistic egoism" such as the one I shall try to outline later. They followed it instinctively. Their work usually enabled them to live comfortably, but the respect and gratitude of the community brought equal satisfaction. It is my hope that these times – which I remember with bittersweet nostalgia – are not gone forever, that medicine will not become just another business.

Scientific work can bring a type of pleasure almost comparable to sensual or sentimental satisfaction. It may come from the patient who says, with tears in his eyes, "If you had not discovered the root of my illness, I would be dead." Satisfaction may also come from finding motivation in ultimate goals quite different from the immediate material satisfactions or carnal pleasures of this world. Immense gratification can be derived from the ability to use knowledge about the workings of the body – acquired through various somatic or psychological techniques – and from the ability to apply this knowledge, thereby improving the fate of society.

It is often said that if the science of medicine is what cures disease, then the physician is not only responsible for the proper use of medicines and surgery, but through his encouragement and understanding must also inspire the desire for health and well-being. This is really the basis of psychosomatic medicine. Undoubtedly, the ideal physician or nurse must have adequate scientific knowledge, but to be fully useful he must also possess great understanding of the personalities of those who turn to him for advice.

A good physician must have empathy, a moral affinity for the feelings of his patients; to help them he must be able to feel what they feel. Despite the great importance I attach to the general rules of my code of behavior, no code can ever give a magic recipe for each person in every situation. The guidance of the physician or nurse is indispensable.

Think, for a moment, about man's ability to speak. All normal human beings can talk. Animals can emit certain sounds and even use them as signals, but they could never learn to speak a human language – say, French or Japanese. It is the ability to talk that is inherited, not the ability to speak English or German. The same situation exists in psychology, geometry or mathematics. Science can supply the general rules to follow, but simple knowledge of the rules will not enable you to apply them to each particular problem. That is why I think that everybody is still his own best physician when it comes to behavior. It helps to be guided in this effort by a physician, a psychologist, a theologian, a philosopher or any other counselor; but these can only discover and transmit the general laws to you. You are the only one fully qualified to know how to apply them to yourself. Medicine is concerned with people or, more exactly, with humanity; and therefore its value does not come from science alone but also from love. "All of medicine is love," said Paracelsus as early as the sixteenth century. This dictum no longer applies, but there still remains a great deal of truth in it.

Today may people abuse drugs; and unless a physician prescribes some kind of pill or surgical intervention, he loses his patient's trust. Yet medicine and surgery are not the only means available to maintain the well-being of humanity. The great majority of diseases for which patients seek medical help are, at least in part, psychosomatic. If someone suffers from a peptic ulcer, for example, it is not only the ulcer that should be cured but also the patient's reaction to the life events that caused his susceptibility to this particular stress-induced disease.

I knew a very good gastroenterologist who was clearly aware of this relationship, but interpreted it in a rather unusual way. When he made the diagnosis of a peptic ulcer and heard the patient complain about his mental difficulties, he reacted by saying, "Look, I am a physician. I can treat your ulcer but I cannot give you another boss, father or mother-in-law." His response was automatic because he saw the relationship so often in his practice, but his attitude revealed his complete misunderstanding of what his role should have been. If a doctor is emotionally or scientifically incompetent to treat a psychosomatic illness, he should refer the patient to another physician who is better prepared in this respect. It is possible to treat psychosomatically-induced peptic ulcers, high blood pressure, migraine headaches, asthma attacks, mental disturbances and many other diseases merely by drugs or surgical interventions. However, to use only those methods would be wrong, just as wrong as treating "the fevers" with antipyretics; these will reduce the fever but will not cure the typhoid or tuberculosis that has caused it.

With most psychosomatic diseases it is the philosophy of life, the code of behavior of the patient, that is really at fault. He must either learn to adopt a "syntoxic" attitude – that is to say, he has to learn to live with the people responsible for his troubles if it is not worth his while to fight; or, if he is convinced he can and must win, he should behave in a "catatoxic" manner and force a showdown. In any event, the conflict has to be terminated. Although these concepts of "syntoxic" and "catatoxic" manners are here being applied to interpersonal relations, it was actually observations on tissue reactions to "syntoxic" and "catatoxic" chemicals (particularly hormones) that called my attention to this law governing human behavior.

Among all diseases, terminal cancer is perhaps the most feared. Yet so much progress has been made in the treatment of certain types of cancer that it is not an exaggerated optimism to believe that medicine will probably soon find remedies against even this little-understood disease. At present, only relatively few types of advanced cancer are completely curable by surgical removal, radiotherapy or chemotherapy. But in the great majority of diseases, the psychic element plays such a predominant role that one can achieve relief and, sometimes indirectly, perhaps even a cure by merely influencing the mentality of the patient.

The old spirit of physicians like my father is still alive, at least in some outlying communities, where "the doctor" has managed to maintain his traditional role in society, even if perhaps his technical competence is not always up to that of the eminent metropolitan specialist who has all the mechanized health machinery of the large university hospitals at his command. Let us admit it, the latter is much better at curing certain diseases but much less able to help people. To me the personal approach is at least an equally important part of the "art of healing." That is why I devote so much of my time now to the study of human behavior.

In an overcrowded university clinic nowadays, the doctor hardly has more than a few minutes to visit each patient. It is true that with his greatly perfected technical knowledge and all the medical instruments at his command he can usually cure the disease with a prescription of appropriate drugs and other therapeutic measures; but often the patient comes back with another problem, because no one looked into why he developed such an ailment in the first place. Perhaps future generations of physicians will have (or at least will attempt to make) time to become familiar not only with the illness but also with the patient.

I hope that, with the courses in stress now given to nurses in many schools, they will be able to take over this personal aspect of the "art of healing." Unfortunately, when I speak to nurses they often complain that as soon as the head nurse sees them chatting with a patient she feels that they are just wasting time in idle conversation when they should be measuring blood pressures and temperatures or administering the drugs according to the physician's prescription. Still, I am much encouraged by the present tendency to introduce courses on stress into the formal curriculum of nurses. In some conferences called to draw up modernized plans for the training of nurses the possibility has even come up of graduating special "stress nurses" – just as, at present, we have the operating room nurse, X-ray nurse or psychiatric nurse – as a recognized speciality within the profession.

Before the moon shot, I spent a few inspiring days with Wernher von Braun on Grand Bahama Island. Among other things, we spoke about the relative distribution of national funds for space travel and medical research. When I complained about the comparatively meager support for medical research, he looked at me with dreamy eyes and said, "You do not have the moon to offer."

But don't we? What could be of greater concern to man than the agony of excruciating pain and the humiliation of impending death which wipes out all other motives? There may be something worth having on the moon. Yet there is no reason to doubt that, with an equal investment of money and talent, a successful attack on cancer, heart disease or premature aging could be launched. As I said many years ago in my book *From Dream to Discovery:*

You give little thought to disease and death while you are
young and strong, but your outlook changes after you have
spent a great deal of time in hospitals. Everything else seems
so terribly unimportant by comparison when you see those
patients with the signature of death on their washed-out, hazy
eyes. Try to remember their expressionless faces which reflect
only total indifference. They do not even bother to answer a
friendly smile – it isn't worth the effort. Try to imagine that
worst thing in the realization of impending death: the humiliation of it. It is so terribly degrading for them to learn that
they are suddenly excluded from all the strivings, the competitive games of life, from all the preparations for the future
which normally guide our every action. Their progress along
the road was so exciting. It was such fun always to anticipate
the pleasures of the next step – and now there is no next step,
just a precipice. They were so used to fighting for knowledge,
money, fame, power, things that can be stacked away for the
future. And now suddenly there is no future.

Our colleagues in the exact sciences, in physics, chemistry or
mathematics, share with us and, in many respects, surpass us
in everything I have said about the beauty of science for its
own sake. But no matter how hard I try to remain objective
and to appreciate the importance of other professions, I cannot
see what else I could do with my life that would be more meaningful and satisfactory than medical research. Even the grandeur of conquering the universe, or the fear that war may
break out, or that our world may become over-populated,
seems to pale at the bedside of a patient who will die because
we were remiss in our efforts to learn more about disease.

I could never have chosen any other profession than medicine.
It was love at first sight more than half a century ago, and nothing
has changed since!

Because I had the advantage of a private tutor in Vienna, I
was academically qualified to enter medical school at seventeen,
but still too young to meet the standard entrance requirements.
Luckily, though, the rector of the university happened to have
served as an officer under my father's command during World

War I, and he obligingly failed to examine my birth certificate with great care. Owing to that oversight I managed to begin my studies at this tender age.

As soon as I entered medical school at the University of Prague and could finally satisfy my curiosity about Nature while, at the same time, completing the requirements for my education, I suddenly began to enjoy studying. My poor grades turned to top marks as my enthusiasm grew. During these years I developed an unusual power of mental concentration which allowed me to block out all distractions and devote myself entirely to the matter at hand. In fact, I often deliberately studied on streetcars or in noisy coffeehouses as a form of training. While this practice certainly helped me to develop my ability to concentrate, I cannot honestly say that I would recommend the habitual selection of the most uncomfortable surroundings for intellectual work.

During the period of 1925–1927 it was permissible, and even encouraged, for medical students at the University of Prague to spend one or two years in first-rate foreign universities, for which full credit was given by our school. Under this system, I studied for one year in Paris and one in Rome. In doing so, I was fortunate enough not only to familiarize myself with other types of teaching and different cities, but also to polish my French and learn Italian.

Although my father was willing to pay my expenses, I tried to save as much money as I could by living modestly. But at the end of my year in Paris, I blew my entire small fortune on a New Year's Eve celebration at the Crillon Hotel, an event which – like most of my youthful follies – I have never regretted to this day. I remember that I sported a white tie with a formal swallow-tailed coat and top hat, and that we drank a lot of champagne; but I have only the faintest recollection of all the parties that continued on until noon the following day, and I haven't the foggiest idea how I ever got home again.

My father came to visit me once during my year in Paris. He sat next to me in the operating theater of Professor H. Hartmann at the Hôtel Dieu Hospital, and the distinguished surgeon turned toward us in the middle of an operation, saying, "Obviously father and son. Both surgeons?" We proudly answered simultaneously,

"Yes, sir." Apparently, we did look strikingly alike, despite the great difference in our ages.

I also recall another event that might be interpreted as an early sign of my awakening "experimental mind." Whenever I returned to Paris from holidays, I tipped the porter at the train station more and more, in an effort to determine the amount required for him to say "thank you." I never found out. No matter how much I gave, he always looked at the tip with an expression of disgust, presumably in the belief that this would encourage travelers to become more generous. I had a similar experience with taxi drivers in Paris; but when I finally gave one driver a tip equal to the fare, I simply admitted defeat rather than invest even more heavily in this experiment. However, when I arrived in Rome for my junior year as a medical student and a porter addressed me as "Eccellenza" (Your Excellency), this compliment made an impression sufficient for me to raise my tip to the top level without having to go through the intermediate stages.

Incidentally, a similar trick was used by a pretty young girl who sold frankfurters to students between classes, in front of the university clinic in Prague. She increased her clientele significantly by addressing us all as "Professor." However, that was not her only virtue, because her frankfurters were the most succulent I ever ate anywhere, and the mustard spread on them was of the best quality. I hear that today this very old woman is still in business, stationed in the same place, on the sidewalk in front of the main entrance.

While I was a student at the college of the Benedictines, Father Bognár convinced me of the wisdom expressed by the Latin phrase *Vitae non scholae discimus* (We learn for life, not for the school); and perhaps it is because of this that I never got into the common habit of postponing studying for examinations to the last possible moment. Knowledge quickly acquired is quickly forgotten so I always tried to keep up with the courses as we took them. Consequently, when we came to the end of the medical course, I was ready to take examinations in any subject. It was customary to set aside a full year to do them one by one; this allowed students to review each subject carefully. The final tests could be taken at any time but they were usually tackled at the rate of one per month.

I do not know whether it is my natural swashbuckling instinct which makes me always want to overcome every difficulty, proving to myself and to others that "I can beat anybody in this tavern," but when we were ready to start, I bragged shamelessly that I could pass one a day. I was dared to do so by a classmate who bet me 200 Czech crowns that this was impossible, as it had never been done before. Being too proud to back out, I went through with the bet – and won. Incidentally, my friend never did pay me!

In spite of that frenzied schedule, I managed to obtain the highest marks, except in dermatology where the moody Professor Kreibich actually flunked me. I felt that he did so with some justification because my answers were totally unsatisfactory; but after discussing his shattering verdict with his assistants, he found out that I had the highest standing in all other subjects and returned to me, saying apologetically that he had obviously made a mistake, the mark he wanted to give me was "excellent." I guess he merely hated the idea of spoiling my otherwise exceptional record that – thanks to his benevolence – earned me the honor of presenting the valedictory speech of the class (in Latin!). On that solemn occasion I modestly pointed out that I was happy to have been awarded the M.D. along with my classmates but that, unlike most of them, I intended to use this merely as a starting point for a much more imaginative career of research and teaching as a university professor. The statement was received with benevolent smiles by my teachers; fortunately, my colleagues did not grasp most of the Latin, especially in the excitement preceding the distribution of diplomas. In retrospect, I do not think it was in good taste but it was in carefully worded Latin and was undoubtedly characteristic of my personality; it reflected my intense motivation to seek a life with a purpose at the top border of my natural stress endurance. Upon thinking it over, I have not really changed much.

I was a medical student when I first became infected with the bug of research. At that time my father let me assist him with minor surgical operations. He also helped me with my innumerable surgical experiments on frogs and chickens which I performed in the basement of our family home, to the great consternation of my mother. I remember that I tried hard to secure permission from the city councilors of Komárom to obtain abandoned dogs from the city pound ("for the good of the future of medicine!"), but my repeated requests were steadfastly refused for fear of adverse opinion about animal experimentation.

This type of resistance has continued to plague me throughout my career. I still receive anonymous letters from various anti-vivisectionists. They do not object to killing animals for food or the sport of hunting, or even for elegant furs and leather. However, they cannot see why medicine could not progress even one step further without animal experimentation.

Of course, these well-meaning people do not hesitate to take insulin, adrenalin, antibiotics or any other drugs when they are sick; but they do not think about the fact that all these remedies were the result of animal experimentation, or that it is actually against the law in most civilized countries to try new drugs or surgical procedures on man without first having established their safety on laboratory animals. Curiously, the most outspoken antivivisectionists protest mainly about dogs, cats and monkeys. They are not nearly as concerned with cruelty to plants, microbes, parasitic worms, or even to frogs, chickens or rats. They have never compared themselves to a microbe or a lovely magnolia spreading fragrance in the garden, and they lack the imagination to extend the concept of enjoying life undisturbed to living beings not closely resembling themselves.

Having purchased a few laboratory rats, I managed to perform the first experiments on the effect of vitamin-D compounds upon blood coagulation. The findings were published in a highly reputable German journal, the *Klinische Wochenschrift* in September, 1928, and bore the notation "from the Surgical Clinic of Dr. Hugo Selye, Komárom." This was actually my fifth publication but it was the first experiment I performed entirely alone, without any supervision from my professors. I was particularly proud that the work had been carried out with absolute scientific rigor although it came from the basement of our home and was done under the most difficult circumstances against the desperate protests of my mother.

My parents obviously would have preferred that I take over the lucrative Selye Surgical Clinic – a career open to an only son without the need for competition – rather than risk failure in the badly underpaid career of basic research. Still, I was leaning toward research rather than a medical practice. Immediately upon obtaining my doctorate, I had to decide which direction I would pursue, and this was not an easy choice.

I knew when I chose pure research I would never have the satisfaction of seeing the grateful eyes of a mother whose child has been saved from certain death. Giving up this reward of medicine represented a great sacrifice for me. But as time went on, I never had reason to regret my choice. Like most physicians who decide in favor of research over private practice, I told myself if in the solitude of my laboratory an experiment will work out well, I will have the enormous satisfaction of knowing that, had I not helped unveil a law of Nature, no practicing physician could have used it for the good of his patients. The discovery of one new treatment can help many more people than any individual doctor could ever treat.

For me, the most noble way of practicing the "art of healing" is to find new methods of curing a disease – say, cancer or mental illness.

Ever since I made my choice about the work I wanted to do, I have thought extensively about the nature of research. An article I published in *The Saturday Evening Post* in 1959 summarizes my conclusions as well as I could today. This essay was later included in an anthology together with contributions by Jacques Barzun, Paul Tillich, J. Robert Oppenheimer, Aldous Huxley, Arthur M. Schlesinger, Jr., Dame Edith Sitwell, Bertrand Russell and some of my other favorite thinkers.

Until recently, most of us engaged in basic research saw no reason to explain our work or our motives to the public. We felt there was something vulgar in discussing our peculiar problems with people not fully prepared to appreciate all the fine technical points and that it would be an immodest bid for attention. We felt that the singular world of basic research could be understood only by those who live in it.

To attempt to explain it in lay language seemed hopeless and even childish – as futile and naïve as to expound the current problems of the American automobile industry to an African chieftain who has never seen either America or an automobile. Now, however, as Bertrand Russell puts it, "Not only will men of science have to grapple with the sciences that deal with man but – and this is a far more difficult matter – they will have to persuade the world to listen to what they have discovered. If they cannot succeed in this difficult enterprise, man will destroy himself by his halfway cleverness."

The basic research of today produces both the lifesaving drugs and destructive weapons of tomorrow. Its outcome will affect everybody, and in a democracy whose people decide how wealth shall be distributed everybody shares the responsibility of developing the nation's scientific potential. But how can anybody vote intelligently without some grasp of the problems bearing upon the development?

Bridging the gap between the scientist and the general public will not be easy. The former will have to learn to translate his problems into language meaningful to the layman; the latter will have to realize that, however simplified, the essence of basic research cannot be assimilated without mental effort.

What is basic research? Charles E. Wilson, the former Secretary of Defense, defined it as what you do "when you don't know what you're doing," a sarcasm presumably intended to justify the inadequacy of financial support for basic research. More commonly, basic research is thought of as the opposite of "practical" research, the kind that can be immediately applied. This suggests its disassociation from man's everyday problems. The development of weapons, television sets or vaccines is obviously practical. Studies of the inner temperature of distant stars, of the habits of infinitely small living beings, of the laws governing the inheritable coloration of flowers, all seemed eminently impractical – at least when first undertaken. They were viewed as sophisticated pastimes, pursued by intelligent but somewhat eccentric, maladjusted people, whose otherwise excellent minds had been sidetracked by a queer interest in the far-fetched and useless.

I remember my own reaction in school when I was taught how to estimate the inner temperature of distant stars. Cunning, I thought, but why should anybody want to know? When Louis Pasteur reported that germs might transmit diseases, he was ridiculed. Fancy a grown man worrying about being attacked by bugs so small no one could see them! When the Austrian monk, Gregor Johann Mendel, amused himself by observing the results of crossbreeding red- with white-flowering peas in the monastery garden, even his most farsighted contemporaries failed to imagine the momentous implications.

Yet, without basic knowledge of the behavior of distant stars, we would not be placing satellites in orbits today; without knowledge about bacteria, there would be no vaccines and antibiotics; and without those observations on the inheritance of color in peas, modern genetics – with its importance to agriculture and medicine – could never have developed.

Such considerations must arouse public interest in basic research. They are bound to make people realize that the more manifestly sensible and practical a research project, the closer it is to the commonplace we already know. Thus, paradoxically, knowledge about the seemingly most far-fetched, impractical phenomena may prove the likeliest to yield novel basic information, and lead us to new heights of discovery.

Some insist that basic research must proceed in the same spirit as "art for art's sake," and should not be appraised by its practical applicability. Yet, in defending this view they usually argue that even the most abstruse research may eventually yield practical results. It is odd that the study of the impractical should have to be justified by its potential usefulness. When the eminent English chemist and physicist, Michael Faraday, first performed his classic experiments on magnetism and electricity in front of an audience, he was honored by the presence of His Royal Highness the Prince of Wales. After watching the demonstration, the Prince asked somewhat sarcastically, "Yes, but what is all this good for?" Faraday's reply which is so often quoted was, "Someday, Sir, you will collect taxes from it." Pasteur reportedly defended his own studies by recounting that Benjamin Franklin had replied to similar queries saying, "What is the use of a newborn baby?" But not everything important to us need be useful in the accepted sense of the word. At the same time, utility is inseparable from man's assessment of what is important. Perhaps in this still unprejudiced, pliable core of a human being we sense a possible future helpful friend. In any case, a baby is useful because we can lavish our love on it – and without love there can be no happiness. Pure art – a great painting, a piece of music – is useful, since it lifts us beyond the preoccupations of everyday life, bringing us peace and serenity. Bearing these facts in mind, I am inclined to define basic research as the study of natural laws for their own sake, irrespective of immediate practical applicability – with emphasis on the qualification "immediate."

But, to me, the need is not so much to define basic research as to distinguish between greater and lesser basic research projects. This distinction is of immense importance, both to the investigator who requires a standard by which to choose his subject and to the public who pays for his work in the hope of profiting by it. The future welfare of humanity depends largely upon the recognition of first-rate basic research in its earliest stages, when it lacks practical applicability. No nation can afford to subsidize every kind of research, and many a fertile, creative thought has had to be buried stillborn because no one wanted to risk money on it until its value was proved.

Let me emphasize that only the kind of research usually designated as "basic" is true discovery. What follows is development. The former kind is basic, or fundamental, precisely because every other kind of research develops from it. It strikes us as impractical and the work involved as haphazard, because wholly original observations cannot be planned in advance. To do so the observation would have to be anticipated on the basis of previously known facts, and hence could not be wholly original. That is why most of the completely new leads are accidental discoveries made by men with the rare talent of noticing the totally unexpected. These form the basis of all premeditated research projects – the kind I call development.

It may be argued that any attempt at early recognition must be foredoomed, since the unexpected cannot be anticipated. To some extent this is true. Of course, there is no reliable yardstick with which to compare the relative importance of basic research projects, but I believe it possible to formulate certain principles which can serve as general directives. Think of them not as rigid measurements, but rather as a kind of course in science appreciation, helping us to recognize and enjoy creative scientific thought.

To my mind, it is characteristic of great basic discoveries that they possess, to a high degree and simultaneously, three qualities: they are true not merely as facts but also in the way they are interpreted, they are generalizable and they are surprising in the light of what was known at the time of the discovery.

It may seem redundant to say that the newly discovered facts must be true, but by this I mean they must be both correct and seen in proper perspective. Otherwise the finding may be misleading because of the inferences drawn from it.

Not long ago a chemist tried to make a compound that would diminish appetite and cause loss of weight. After years of study, he succeeded in producing a drug that conformed to his theories concerning the structure this kind of substance should have. He then tested the compound on rats, cats, dogs and monkeys. As he expected, all the animals ate very little and lost weight. In a paper describing his findings, he explained why he thought a drug of such chemical structure would act in this manner. In the conventional sense, his findings were true. In my sense they were false. We know that almost any damaging substance will diminish appetite, and his substance was damaging. The author neither admitted nor denied this. He did not recommend his drug for human use. Still, his paper implied applicability. Hence, his finding was untrue by implication. Had he realized that his compound decreased appetite only because of its damaging effects, he would not have bothered to write a paper about it. Few scientists knowingly publish untruths, but many scientific papers contain such untruths by implication.

Yet, even if a finding is true by all standards, it may not be important. I once read a paper describing the mean weights of the internal organs of laboratory rats. The author's facts were correct; he had killed hundreds of animals to build up a highly significant series. But the resulting information was of limited importance, being neither generalizable nor surprising. It is not generalizable, because we can deduce no general laws from it; it does not necessarily apply even to rats of a different strain. Indeed, in the researcher's own stock, the organ weights probably would have varied had he changed the diet or the temperature of the laboratory. Nor is the information surprising, because it was evident at the start that the mean weights could be determined by measurement. This sort of work not only fails to qualify as "basic research" but it has not even been practically applied to anything.

The best you can say for it is that it might be applicable by somebody needing these figures as a standard of comparison for original investigation, but then his would be the basic research. Scientific literature abounds in such reports. The authors customarily protect themselves by stating self-righteously that they draw no conclusions from their observations. But this is not good enough. Facts from which no conclusions can be drawn are hardly worth knowing.

This sort of finding may be made accidentally, but usually it results from what we call "screening," and, hence, falls into the class of development rather than of discovery. Such screening might be used by the clinician testing a number of cortisone derivatives, more or less at random, on patients with rheumatic diseases. Cortisone itself is a hormone that has been found effective in such cases and the clinician merely wants to screen related compounds to see whether one of them might prove more effective. Again, all this is development of previously known facts, not original, creative research.

We are guided in such work by so-called "deductive reasoning," which helps us foretell certain things about an individual case from a previously established generalization. If most cortisone-like compounds are effective against rheumatism, any newly prepared member of this group looks promising.

But the deduction itself cannot be generalized. The work may be of immediate practical importance, leading us perhaps to the ideal anti-rheumatic compound, but, in the highest sense, it is sterile, because the observation is complete in itself, offering little likelihood of further discoveries.

Unfortunately, this drab kind of research is the easiest to finance, because of its immediate applicability to practical problems which can be precisely described in a routine application for funds.

Other observations lend themselves to "inductive reasoning," the formulation of general laws from individual observations. But this feature does not suffice either. To illustrate, it was shown that the first ten hormones, the products of endocrine glands, that could be prepared in pure form were all white. From this, we could generalize. We could foretell, with a high degree of probability, that the next five hormones to be synthesized would also be white. So they were. But what of it? Who cares what color future hormone preparations will be? The appearance of the substances is irrelevant.

Here, then, was an observation both true and generalizable, but lacking the third essential quality of important basic research, the quality of surprise; that is, the unexpectedness of the discovery at the time of making it. Most body constituents are white when purified; hence, it is not surprising that hormones should be white.

I recall my astonishment on learning in medical school that certain pathological growths in the human ovary, the so-called "dermoids," may contain teeth and hair. A medical curiosity, but not generalizable – at least not at present. All we can say now is that occasionally, even without fertilization, an egg in the human ovary may develop into a monster consisting mainly of hair and teeth. This much has been known ever since the seventeenth-century German physician, Scultetus, gave the first complete description of what he called *morbus pilaris mirabilis*, the astonishing hair malady. Martin Luther referred to it as the "Offspring of the Devil."

For centuries, physicians and laymen alike have been fascinated by the anomaly. But it opened up no new vistas of research.   The reason is, I think, that the observation was made too early.   Even today we are not equipped to evaluate it.   It is like a strange island remote from the chartered areas of human knowledge.   Perhaps, later – when we know more about fertilization, about reproduction without fertilization and about the "organizers" that direct the formation of human structures – the "Offspring of the Devil" will become an angel guiding us to the solution of Nature's mysteries.   But merely being aware of the oddity avails us nothing.   Scultetus saw, but he did not discover.

Laymen rarely appreciate the fundamental difference between seeing and discovering.   America was not discovered for mankind by the Indians, nor by the Vikings who came in the tenth century, but by Christopher Columbus, who established a permanent bridge between the new and the old worlds.   It is the process of unifying, the "creative synthesis," be it even of long-known facts, that alone can promote true understanding and progress.

As Hans Zinsser, the great American bacteriologist, put it: "So often, in the history of medicine, scientific discovery has merely served to clarify, and subject to purposeful control, facts that had long been empirically observed and practically utilized.   The principles of contagion were clearly outlined and invisible microorganisms postulated by Fracastorius about a hundred years before the most primitive microscopes were invented; and the pre-Pasteurian century is rich with clinical observations that now seem a sort of gestation period leading to the birth of a new science."

This essential distinction between seeing and discovering is illustrated by the development of insulin, the pancreatic hormone with which we treat diabetes.   In 1889, the German physiologist, Minkowski, and his associate, Von Mering, surgically removed the pancreas in dogs and thereby produced diabetes.   They did not, however, realize that the disease resulted from a lack of pancreatic insulin, and their finding did not stimulate much progress until 1922, when the Canadian Frederick Banting, and his co-workers extracted insulin from the pancreas, and showed that this hormone can actually abolish not only the Minkowski type of experimental diabetes but also spontaneous kinds.

It subsequently turned out that, some seventeen years earlier, the French physiologist Marcel Eugene Emile Gley had performed experiments similar to Banting's. He had even described them in a private communication, deposited in a sealed envelope with the Société de Biologie. Only in 1922, after Banting's publication, did Gley permit his letter to be opened. It fully supported his claim to have first found insulin. But he received little credit. As Minkowski remarked during an international symposium on diabetes, after Gley violently protested against the injustice of it all, "I know just how you feel. I could also have kicked myself for not having discovered insulin, when I realized how close I came to it."

Obviously, Gley did not recognize the importance of what he saw. He failed to generalize from it, to tie it in with clinical medicine; otherwise he would not have been satisfied to deposit his findings under seal. In fact, it would have been criminal to do so, had he realized that he thereby signed the death warrant of the thousands who succumbed from diabetes for want of insulin. None of Gley's work was comparable in importance to the discovery of insulin. Why did he put it aside, if not because he failed to understand its significance? It is easy to deposit private communications about things we are not sure of, and unseal them when somebody else proves that we were on the right track. To my mind, Gley not only failed to discover insulin but he also proved that he could not do so. By chance he saw it, yet he did not discover it.

The element of chance in basic research is overrated. Chance is a lady who smiles only upon those few who know how to make her smile.

Let us consider a really great achievement of basic research: the observation by Alexander Fleming that penicillin can kill varieties of disease-producing microbes, at dose levels tolerated by man. This is true both in the fact itself and in the obvious inference that penicillin can protect against infections. It is also a generalizable observation. It has enabled other investigators to discover many useful drugs derived, like penicillin, from molds. And, finally, it was surprising to find that molds, which we regarded as contaminators, can have a curative value. Only a highly creative, original mind, one that can completely free itself from established ways of observation, can make such a discovery. Many bacteriologists had seen that cultures of microbes are spoiled when exposed to molds, but all they concluded was that molds must be kept out of such cultures. It took a stroke of genius to see the medicinal promise of the basic observation.

Basic research must, of course, penetrate deep into the unknown without losing contact with known realities. To accomplish this, the scientist must have a peculiar kind of intuition. Perhaps his most important characteristic is a negative one. He must lack prejudice to a degree where he can look at the most "self-evident" facts or concepts without necessarily accepting them, and, conversely, allow his imagination to play with the most unlikely possibilities. In the process he requires serendipity, the gift of finding unsought treasures. (The word was coined by Horace Walpole, in allusion to the fairy tale of The Three Princes of Serendip, who were always discovering, by chance or by sagacity, things they were not seeking.) He must have the power of abstract thinking. Planned steps into the unknown must first be made in the mind, without the concrete support of experience.

The basic researcher must also be able to dream and have faith in his dreams. To make a great dream come true, the first requirement is a great capacity to dream; the second is persistence – a faith in the dream. As for intellect, I repeat what I said in The Stress of Life, "Pure intellect is largely a quality of the middle-class mind. The lowliest hooligan and the greatest creator in the field of human endeavor are motivated mainly by imponderable instincts and emotions, especially faith. Curiously, even scientific research – the most intellectual creative effort of which man is capable – represents no exception in this respect. That is why the objective, detached form of an original scientific publication or of a textbook falls so ludicrously short of really conveying the spirit of an investigation."

Finally, the basic scientist must have all these qualities in the proper proportion. Too great a propensity for abstract thinking may turn him into a bookworm addicted to sterile ratiocination. Too much faith in his dreams can hinder the verification of concepts by experiment. That is why the line of demarcation between the rare genius and the eccentric inventor is often seemingly so indistinct. To the uninitiated, there is much in common between crack brains and cracked brains. Yet it is important to recognize the promising basic scientist early, when he needs support for the development of his singular gifts. The nation's culture, health and strength depend primarily upon its creative basic scientists – the "eggheads."

What is really meant by this now-so-popular term? To my mind, an egghead's main endeavor is to search for the kind of truth that can be verified by experience. The researcher employed by industry may be excellent at his particular job, but usually he does it for a living; rarely is it his main purpose in life. (Of course, if it is, he qualifies as an egghead.) An intellectual may accept a fact unquestioningly on the authority of books or scholars, without feeling the urge to verify it by experience. The theologians who must accept dogma on faith, the teachers who try to disseminate knowledge, the lawyers, engineers or physicians, who apply truths, are all intellectuals and may be very valuable people. But they are not eggheads.

We can no longer afford to allow scientific genius to remain idle for want of money. Nor can we afford to concentrate all our attention upon the physical sciences because of Sputnik. Nuclear war may or may not come, but the war against disease and death from "natural causes" is on now.

The problem, however, goes beyond the mere provision of financial aid to our scientific elite. To adapt ourselves to the spirit of this century we must reassess our whole philosophy and our sense of values. Just as the Stone Age, the Bronze Age and the Iron Age were characterized by the use of stone, bronze and iron, so our era will undoubtedly go down in history as the Age of Basic Research. Man has gained unprecedented power through investigation of natural laws. This power can lead us to the brightest chapter in human history – or the final chapter.

We must ask ourselves one supreme question, and act accordingly to our answer. Shall we fight each other or shall we fight Nature? Men attack men in bitter competition for profit. Nations attempt to exterminate other nations in the struggle for dominance. The real enemy is Nature. Yet we can make Nature our servant. Let man measure his strength against an adversary worthy of the strongest contender, an adversary at once powerful enough to challenge us all and rich enough to providue us all with priceless treasure as long as the universe endures.

There are those who create wealth and those who fight over it. The former are undoubtedly the happier. Wealth is the by-product of their passion. The scientist loves research. The great industrialist does not create jobs for his workers and products for his customers merely to enrich himself, nor does the artist paint chiefly for fame. To these creators the pursuit is not tedious toil, nor are the rewards the ultimate aim of existence. To them wealth and recognition are largely the unexpected, though gratifying, secondary result of what they do for its own sake.

Nature seems to have so arranged matters that her essential objectives are camouflaged, as it were, so that they impress us as the unplanned consequences of something we enjoy doing. (Few people enter the nuptial chamber with the production of a child as their main preoccupation.) That is why the public at large, and often the scientists themselves, do not feel that honors or material rewards are called for. Yet, the man of creative mind must be accorded a privileged position, not as payment, nor because he needs encouragement, nor even to help him in his work, but as the most effective means we have to demonstrate our appreciation of human values to the next generation.

We must educate our children to understand that from now on man's great wars will not be fought with muscle. His battles will not be won by the glorious, intoxicating, momentary courage to face danger and die for a cause. Our children must learn that the great victories in peace and war will be won by warriors of a different stamp, men of intellectual vigor, and by the sober, persistent dedication of their entire lives. They will have to learn that it is far more difficult to live than to die for a cause.

CHAPTER FOUR

Becoming an Immigrant

I obtained my Ph.D. in organic chemistry two years after my M.D., but I never intended to use it, except as an additional qualification to conduct modern medical research. Because I earned my doctorates at such an early age, I was fortunate enough to be granted a Rockefeller Research Fellowship to study in the United States. So few of these opportunities were granted to Czechoslovaks that I know what a large part my chief, Professor Biedl, must have played in securing this extraordinary opportunity for me. I shall always be immensely grateful to him for the persistent enthusiastic efforts he put into sponsoring my application, as this trip decisively influenced my subsequent career.

Those who were born and will die in the same country, or who emigrated because they came to dislike their native land, may not understand the feeling of the perpetual immigrant. When I came to North America I had already been Austrian, Hungarian and Czechoslovak. Although this did not mean changing countries in a geographical sense, it affected my way of looking upon nationality, patriotism and chauvinism. I have always felt a profound urge to belong to a nation that I could be proud of, and it is part of my basic code that I should behave in a way that would make me an asset to my nation. But which nation? Austria? Hungary? Czechoslovakia? Canada?

As a schoolboy under the influence of my father, my predominant childhood surroundings and my typically Hungarian last name, I had been quite a militant Hungarian chauvinist, especially when Komárom was handed over to the Czechoslovaks. Inflamed by the secret irredentist revolutionary arguments of our teachers and the local Hungarian adult population, we school kids wanted to defend our country heroically. Even though the government officially prohibited any celebration of the Hungarian national holiday of March 15th, we organized a big demonstration on the town's soccer field and everyone wore Hungarian costumes (the city folk who had none borrowed their outfits from neighborhood peasants). A few of us went even further and wore large silk ribbons with the red, white and green colors of Hungary. There were too many of us to arrest; but those who had the largest, most provocative ribbons were picked up by the police, and I was among them.

I was duly brought before a Czechoslovak military court which, either out of a sense of fairness or for linguistic reasons, included one Hungarian member, a lawyer whose name I have forgotten. Before my trial began, he told me that since I was obviously unable to state my case properly, he would indicate by predetermined movements of his thumb what replies I should give to fool the judges. This gave me some assurance, but I was nevertheless sick with terror during the two weeks between my arrest and the trial. In the great emotional turmoil of that period, many revolutionaries – even school children – were lined up against a wall and shot summarily for using or even bearing firearms. Although I knew that mine was a minor offense in comparison, I expected the worst. My parents gave me little comfort, thinking that my father's service as an officer in the enemy army would cause the Czechs to be particularly vicious toward me. When the trial finally took place, though stern and grim-looking, the judges were not particularly malevolent and, aided by my friend's thumb, I was saved. The court decided that I had been brainwashed by irresponsible elements and that, in view of my youth, I should be pardoned.

Even this dreadful experience did not cure me of my chauvinism. A few weeks later, a group of my classmates decided that the patriotic thing to do would be to write the Hungarian irredentist motto in large letters on the walls of the main buildings. Between two and four in the morning when nobody was around, that is exactly what I did. Armed with a big bucket of black paint and accompanied by a classmate who acted as a lookout, I adorned the principal buildings with the nationalist slogan:

*Egész Magyarország Menyország
Csonka Magyarország nem Ország.*

(A whole Hungary is God's country
A multilated Hungary is no country.)

Contrary to our expectations, this gesture did not change the course of history.

Once I arrived at Johns Hopkins University in Baltimore, where I was to spend a year in the Department of Biochemical Hygiene before returning to take up my duties in Prague, I realized that it was not very easy to be uprooted again. I sailed to New York on the *President Harding,* a little boat of about 15,000 tons that pitched and rolled throughout the lengthy voyage, during which I was almost uninterruptedly seasick. In the few quiet hours when I was able to get a little fresh air on the deck, I had a chance to speak with some Americans. I immediately discovered that Miss Johnson's Oxford English was far from being the best preparation to understand their colorful expressions and particularly their jokes. After landing in New York, I had to report to the Rockefeller Foundation headquarters. I recall that I was immensely impressed by Broadway, 42nd Street and especially by the Empire State Building. Then I proceeded to Baltimore where I rented a cheap little room with a kitchenette near the university. I started doing research intensely, trying to profit by the one year I hoped to spend under laboratory conditions which were economically so far superior to those we had in Europe. At the same time, I went on a campaign to become rich by saving as much as I could of my princely fellowship of $150 a month.

As I never wanted to depend upon my parents for money, and I knew that once I returned to Prague I would have to purchase my own experimental animals and most other materials needed for research, I accumulated as many greenbacks as possible, confident that they would go a long way to get me the necessities for research back home. I never was very fussy about food and soon found out that I could live very cheaply, even in the United States, by doing my own cooking with inexpensive ingredients. I lived mostly on canned foods, particularly on oversized boxes of the cheapest (ten cents a tin) sardines. This was no great sacrifice for me because I actually liked them; but having had them almost every day for months, I still remember my stay in Baltimore as the "sardine period" of my career.

I immediately began to feel at home, being warmly accepted by the American postdoctoral students at Hopkins; but the official "social life" of the university, supervised by the well-meaning wives of our professors, baffled and even traumatized me. These "community spirited" ladies, evidently guided by the best intentions, continually arranged little parties to which they invited the "poor lonely foreign students." They felt terribly sorry for us. After all, we were so far from home, separated from our loved ones; they assumed we were lost in a foreign country, having no one to "socialize with." I must admit that neither I nor my Central European friends had any difficulty in meeting people of both sexes on our own; and while we were extremely grateful for the good intentions of our hosts, it made us feel awkward to be so patronized.

Besides, the conversations we had with our hostesses and with the professors' daughters who were invited to meet us struck me as unusually primitive, not to say ridiculous. We were encouraged to relax and mix by playing all sorts of social games, including charades. I had never played this game nor had I ever heard of it, but when it was explained to me I was horrified. I could not imagine how these people, evidently the aristocracy of American intelligentsia, could make such perfect fools of themselves playing these silly games. In retrospect, I think I suffered what is technically known in stress research as "cultural shock," the traumatic experience of being completely disoriented when you are suddenly placed into a society whose customs are totally different from your own.

Despite Miss Johnson's valiant efforts, I also had linguistic difficulties. I once congratulated a girl on her beautiful complexion, saying that her hide was of the finest quality. For reasons I could not understand, she did not really consider this a great compliment. How could she know that in none of the languages I spoke was there any way of differentiating between skin and hide? On another occasion I met a girl at a party and offered to walk her home. Since I felt that she was really nice, I asked her whether we could meet again, perhaps to go for a walk or a movie. "Yes," she said, "but will you give me a ring first?" I was petrified, believing she meant an engagement ring. At home I had heard many exaggerated stories about the fierce enforcement of "breach-of-promise" laws in the United States, and I was shocked to think that you could not ask a girl out for a walk or a movie without being engaged to her.

Although work at the lab proceeded extremely well, I found the official university social life at Hopkins around the beginning of 1930 intolerable. I became so nostalgic that I could not stand it any longer. I desperately wanted to go home; but after all the trouble Professor Biedl had taken to get me this scholarship, I really could not let him down by abandoning such an unusual opportunity for postgraduate studies at an excellent school, thereby perhaps even spoiling the chances of his other students for similar privileges in the future.

It was at that time that I met a few Canadians at Hopkins who told me that Canada was much more European, with its English and French cultural traditions. As I greatly admired Professor J. B. Collip, one of Canada's most distinguished biochemists, I asked for a transfer to McGill University to complete the second half of my Rockefeller Fellowship under his direction. Much to my relief, this was granted without difficulty. I subsequently found out that some Canadians also play charades, and that not all of American social life revolves around such games. By now I find it difficult to understand my initial reaction.

When I arrived at the Canadian border (by bus, to save money), we were met by the Quebec customs and immigration people. As I had not spoken French for quite a while, I looked forward to exchanging a few words with them in their own language. But, oh horror! It turned out that Madame Totier's French was no better preparation for Quebec than Miss Johnson's teaching was for the United States. I did not understand half of what they were telling me. At first I thought that perhaps they were English-Canadians, but they assured me that they were pure Québecois and gave me the feeling that my French was mere affectation. As I became more sensitive to the situation in Canada, I recognized that the people of Quebec had as much right to speak their own variant of French as I had to speak Viennese German, a dialect that a Prussian would consider most peculiar (in fact, I invariably use "the Austrian language" with defiance, even though I can speak perfect Hochdeutsch).

In any event, I spent the second half of that year in Montreal doing research in the Department of Biochemistry at McGill; and by the time I was ready to return to Czechoslovakia, I had become thoroughly adapted to North America, both above and below the Canadian border.

Soon after my return to Prague, the chief of our institute died. The man who replaced Biedl was a cardiologist and I did not like him or his research field, which he wanted me to adopt; so I had to consider finding another job. By sheer coincidence, just at that time I received an offer from Professor Collip to return to Montreal as a lecturer in biochemistry at McGill and I grabbed this opportunity. Once again, I was on my way to North America.

I was first adopted by English-speaking Canadians when I started my academic career at McGill. I then became integrated into French Canada, where I feel equally at home; perhaps even a little more, as I have spent more time here at the *Université de Montréal.*

I never really had any wish to sever my relations with the country of my birth, even though the Austro-Hungarian Empire no longer exists. When I give lectures in Austria or in Hungary, I am frequently asked, "How can you be a good Canadian if you are a native son of Vienna and had a Hungarian father? Did you sever your roots?" I try to explain that when my second son was born, it did not diminish my love for the first. Today the country to which I am most attached is Canada, where I have spent forty-six happy years, but this does not imply that I like my other countries any less than before my immigration.

Evidently, a change of countries provides new, or at least different, problems to confront. One family incident that occurred years later is still very amusing to me. My daughter Marie was five years old at the time and like most children of her age made mistakes in grammar or pronunciation. We speak French at home and, as I am rather sensitive about the proper usage of language, I always corrected her. She took my criticism quite calmly, until one day when she had a temper tantrum (also not unusual among five-year-olds), and said, "Daddy, I know you're right, but I'm sick of you correcting me!   French is my native language, and you're just an immigrant!"

Looking back on my youth, I feel enriched by my experiences on several counts. When I go to Vienna, no one regards me as a foreigner, especially because I speak the local Viennese German. I am equally at home in Hungary. My own background helps me to understand the problems of both principal Canadian language groups without prejudice, and makes me very conscious of the difficulties resulting from the coexistence between French- and English-Canadians, at the same time allowing me to view the situation with a certain detachment.

I am also grateful for the combined qualities I inherited from my parents. I loved them both, but in very different ways. I admired my father but also pitied him in a way, perhaps because of his introverted personality and timidity which made it difficult for him to give vent to his feelings.

On the other hand, my mother was very impulsive, and I have inherited this feature from her. She was extremely active and intelligent, always wanting to surpass herself, to achieve the excellence she so much respected. After we lost all our belongings in World War I, it was really she who founded and administered the Selye Clinic.   True, she could not have done this without my father's surgical expertise, but he would not have gone very far without the good business sense of my mother.

Even though I left my native land I still maintained ties with my European heritage, because my parents remained behind. My father died in Budapest at an advanced age (although about six years younger than I am now) while taking a walk in a park. It was never established whether he suffered a stroke or a cardiac accident. My mother was killed accidently during the Hungarian uprising of 1956. She watched the entrance of the Soviet troops, and during the ensuing shooting a stray bullet struck her between the eyes. She was seventy-six years old. I learned about her death from the Canadian Embassy in Budapest, and it left me with a feeling of emptiness, but the distance in time and space also helped soften the blow.

Under the same circumstances, many of my former Hungarian compatriots may have been marked by a lasting hatred for the communists. But I do not even know whether the bullet came from the gun of a Hungarian or a Soviet. The behavior of one soldier, who might take pleasure in killing an old woman because he is drunk with the glory of victory, could hardly influence my attitude toward an entire nation or political philosophy.

CHAPTER FIVE

The Birth of the Stress Concept

It was in Canada that the ideas I had begun to formulate at the University Hospital of Prague started to take shape, and a concept was formed that still dominates my life. Wherever I go to lecture or to participate in discussions devoted to stress, I am always asked what made me first think of this concept. The story has been told many times, both in my own books and in those of others; yet this autobiography would not be complete if I did not include it, as it is not only at the basis of research on stress in general but more particularly of the stress of my life.

As far as I can remember, I first thought of what I later called "biologic stress" when I was a second-year student at the University of Prague. During the first two years of our curriculum, we were never confronted with a patient; we followed exclusively pre-clinical courses in anatomy, histology and biochemistry. It was only at the end of the second year that the great moment arrived which is awaited with so much anticipation by all students of medicine, that of being faced for the first time with a patient. I will always remember the first lesson of our eminent internist, Professor von Jaksch, one of the most famous hematologists of that period. The subject of his introductory lecture was diagnosis. He asked his assistants to bring him five patients, specially chosen from different services of the University Hospital, who suffered from completely unrelated maladies. In every case he could arrive at the correct diagnosis by merely asking questions and looking for specific signs and symptoms of disease. I was deeply impressed by the logic of his interrogation and the precision of his observations, based on many years of experience. Almost all the manifestations of illness which he examined and nearly all the questions he asked concerned diagnostic indexes, the very existence of which was unknown to me.

For example, I remember that he looked for the reactions of a patient's pupils to light and for a series of other reflexes. In the case of a child sent over from the pediatrics clinic with a high fever, he examined the inner surface of the cheek, on which he discovered little while spots, and immediately he exclained, "Measles!" He then explained to us that these little spots were first described by Professor Koplik and are known as "Koplik spots." They are neither painful nor likely to turn into anything dangerous, but they are quite characteristic of measles. In a similar manner he managed to identify the cause of the disease in every case. I must admit that he had a little luck, because this is not always possible by mere inspection and questioning; yet it was an awe-inspiring spectacle to see that medicine had progressed so far that it was now possible for an experienced physician to make a correct diagnosis in so many different cases, even without the use of any complicated instrumentation or chemical examination.

However, as soon as I recovered from the first emotional impact of my boundless admiration, I began to wonder why the professor did not say a word about all those signs and symptoms of disease which were perfectly obvious even to me, without any previous knowledge of practical medicine, and which even the patients must have recognized, for they were what induced them to seek medical advice. All five patients, whatever their disease (one suffered from cancer of the stomach, another from tuberculosis, yet another from intense burns), had something in common: *they all looked and felt sick.* This may seem ridiculously childish and self-evident, but it was because I wondered about the obvious that the concept of "stress" was born in my mind.

Just look around and examine sick people. They are all indisposed, they look tired, have no appetite, gradually lose weight, they do not feel like going to work, they prefer to lie down rather than to stand up. Today, we would say they show non-specific manifestations of disease. They all present a syndrome (which means a group of symptoms and signs that appear together) simply indicative of being ill. That is why I baptized this state that so attracted my attention as "the syndrome of just being sick."

I wondered why nobody had ever given this syndrome any special attention. With all the methods of modern medicine, physicians had looked for and analyzed the more subtle and unexpected signs of disease, but nobody seemed to pay any attention to the most common malady, "the syndrome of just being sick." Why didn't anybody study its biochemical manifestations, try to establish its mechanism, and perhaps even attempt to find some treatment likely to combat the most frequent morbid changes that all maladies have in common? This struck me as the most fundamental problem in medicine.

In my youthful enthusiasm (I was nineteen at the time), I rushed to our professor of physiology, explaining my ideas and asking him for permission to work on developing them in his laboratory during free weekends or after study hours.

The most humiliating conversation ensued, one that I shall never forget. Our professor's full name, including his titles, was Hofrat Professor Doktor Armin Tschermak Edler (Nobleman) von Seysenegg. It was a little awkward to repeat this whenever we addressed him, so it was generally agreed that at least his highest title, "Hofrat" (Counsel to the Imperial Court), should be used, and he expected to be called "Herr Hofrat." Unfortunately, I did not know this and simply addressed him as "Herr Professor." This was apparently the only part of my long, enthusiastic speech that caught his attention because when I finished extolling all the merits of my new concept of disease, his only remark was cuttingly sarcastic: "Well, if you are that chummy, why don't you just call me by my first name, Armin?"

Even after profuse apologies for my ignorance and sincere assurances of my profound respect, the great man remained unresponsive to my request. He advised me to prepare for exams instead of wasting time on futilities. In fact, he said that this idea was so childish that it wasn't even worth discussing. "Obviously," he said, "if a person is sick he looks it. What is so special about this? If a man is fat he looks fat." I felt that the comparison was not valid. A fat person naturally looks fat; in making such a diagnosis you merely state a single fact that you see. But it is quite different to make the generalization that the most diverse diseases have certain characteristics in common; in other words, that there exists a stereotyped syndrome which characterizes disease as such.

During this whole period I was obsessed with the thought that there existed specialists in every branch of medicine – there were physicians who looked after diseases of the eyes, the ears, the joints – but no one had yet tried to specialize in the most common and hence most important syndrome: that of sickness as such. I wondered why the already well-known methods of exact scientific investigation, of looking for quantitatively measurable biochemical, microscopic or functional changes, could not be employed to clarify the mechanism of "the syndrome of just being sick." Once this mystery was solved we might even succeed in suppressing the stereotyped manifestations of illness in all patients, whatever the specific underlying cause of their particular malady. We might prevent the loss of weight, the feeling of weakness and other less uniformly displayed but still quite common disease manifestations, such as generalized aches and pains, inflammation or loss of energy.   After all, we already knew that antipyretics could restore body temperature to normal in different kinds of fever, and we had found that analgesics would diminish pain due to diverse causes.   It seemed plausible, therefore, that treatment could be directed against the nonspecific manifestations, rather than against particular disease producers.

However, passing my examinations was in fact a more immediate necessity and since our professor, and even my classmates, discouraged me and ridiculed my ideas, I returned to the routine of daily studies in the standard courses of our medical school.

CHAPTER SIX

The First Experiments

It was ten years later that I again encountered "the syndrome of just being sick." This happened in 1936, two years after my arrival in Canada. At that time I worked at McGill as an assistant to Professor J. B. Collip, whom I so admired as the discoverer of the parathyroid hormone and one of the early co-workers of Sir Frederick Banting, who played an instrumental role in the first purification of insulin preparations. It was then that I hit upon my "obvious" yet unacceptable syndrome for a second time but in an entirely different form, at first without even remembering my original observations in the classroom of Professor von Jaksch in Prague.

In those days, only two types of female sex hormones were known, but Professor Collip suspected that there might be a third one yet to be identified. He assigned to me my first academic task in Canada: I was to go out to the slaughterhouse with a large bucket and bring it back to him as rapidly as possible, filled with the ovaries of freshly slaughtered cows. I may say that I accomplished this with singular distinction. I got back in record time: the ovaries were still hot and the bucket was full to the brim. He made various extracts of this material and, as I was the youngest member of the academic staff, I was assigned the tedious task of injecting these into female rats and looking for any kind of change produced that could not be ascribed to one of the known hormones of the ovary. When it came to performing autopsies on these animals, I expected to find changes in their sex organs. Instead, to my surprise, I observed a curious syndrome that no other ovarian hormone was known to produce, namely an enlargement of the adrenal glands, with signs of increased endocrine (hormone-producing) activity; atrophy of the lymphatic system, including the thymus (which at that time was not yet known to have a defensive function in the production of immune reactions); and peptic ulcers of the stomach and upper intestine (especially the duodenum).

Was this syndrome characteristic of some new ovarian hormone or merely the result of the toxicity of the extract? In order to answer this question, I injected more rats with extracts prepared from various organs other than ovaries as well as with highly toxic substances such as formalin. Curiously, all these exerted the same changes that I have previously referred to: adrenal hyperactivity, lymphatic atrophy and gastrointestinal ulcers.

Evidently, I thought, we were on the wrong track in our efforts to identify a new ovarian hormone. Then, suddenly, I remembered my early observations as a medical student in Prague. Maybe all my injections merely damaged the rats, producing "the syndrome of just being sick." It was then that I thought of putting some rats on the wind-swept roof of the medical building at McGill during our cold Canadian winter. They were obviously uncomfortable and shivered in their cages; but after surviving in this unnatural habitat for about a day or so, they again all showed the same signs that I had seen after the injections. In further pursuring these experiments I placed animals in barrel-like revolving treadmills driven by an electric motor; there they had to run constantly to stay upright. This forced muscular effort again produced the same syndrome.

It gradually turned out that no matter what type of damage I inflicted upon an experimental animal, if it survived long enough and the stressor was sufficiently strong, the typical combination would be produced: adrenal hyperactivity, lymphatic atrophy and peptic ulcers. Evidently, what I saw was the nonspecific response to any kind of challenge, a phenomenon which I later called "biologic stress." I first published these findings (at the age of twenty-nine) as a short letter to the editor in the British journal *Nature*, under the title *A Syndrome Produced by Diverse Nocuous Agents.*

I began to wonder what might be the cause of other changes which, although not totally nonspecific or common to all maladies, seemed to affect such a considerable portion of the population. I asked myself, for instance, why so many people suffer from heart disease, high blood pressure, arthritis or mental disturbances. These are not completely stereotyped signs of all illness, yet they are so frequent that I could not help suspecting some nonspecific common factor in their causation.

These problems continued to intrigue me. Could it be possible that all these maladies were only expressions of the common signs of stress and aggression, modified by individual predisposition for one or the other type of response? For example, the stereotyped nervous and hormonal reaction during stress might hit one or the other organ selectively, depending upon an inherited or acquired predisposition which made this the weakest part of the body. Consequently, this organ would be most likely to break down under the strain of a general effort to meet the demands of life.

I discussed this probelm with various professors and colleagues at McGill, but did not succeed in "selling my idea" that there was something to be gained from studies along these lines.

Nowadays it is perhaps difficult to appreciate just how absurd my ideas about stress seemed to most people before I had more facts to substantiate them. For example, I admired J. B. Collip very much and respected his opinion and, even though he was my chief, I thought of him as a real fatherly friend who seriously wanted to help me with my research efforts. One day – during these hectic weeks – he asked me into his office for a good heart-to-heart talk. He reminded me that for months he had attempted to convince me that I must abandon this futile line of research. He assured me that, in his opinion, I possessed all the essential qualifications of an investigator and that I could undoubtedly contribute something, even to the generally recognized and accepted fields of endocrinology, so why bother with this wild-goose chase?

I met these remarks only with my usual outbursts of juvenile enthusiasm for a new point of view; I outlined again the immense possibilities inherent in a study of the nonspecific damage which must accompany all diseases and all but the mildest treatments.

When he saw me thus launched on another enraptured description of what I observed in animals treated with this or that impure toxic material, he looked at me with desperately sad eyes and cried: "But, Selye, try to realize what you are doing before it is too late! You have now decided to spend your entire life studying the meaningless side-effects of disease. I am even tempted to look upon your work as the pharmacology of dirt!"

Of course, he was right. Nobody could have expressed it more poignantly; that is why it hurt so much that I remember the phrase after some forty years. Still, to me the "pharmacology of dirt" – that is, the response to anything that makes a demand for adaptation – seemed the most promising subject in medicine.

Yet, as time went by, I often doubted the wisdom of my decision. So few among the recongized, experienced investigators, whose judgment one could usually trust, agreed with my views and, after all, was it not silly and pretentious for a beginner to contradict them? Perhaps I had just developed a warped point of view, perhaps I was merely wasting my time?

In such moments of doubt, I derived considerable strength and courage from the fact that, right from the beginning, one of the most respected Canadian scientists, Sir Frederick Banting, expressed interest in my plans. At that time, he was often visiting university laboratories throughout the country since he acted as an advisor to the National Research Council. When in Montreal, he often dropped into my somewhat overcrowded little laboratory. There was not much space and he usually settled down on top of the desk, listening with interest to my day-dreaming about "the syndrome of being sick." Nothing could have done me more good! He also helped to secure the first modest financial aid ($500) for this kind of research, but that was comparatively unimportant. More than anything in the world I needed his moral support, the reassuring feeling that the discoverer of insulin took me seriously. I often wonder whether I could have stuck by my guns without his pat on the shoulder.

The stress concept continued to be attacked for various reasons for the next few decades. Even now there are scientists who disagree with special aspects of it, but most of its principal tenets are no longer under debate. Indeed, the concept of biological stress has been included in medical and psychological textbooks throughout the world and, since it affects everybody, it has become one of the most popular problems of modern medicine.

I have told these anecdotes about the early background to my work many times since they were first published in my book, *The Story of the Adaptation Syndrome,* in 1952. I relate them frequently nowadays during lectures to students, because they show how difficult it is to convince people of new ways of looking at things, and they help others to understand the very essence of the stress response. I have included them again in this book because these events are perhaps the most essential parts of the stress of my life.

In continuing my work, the first task I set myself was to identify the mechanisms through which so many demands requiring adaptation could produce the same characteristic stereotyped manifestations of the stress response.

I had reason to believe that a common pathway goes through the hypophysis, an endocrine gland situated just below the brain, so I developed a reasonably simple surgical technique permitting the removal of this gland. It turned out that animals deprived of their hypophysis become comparatively more susceptible to a great variety of demands and cannot cope through the usual defensive mechanisms – for example, adrenal enlargement. However, other stress manifestations are apparently independent of the hypophysis since they persist even in its absence.

At a recent international congress on stress sponsored by the World Health Organization, I proposed the following definition: *Stress is the nonspecific response of the body to any demand.*

Through improved technology it has become possible to show that not only "nocuous agents," disease and damage, but even demands for adaptation to pleasant or healthy new circumstances will evoke the objective, measurable characteristic indexes of stress, especially a rise in the blood concentration of certain endocrine products which I have called stress hormones. Particularly important among these are:

1. ACTH (the *a*drenocortico*t*rophic *h*ormone of the hypophysis).
2. Adrenalin and noradrenalin (more correctly referred to as epinephrine and norepinephrine respectively.) These are secreted by the inner core portion of the adrenals, two little endocrine glands situated just above the kidneys on each side.

3. The substances which I have designated as corticoids. These are hormones produced by the peripheral portion or cortex of the adrenals; of this group, cortisone is perhaps the best-known representative.

4. CRF, a neurohormone – that is to say, a hormone produced by nerve cells. This was discovered by my former postdoctoral student and now professor at the Salk Institute, Dr. Roger Guillemin, conjointly with Drs. Schally, Saffran and others. CRF performs a key role in the stress response. Nervous impulses (arriving at the base of the brain in the region called the hypothalamus) elicit this comparatively simple chemical compound which can now be isolated, the main function of which is to instruct the pituitary (hypophysis) to produce ACTH. The latter, in turn, stimulates the adrenal cortex to secrete corticoids. Other hypothalamic nerve stimuli which do not pass through the pituitary stimulate the adrenal medulla and certain nerve endings in the body to produce epinephrine and norepinephrine. All of these are hormonal substances necessary for adaptation and defense.

Incidentally, Roger Guillemin, in collaboration with several other investigators, discovered another type of hormone in brain tissue, particularly in the hypothalamus but also in the pituitary. These "endorphins" are chemically similar to ACTH, being *endogenous* and having *morphine*-like anti-pain properties. They probably also play an important role in the stress response. Guillemin shared the Nobel Prize in Medicine for this discovery in 1977 and has just sent me a special chapter on endorphins and stress, co-authored with some of his team members, for inclusion in *Selye's Guide to Stress Research,* which, will be published by Van Nostrand Reinhold. It will be an annual anthology of scientific data in all fields related to stress, with chapters written by specialists selected on the basis of their particular competence in the most timely aspects of the stress concept as it develops.

To clarify the role of these and many other mechanisms that are involved in the stress response we had to do a great deal of experimental work.

First of all, I removed the adrenals of experimental animals (leaving the pituitary intact) and then exposed these animals to well-known stress-producing agents.   In the absence of the pituitary, stress was no longer associated with any visible structural or biochemical change in the adrenal cortex.   Obviously, the pituitary was necessary to send the message of stress to the adrenal cortex.

Then gradually the other pathways were clarified.   In animals subjected to various agents demanding adaptation, the first stress response was what we called the "alarm reaction," during which the pituitary produced an unusually high amount of its ACTH, and this resulted in considerable corticoid secretion.   However, under the influence of prolonged exposure to similar agents the alarm reaction was followed by the "stage of resistance," during which the animals could meet demands with little increase in their basic ACTH and corticoid production.   Finally, the "exhaustion phase" set in and eventually the animals succumbed to stress, having exhausted their adaptive capabilities or "adaptation energy."

Under certain circumstances animals in a state of stress develop diseases which I have called "stress diseases" or "diseases of adaptation" – for example, heart accidents, nervous exhaustion, etc.   All of these are reminiscent of the maladies occuring during constant intense stress in people.   It became clear that many of these diseases were the result of inappropriate functioning of the pituitary and adrenals during emergencies arising from demands for adaptation to changing circumstances.   To better understand the implications of these findings, let us keep in mind that the same phenomena can be observed every day all around us.   For years most of us resist the stress caused by preoccupations, frustrations, physical fatigue, tension, overwork, chronic infections and innumerable other factors that demand adaptation.   Finally, however, there comes a day when a normally well-balanced person begins to show signs of increased blood pressure, the overworked businessman suffers a heart attack, or the mother with the responsibilities of a large family and a demanding husband begins to notice the signs of a gastrointestinal peptic ulcer.

There is no point in discussing the technical details of the countless experiments I had to perform in order to furnish scientific evidence for all this. Suffice it to say that at this stage of research my main endeavor was to prove that an excess of certain stress hormones was producing the majority of all the experimental diseases in my animals. If this were so, at least in suitably pre-pared and thereby predisposed animals, injection of the same hormones would have to produce lesions comparable to those induced in them by stress itself.

Among the many hormones normally secreted by the pituitary (in addition to the previously mentioned ACTH, which stimulates the adrenals) a substance which I called STH appeared to play an important role in modifying the changes characteristic of "the syndrome of just being sick." Also known under the name *so-matotrophic hormone*, STH was long recognized as the "growth hormone" since it stimulates the growth of young animals and children. Among the corticoids, *d*esoxy*c*orticosterone, normally given as the *a*cetate (DCA), appeared to be particularly involved in causing high blood pressure and certain renal lesions that I thought to be associated with stress. I administered enormous doses of DCA to rats and, in agreement with my expectations, within a short time they did in fact develop high blood pressure and such lesions in the heart, vessels and kidneys as are normally seen in certain common types of human hypertension (high blood pres-sure). Similarly, under very special conditions, DCA also induced inflammatory lesions in the joints not unlike those seen in cases of rheumatism.

In 1944, I published the results of these experiments in *The Journal of the American Medical Association*. By that time it was evident that hormonal disturbances play an important role in the development of various diseases normally related to the stress of life. Such hormonal disturbances might be an excess, a deficiency or a faulty proportion between the production of two antagonistic hormones. If so, this would offer interesting therapeutic possibilities.

During all this time, one date retained a special importance for my work: 1936. It was then that I sent my previously men-tioned letter to the editor of *Nature* under a title which already gave the approximate definition of what is now called "biological stress." It was a syndrome attributed to damage, toxicity and the demand for adaptation to all kinds of injury. Before that time nobody suspected that there might exist such a stereotyped syndrome caused by damage as such. Of course, there are syndromes characteristic of leprosy, of typhoid, of cancer, or any other disease, but it was difficult to imagine a syndrome that characterizes no particular disease. This short article of a single column was the first on the subject. It is interesting to note, in contrast, that now an average of about eight thousand publications (technical articles, books) are printed on this topic each year.

New developments since that time have forced me to modify the definition implied in that first paper. Instead of my phrase "the syndrome produced by diverse *nocuous* agents," the present definition of stress emphasizes that the syndrome can be produced by *any* agent. We now know that demands for adaptation can also be made by agents which are not nocuous; but with the coarse methods (primarily inspection of the organs with the naked eye) available to me in 1936, it would have been impossible to recognize the moderate stressor effect of healthy, pleasant agents.

Nowadays we have sophisticated biochemical tests that can detect minute elevations in the blood concentration of certain substances, mainly stress hormones (ACTH, corticoids, adrenalin, etc.), which the body produces even when it has to adapt itself to very mild stress situations. In a sense, one might say that these stress hormones are furnished upon demand, through cybernetic self-regulation by the "pharmacy" of our own body. In any event, with today's techniques we can even detect stress caused by adaptation to agreeable and healthy new circumstances. We can now provide concrete evidence that great joy can produce the same nonspecific biochemical changes in the body as intense pain.

What impressed me as most typical of the stress syndrome, and what proved to be its most essential characteristic, was this feature of *nonspecificity*. Once you have understood this you have grasped the very essence of the stress concept as applied to medicine, psychology, sociology or any other field.

It is not difficult to diagnose such diseases as leprosy or typhoid by their specific features. But it seems impossible to recognize the particular signs of something that has none. Yet the concept of nonspecificity is useful even apart from what we call disease. For example, when you are cold you shiver; that is a specific response to cold, and it helps you to generate heat by muscular work. In the heat you perspire, because evaporation of fluid helps you to cool down. These are specific responses to heat and cold. However, superimposed upon them is the ever-present nonspecific syndrome that is produced by the most diverse agents.

Even the stress caused by the same experience may produce different specific responses in different people. Of course, all agents elicit specific results: insulin decreases blood sugar while adrenalin increases it. Apart from these specific effects, the agents also create a general demand for adaptation, a need to reestablish a normal state. It is this need that is nonspecific.

Explaining the concept of nonspecificity to scientists has been one of the most frustrating parts of my research career. Oddly enough, the general public never had difficulty with this notion, but among highly competent scientists – including those specializing in stress – there has always been a disturbing amount of confusion about this point.

I try to explain nonspecificity by comparing it to energy utilization. The same amount of energy – say, electricity – is required, whether formed by mechanical means (a waterfall, fire, burning coal) or by the liberation of nuclear power. And no matter where that energy comes from, it is nonspecific as to its final effect: we may use it for cooling or heating, lighting a room or ringing a bell.

I never fail to convince my colleagues of this as long as I have them sitting in front of me, listening as I present this analogy step by step. They all agree that although leprosy, typhoid and ecstatic pleasure have their own individual features and are due to different causes, they nevertheless result in the common need for the body to adjust to a demand for adaptation. However, as soon as they return to their offices and come across a patient, these same physicians will again say, "But can't you see that no matter how we argue theoretically, the fact is that every disease is different, and that leprosy is not the same as ecstatic joy!"

I can only assume that something is wrong with my mode of teaching because this confusion about nonspecificity exists even today. Whatever the reason, it has often driven me to despair that what I consider to be the very simplest, and yet the most fundamental, aspect of the stress concept is so frequently misunderstood.

A great friend and former colleague of mine at McGill, David Landsborough Thomson, once discussed a similar problem in an address on "Science and Poetry" published posthumously in the *Aberdeen University Review*. Simplification, he says, is one of the most important characteristics of science; complex problems must be taken apart, each piece being examined separately.

> In high school physics we are told about gravity and the laws of falling bodies – thirty-two feet per second "neglecting the resistance of the air." The situation in real life, where there is air and it does create friction, is much more complicated; but the fundamental law can be worked out only be setting the complications on one side, to be dealt with later. This device runs all through science; we talk of a "perfect" (and nonexistent) gas, we carry our experiments at a constant temperature, and so on . . . The mechanics of the heavenly bodies really could not be worked out in terms of real objects in a real context; it was not until Galileo and Descartes taught us to think first of imaginary, ideal objects, in empty Euclidean space, that the true laws became clear.

Without the ability to extract the abstract concept of nonspecificity from particular cases, the mechansims of stress would never have been worked out.

I selected the term "stress" because in science there is a certain reluctance to introduce new words for a new concept if an existing one can be adapted to a special scientific usage. As the highly respected father of modern genetics, Eugene Opie, Professor of Pathology at Cornell University Medical College and later at the Rockefeller Institute in New York, put it: "A new name is like a window in a vacant house. Every boy who passes has an urge to throw a stone at it."

Since you cannot always characterize a new concept by enumerating all its features, there are only two solutions: either you invent a name, opening yourself to criticism for your seemingly immodest bid for originality, or you use an already accepted word in a newly defined sense.   Instead of creating even more antagonism by a neologism, I opted for the second choice, having many eminent precedents to lean on.

Pavlov, for example, used the term "conditioning" for the new concept of conditioned reflexes, although the word, in the sense of "creating the conditions for something," had long been in existence.   In fact, the same word continues to take on many new connotations – for instance, in the case of "air conditioning," which obviously has nothing to do with the Pavlovian idea. We use the term ourselves in stress research, to mean "setting the conditions for a certain type of response to stress," in the form of a disease or a physiological phenomenon.

In seeking a name for my theory, I borrowed the term from English physics, where "stress" refers to the interaction between a force and the resistance to it.   I merely added an adjective to emphasize that I was using the word in a special sense, and baptized my child "biological stress."   But, frankly, when I made this choice I did not speak English well enough to know the difference between "stress" and "strain."   In physics, "stress" refers to an agent which acts upon a resistant body attempting to deform it, whereas "strain" indicates the changes that are induced in the affected object.   Consequently I should have called my syndrome the "strain syndrome."   However, I was not aware of this subtle difference; besides, at first I did not clearly distinguish between the causative agent and its effect upon the body.

It was not until many years later that the *British Medical Journal* called my attention to this regrettable oversight in an editorial comment stating somewhat sarcastically that, according to Selye, stress is its own cause. They were right! I should have distinguished between stress and that which causes it. I should have spoken of biological "strain" elicited by biological "stress." However, by that time it was too late to change my term, as it had been generally accepted, not only in English but also in all foreign languages. Now I was really in trouble!

It was then that I decided that, after all, I had to introduce a neologism into the English language – namely the term "stressor."

This permitted me to retain the term "biological stress," to mean the response for which it had been most generally used, and "stressor" for the agent that induces it. To try to make this common source of misunderstanding clear, let me repeat that what corresponds to "strain" in English physics is called "stress" in biology; what is designated as "stress" in physics is known as a "stressor" in the life sciences. This terminology has been generally accepted.

After this first linguistic problem was resolved, I became aware of another unexpected complication in terminology, for I learned that no word corresponded exactly to "stress" in other languages. Hence, these merely adapted my original English term; some without hesitation, others only after endless and often bitter efforts to replace it by a native word. When I transferred my activities from the English McGill University to the French Université de Montréal, a professor of physics told me that the word stress was not employed in the French literature of physics and engineering. This caused me little trouble in dealing with students, because, after I explained the word, they accepted it without hesitation. The problem became traumatic – not to mention stressful – when I had the great honor of being invited by France's most venerable institute of learning, the Collège de France, to give a series of lectures in Paris on this new topic. As I was being led to the podium, my friend Robert Courrier, permanent secretary of the French Academy of Medicine, whispered into my ear what he thought to be a most innocuous remark: "I do not know, Professor Selye, whether you are aware of it, but in this institution for several decades, it has been accepted as a tradition that all professors participate in the first lecture of an invited foreign speaker, and sitting in the first row before you, you will have the most eminent Frenchmen of letters, the custodians of the purity of the French language." Well, it was too late to think about it and I used the Anglicism throughout my address, but in the discussion, the linguists who wanted to contribute something attempted to find a suitable word for stress in French. As we went along, the discussion became so scholarly I did not understand very much of it – except that, at the end, they did agree on a proper, generally acceptable French designation. They pointed out that in French the word *agression* had been – and to some extent still is – violently defended as an alternative for stress in my sense, although a passionate kiss or a game of tennis could hardly be so designated. The same objection must be made to *stimulation*. Stimulation can be highly specific; for example, the sensation of green is caused only by a certain wavelength of light acting upon the retina and, hence, it could not be included in the definition of a nonspecific response to any demand. So my term won the linguistic battle, and *le stress* can now be found in any French medical dictionary.

The word "stressor" caused less of an argument, although it had to be slightly changed to adapt to French usage, and a stressor agent is generally referred to as *agent stressant* or *stresseur*. In any event, whatever the value of my scientific work, I do have the satisfaction of having enriched virtually every language in the world by at least one term.

The relationship between stress in physics and biological stress is easily appreciated if we think, for instance, of a chain placed under physical tension – that is, stress. No matter what pulls on the chain and no matter in which direction, the result is the same – that is, nonspecific. The chain is faced with a demand for resistance. Just as in the chain the weakest link (or in a machine, the least-resistant part) is most likely to break down, so in the human body there is always one organ or system which, owing to heredity or external influences, is the weakest and most likely to break down under the condition of general biological stress. In some people the heart, in others the nervous system or the gastro-intestinal tract, may represent this weakest link. That is why people develop different types of disease under the influence of the same kind of stressors.

These were the considerations that led to the concept of the "diseases of adaptation," which are primarily elicited by stress and yet can take on the most difficult forms in different people.

To prove all this, many years of experimentation were necessary. In one series of tests, I placed rats on different diets and noted that a high intake of sodium (present in kitchen salt) or a deficiency in potassium predisposes the heart to infarcts (cardiac accidents) under the influence of stress, whereas fasting predisposes the stomach to peptic ulcers. The influence of this predisposition or conditioning has been demonstrated since then by so many scientists in so many experiments that hardly any doubt can remain about its importance.

CHAPTER SEVEN

"Selye's Syndrome"

Stress is present in us during the entire course of exposure to a nonspecific demand, be it of short duration or prolonged over many years. But we have to distinguish between stress at any one moment and the total response to chronically applied stressors. This total response evolves in the previously mentioned three phases: the alarm reaction, the stage of resistance and the stage of exhaustion. This entire triphasic response is called the "general adaptation syndrome" (G.A.S.) and is sometimes referred to in the literature as "Selye's syndrome."

It is general because it affects the body as a whole and not just one particular region. In this, it differs from the "local adaptation syndrome" (L.A.S.), the nonspecific response of the body to a localized demand – for example that made by a burn, an insect bite or the fatigue of an overstrained muscle group. Although this L.A.S. is very important to physicians, it is comparatively less interesting to the public at large, because its implications in everyday life are few; hence, we shall not deal with it here. Suffice it to point out that local stressors are specific to the extent that they primarily affect one or the other organ system, not because it is the weakest link (as in the G.A.S.) but because in the L.A.S., the stressor is only applied to a group of muscles, a region of the skin or some other circumscribed part.

Stress can result from tensions within a family, at work, or from the restraining influence of social taboos or traditions. In fact, any situation in life that makes demands upon our adaptive mechanism creates stress. From a psychological point of view, the most stressful experiences are frustration, failure and humiliation – in other words, distressing events. On the other hand, we derive a great deal of energy and stimulation, considerable force and pleasure from victories and success. These give us ambition for work, a feeling of youth and of great vitality. As the saying goes, nothing generates more success than success, or more failure than failure. We are encouraged and invigorated by our victories, whereas constant defeat eventually deprives us even of the motivation to try.

Although these obvious differences exist between the effects of pleasant and unpleasant experiences, in biological terms both have a common effect – they cause stress. Even such happy sensations as great joy or ecstasy cause stress, for we must adapt to *any* demands made upon us, be they favorable or unfavorable. This kind of good stress is known as *eustress* (from the Greek "*eu*" = good, as in euphoria, euphonia). Distress is much more likely than eustress to cause disease, although there is evidence that both can be harmful under certain circumstances. There is still no compelling scientific explanation for this, but perhaps eustress (for instance, ecstasy) is less likely to be harmful because it rarely equals the intensity and duration of suffering. Besides, it is merely a matter of conditioning that determines whether we perceive a particular experience as pleasant or unpleasant. The event itself is always a stressor causing the same stress. Conditioning can only modify our perception of the event as being either pleasing or displeasing. This principle can be illustrated by an air conditioner – by setting the thermostat, we determine whether the same amount of electric energy will produce cold or heat.

There can be no doubt that both eustress and distress have certain measurable biochemical and nervous elements in common. The following is an example I have often used to explain this apparently paradoxical fact: a mother receives a telegram announcing that her only son has been killed at war, and one year later he steps into her living room in perfect health because the news was false. The first experience is extremely painful, the second fills her with joy. Her tremendous grief is significantly different from her great pleasure. If you ask this mother if both experiences were the same she will obviously answer, "No! Quite the contrary!"

Nevertheless, from the viewpoint of nonspecificity, the demands made upon her body may have been essentially of the same degree: a need to adjust to a great change in her life. From a medical and biochemical point of view, the concept of stress implies only an adaptive reaction to change, whether change is for the better or the worse.

Even if we disregard the finer biochemical or microscopic changes associated with these two events that affected the mother, there are plenty of signs that anybody can observe. For example, if the mother happened to be reading the evening paper while about to fall asleep in her armchair, she would certainly not continue to read or to doze off; in fact, she might suffer from insomnia for several days. She would jump up and move about, though not intent on going anywhere in particular. She would be unable to concentrate on any problem and would become extremely accident prone. Her heart would pump more strongly and rapidly, her blood pressure would rise. Yet all these changes would be just about the same, both when she had to face the distress of losing her son and when she experienced the eustress of having him back again.

It is this objective analysis of the previously vague concept of stress that made it subject to modern scientific investigation on the basis of measurable indicators. This is what permitted the clear distinction between "specific" and "nonspecific," a cardinal point in the doctrine of stress and of the diseases of adaptation. Despite the apparent simplicity, even today some people find it difficult to make this distinction, especially as there are many transitional types between absolutely specific and absolutely nonspecific reactions.

The difficulties of comprehension that arise from what seems to be such a simple distinction are not as surprising as may appear at first sight. We must remember that modern medicine was based on the concept of specificity. No other approach has been seriously considered ever since Pasteur and Koch found that each one of the contagious "fevers" has its specific germ and that one type of bacterium can only produce one type of disease. Even before the bacteriological era it was known that each type of vitamin deficiency (scurvy, beriberi, rickets) is due to the lack of one specific food factor.   It seemed obvious that in order to cure a disease, its specific cause must first be established, so that a remedy for the malady may be prescribed.   The more specific the actions of a drug, the better it is considered to be.   Non-specific side reactions represent definite disadvantages.   If you want a good anesthetic you do not select one which at the same time diminishes blood pressure or has other unplanned effects. Yet my interest focused precisely on the most nonspecific side-effects of disease-producing agents, the "noise" accompanying pure tones, the dirt contaminating pure colors.

I am glad to have been so stubborn about this orientation of my work because the side-effects have considerable importance, once recognized and studied as such.   Think of the pollution of our air and water.   When I started out I also focused my attention on a particular form of pollution – that of life – because stress in many respects is a type of pollution, a by-product or waste of life.

It took me a long time to learn the little I know about the mechanism of stress and ways to defend ourselves against its damaging actions.   In order to understand this mechanism well, it is important to realize – in addition to what I have already explained – that there are two types of stress hormones; they may also serve as the prototypes of the reaction forms with which we can meet the stress of daily life.   These two types of hormones are respectively called "syntoxic" ("*syn*" = together) and "cata-toxic" ("*cata*" = down, against).   The syntoxic hormones generally belong to the chemical group of steroids; their nuclear structure is common to corticoids, male and female hormones.   However, by minor changes in the basic chemical formulas, it is possible to transform these hormones into each other; for example, a femi-nizing into a masculinizing hormone or into a corticoid that com-bats inflammation and increases resistance.   There exist steroids which, apart from their more specific hormonal actions, also exert syntoxic effects; that is to say they permit coexistence with a potentially damaging substance.   They are messengers of peace-substances which, in chemical language, order our tissues to stay quiet.   From this point of view, cortisone and its derivatives are most effective in acting as "tissue tranquilizers."

Many diseases, especially those due to excessive inflammation or immune reactions, should be treated by such chemical messengers of peace. Take a mosquito bite. It is not the poison of the insect that causes most of the trouble but the response of our tissues, which put up a tremendous inflammatory defense reaction resulting in swelling, itching and discomfort. Inflammation is basically a useful response. It attempts to seal off or quarantine an intruder by a wall of inflammatory tissue, which separates the directly affected area from the surrounding healthy tissue; in this way it can prevent a disease producer from multiplying and spreading throughout the blood. This would be useful, for example, in the case of a focus of tuberculosis, because without a surrounding inflammatory wall the microbes would be disseminated throughout the body and would kill. However, such an extreme reaction is excessive and useless in the case of mosquito bites.

On the other hand, there exist disease producers which are in themselves dangerous and must be suppressed. That is why we have to distinguish between so-called direct and indirect pathogens. The first type is damaging in itself. My hand will be damaged if I happen to put it into boiling water or strong acid. It is not my own reaction which is damaging but the agents themselves. Even the hand of a dead man would be attacked by boiling water or strong acid. Obviously, here we cannot ascribe the damage to any vital response. Certain types of inflammatory and immune reactions, however, are caused by indirect pathogens; here it is not the agent, but rather our response to the agent, that causes the trouble. Allergic hyperreactivity to pollens is one good example. Plant pollens are in themselves quite harmless, but certain people overreact to them. Herein lies the difference between direct and indirect pathogens.

Suppose you are a multimillionaire and suddenly you learn that you have only ten thousand dollars left. Your reaction could be so shattering that it might push you to suicide because you consider yourself "ruined" and this appears unbearable. Now, let us change the situation: instead of being a multimillionaire, suppose you are a vagabond who never managed to save more than a few cents at a time. If you are told that you have ten thousand dollars in your bank account, you can hardly believe your luck; you are overjoyed by this unexpected windfall of wealth. Yet in both cases the news was exactly the same. Only your reaction was different. In other words, it is not so much what happens to you, but the way you take it that is crucial.

In certain cases the pathogen is direct and our body must send out a catatoxic message. We have to destroy the agent, avoid it or flee from it, because here coexistence is impossible. In the financial situation just described, the pathogenic agent is indirect. The dangerous factor is not the agent (that is, the information about the amount of money we possess), but our excessive or inappropriate reaction to it. In such cases we need directives encouraging syntoxic behavior.

In our laboratories at the University of Montreal we have learned to distinguish between these two groups of chemical messengers. We have studied 1,200 steroids synthesized around the world to assist us with this work. We have been able to identify the most active among the available syntoxic and catatoxic compounds. At present we are particularly interested in the catatoxic substances, because those with syntoxic effects, such as cortisone and its derivatives, have already been extensively studied, whereas the catatoxic variety became known only during the last few years.

It was in the course of these later investigations that a synthetic hormone derivative was found which, among all those studied to date, proved to be most potent in destroying dangerous foreign substances in the body. Its chemical name is very long and complicated, so we usually refer to it by the acronym composed of the initials of its most important constituents: PCN. At the present time this is the most active catatoxic substance known. If you administer PCN to a rat and then give it a normally fatal dose of digitoxin, strychnine, certain cancer-producing substances, LSD, or any among a large number of poisons, it will survive, often without showing the slightest sign of damage. This is not due to increased tissue resistance or depressed tissue reactivity to the damaging agents but to the fact that the poisons are simply destroyed by complicated enzymatic reactions in the liver. This is the mechanism characteristic of catatoxic agents. On the other hand, a syntoxic substance such as cortisone does not attack the chemical aggressor, but merely makes the body insensitive to its irritating or damaging action.

Up to now, the clinical value of PCN has not been satisfactorily proven, but there are undoubtedly some steroids which exert catatoxic effects. Besides, other substances, such as antibodies, act in a catatoxic manner by destroying bacteria. Hence, the basic concept is already well-established.

These experimental studies formed the basis of my present philosophy and code of behavior in dealing with the stress of life.

CHAPTER EIGHT

First Hurdles
and Rewards

Ever since my early days at McGill I have wanted to learn all I can about stress, and my colleagues have often wondered about my single-minded tenacity in scrutinizing its mechanisms and effects. The truth is that, from time to time, I did consider changing my orientation. When research led me to conclude that, depending upon conditioning factors, stress (for example, that caused by muscular exercise) can either produce or prevent cardiac death, I considered redirecting my career and returning to clinical or biochemical work to see the problem through to the stage of practical application. Again, when I stumbled upon unplanned observations, particularly on calciphylaxis (an induced hypersensitivity in which tissues respond to various challenging agents with a sudden calcification), I thought of switching to that topic primarily. Eventually I reconciled myself to my human limitations. I realized that the best I could do would be to describe the experimental basis for any one work sufficiently to give it that "critical mass" for competent specialists to carry it further, and then start something else.

In my last years at McGill I published my first book – or, rather, books – a six-volume *Encyclopedia of Endocrinology*. I also began to lecture publicly, not always enjoying it at first, but anxious to gain public understanding of my work. One often-told incident (which was sufficiently dramatic to be reported in the *Journal of the American Medical Association*) shows how very badly I needed more general support at that stage.

It happened at the time of World War II, during the reign of His Most Gracious Majesty King George VI, that I was desperately looking for the urine of patients suffering from periarteritis nodosa.

I suspected that this disease might be due to a derangement in the adaptive activity of the adrenals and associated with an increased corticoid excretion. Now I wanted to verify this hypothesis, but at that time the disease was not yet very well known and probably not often diagnosed. In any event, we could not find a single case either in Montreal or the vicinity; eventually I located two cases in Burlington, Vermont, just across the border. Because of the war, we were on a strict austerity program, and it was considered unpatriotic to import valuable materials from the United States; but, pushed by curiosity, I decided to proceed anyway. Arrangements were made for shipment of the urine by plane in sealed containers so that it might arrive fresh. One of my associates was to meet the plane as I waited in my lab ready to extract the specimen before any decomposition could set in.

During this vigil I received a desperate phone call from my assistant at the airport informing me that urine was simply not listed in His Majesty's Customs Book, either as duty-free or as dutiable, so it could not pass the border. Irritated by this silly red tape, I asked our dean to write an official letter to the highest customs authorities of the land, explaining that, in basic research, we sometimes need items which might impress people as odd, but we need them just the same. The customs officials of a cultured nation should know more about the needs of a university engaged in basic research.

This strongly worded letter, coming from a dean of McGill University, worked. Only a few days later we received an answer informing us that, of course, the federal authorities had foreseen such cases; it was only the inexperienced customs official at the airport who didn't know where to look for this item in the book. It was clearly duty-free, as it came under the category described as "used personal articles."

Now this was fine, but I knew the shipment had decomposed by then anyway, so I did not collect. During the following days, we received more and more urgent telephone calls from the airport, begging us to remove the merchandise which apparently had become somewhat offensive. I didn't budge, because by that time I had lost interest. Finally, the postman brought a printed statement; evidently such cases had also been foreseen, or there would not have been such a form to fit the occasion. Only the number of my shipment was inscribed in handwriting and the printed text read as follows: "Unless within five (5) days after receipt of this notice you collect the merchandise mentioned above, the shipment will be opened and contents sold at public auction."

I must admit I failed to follow the case further and, to this day, I do not know who the happy owner was.

Eventually my research gave me ample opportunity to lecture outside the university. I was fortunate enough often to be invited to speak abroad on scientific matters. In this way, I met many interesting people, including Joseph Stalin in Moscow and Juan Perón in Buenos Aires, both within an interval of a few eventful weeks.

What struck me as most curious was that Stalin and Perón, whose political ideas were so diametrically opposite, spoke in essentially identical terms about the academic progress brought about by their respective regimes. Both compared the governmental subsidies for teaching and research before and after they took power, and in both cases the increase was impressive. The only difference was that one spoke of rubles, the other of pesos.

Juan Perón was much more extroverted than Stalin. My former wife and I had made reservations at a very good hotel in Buenos Aires. We arrived at two o'clock in the morning, completely exhausted and ready to sleep. Our flight (on one of those old propeller planes) had lasted more than seventy-five hours with several stops, and we were anxious to settle in for some rest. But at the hotel we were intercepted by a presidential aide. He informed us that he had canceled our reservations and, despite our protestations of extreme fatigue, he brought us to the presidential guest house where a most luxurious suite awaited us, with an almost life-sized painting of the President and Evita Perón above our double bed.

Later, Perón received us at the Casa Rosada, the presidential palace, where he spoke of the ever-increasing contributions to universities made by his government. I found it difficult to avoid calling his attention to the fact that similar progress had been made during the same period in Canada, and that governmental aid to universities was actually progressing rapidly all over the world. In fact, Stalin later took pride in these very same advances.

During this visit to Argentina, I hit the jackpot in academic honors. This came to my great surprise, and for reasons that I still have not been able to determine. We arrived at the guest house one evening after a dinner with friends and found in our room a message telling me to appear the following morning at a certain lecture hall. There, in front of an overflow audience seated in an enormous auditorium, President Perón made another speech and presented me with a diploma from each of the five state universities in Argentina.

After this he embraced me in the Latin manner, to the accompaniment of flashes set off by innumerable newspaper photographers. I was highly flattered by this totally unexpected and undeserved honor, but also somewhat worried to think that the picture of this embrace might be reproduced in any of the newspapers or journals at home. In view of the somewhat tense political relationship between Canada and Argentina at that time, this might have been quite embarrassing. Fortunately, the picture was not picked up by the Canadian press.

I was then sent to Moscow to represent the Royal Society of Canada at an extensive international scientific meeting called ostensibly to celebrate the 120th anniversary of the Imperial Russian Academy of Sciences (now the Soviet Academy). However, I strongly suspect that the real reason was to demonstrate that, in the aftermath of World War II which was still very much in evidence everywhere, the Soviet regime was the first to give any special attention to the development of science.

I remember having undertaken the first leg of this journey in a small Royal Canadian Air Force plane with just enough space for the pilot and myself. It was during the winter of 1945, and just about every hour or two the pilot told me, with an air of complete indifference, "Well, ice is accumulating on the wings and makes us very heavy, but we're still at 5,000 feet. . . . We're continuing to drop, now we're at 1,000 feet. . . . We must land quickly to get the wings defrosted because the engine can't carry our weight anymore!"

After many stops, I finally arrived at Fairbanks, where the Russians took me to an air base provided for them by the Americans on a lend-lease basis for the duration of the war.   There I met two other Canadians and we were placed on a luxuriously furnished American lend-lease Soviet bomber which was to take us through the entire continent of Asia over Siberia, because it was still judged too dangerous to fly the Atlantic route.   Our plane, though completely lined with blue plush and furnished with three comfortable beds for the members of the Canadian delegation, was still heavily armed in case of possible attack by enemy aircraft whose pilots stubbornly refused to surrender.   I felt like Genghis Khan traveling in his luxurious, ceremonial wagon with a heavily armed escort.   Seven centuries later, here I was, going through approximately the same region!

One particularly striking member of our crew was a very beautiful, doll-like Russian girl.   She wore an air force uniform covered by decorations, but still retained a charming – almost feline – femininity.   Everyone in the group treated her with the greatest respect, and we learned that she was a national heroine, having shot down sixteen enemy planes during the war.   On our mission she acted the role of rear gunner although, in fact, we did not meet any enemy planes.

At the banquet given in the Kremlin for the heads of the foreign delegations, Stalin sat between Zhukov and Molotov, with whom he conversed in a very relaxed manner. He sat quietly smoking his pipe and, curiously, did not address any of his foreign guests directly.   He heard me speak Russian with Molotov, who was seated next to me, so it was evidently not any linguistic barrier that caused his reticence. After the party, we all wondered why he had been so reluctant to talk to his guests. Sir Robert Robinson, who represented the Royal Society of England, suggested that he perhaps did not wish to give anyone the opportunity of quoting (or misquoting) him on the basis of personal conversations.   Whatever his motives, I found the evening quite amusing.

When I returned to Montreal after another exhausting transcontinental flight in a small fighter plane, reporters were waiting in our living room. I told them briefly about the congress, adding a few tales of my personal experiences abroad.   One day, while sitting in a park, I had been approached by a young man who introduced himself as an engineer.   The country, he explained, was desperately in need of gold for use in dental work. Although at the time the austerity program allowed us to take only a few dollars out of Canada, and even these could not be exchanged for many rubles, I had found quite a few Russians anxious to trade goods. It turned out that he wanted to purchase my wedding ring. I did not accept his offer, but it did lead to an interesting discussion of Western politics, in which he was well versed.

By two A.M. the reporters had withdrawn, except for one woman who stayed for a cup of coffee with the family while I was unpacking. She expressed interest in some rather nice pieces of antique church embroidery that I retrieved from my suitcase. I explained that they were far beyond my means, but the dealer had offered them in exchange for a pair of striped pants for which I had little use on this trip after the official receptions were over. (Apparently, striped pants were much in demand then to caricature capitalists on the stage.)

The arrival of the paper the next morning rudely shattered any illusions I might have kept about having a knack for public relations. My interview was captioned: "McGill Professor Loses Pants to Reds." The text reported almost none of my enthusiastic comments on the activities of the Soviet Academy and dealt mainly with my one barter transaction. No wonder this document gave a somewhat one-sided picture of how I spent my time in Moscow. To make things worse, several other dailies reproduced this version of my interview, with which my Russian hosts were understandably disgusted. Soon, both *Izvestiya* and *Pravda* registered great disappointment about the Canadian delegate who, instead of attending scientific meetings, spent his time buying and selling old junk. Conversely, several American papers gallantly sprang to my defense. *Time Magazine* remarked in its column on international affairs that "*Pravda* screaming like a fishwife soundly lambasted Selye" because his "homecoming contained nothing about the outstanding scientific event" and dealt exclusively with the "pants-tapestry deal." I certainly did not foresee that such a storm would be raised by one playful remark made over a cup of coffee, long after the reporters' ominous notebooks had been sheathed.

This was not the last time I had reason to be mindful of the power of the press. In 1959, *Maclean's,* a popular and respected Canadian magazine, decided to publish an article about my work, and I consented with pleasure to an extensive interview. To my surprise, the pieces appeared under the misleading title, "A Scientist's Startling Claim: Death is NOT Inevitable." I responded to that distortion of my words with the following letter to the editor, using a corrected photocopy of their title:

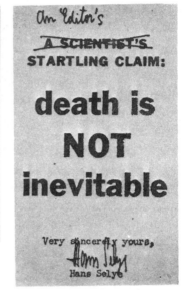

Incidentally, the foregoing signature, though mine, did not reflect a naturally acquired style. When I was a child my father had a stamp with his signature, "H. Selye," because as an administrative officer he had to approve countless documents and had no time to sign them individually. I was fascinated by the gadget and it seemed extremely distinguished and adult to be important enough to have a stamp for your personal signature. It struck me as a good omen that the "H" for Hugo was also applicable to my own name.

When the stamp, which had suffered somewhat from overuse, was ready to be discarded my father offered it to me and I was delighted to accept this wonderful gift. To make it really mine, I consciously set out to make my handwriting match the stamp, practicing the narrow Gothic "H" for hours. Even today I write in that oddly characteristic style – characteristic of my father, not of me. I wonder what a graphologist would make of this?

My letter of protest might have made enough of an impression for *Maclean's* to publish it, but it did not prevent similar misinterpretations in later years. Soon after the publication of my book *Stress Without Distress,* a 1975 issue of *Family Circle* featured an article on my code of altruistic egoism with the baffling announcement on the cover of the magazine: "Rx for tension and stress: be selfish!" Quoting only this second half of my prescription, a completely different implication was given to the code. The woman who had interviewed me apologized that her article had fallen prey to an editor's ax. It may not have been a conscious bid to overdramatize by shocking the readers, but unfortunately the text of the article itself had also been greatly shortened, presumably to save space, so it now emphasized only egoism. As a result, the final version implied that I really favored crass selfishness as a biologically sound way of life for man.

As this journal has a very good circulation, I was flooded with letters and telephone calls from women outraged about my morals who had never read my book but assumed that the article contained the essence of my philosophy. I begged them to borrow my book from a local library and at least read it before forming an opinion.

To return to the postwar years, in 1945 I was offered the opportunity to found and direct the Institute of Experimental Medicine and Surgery at the University of Montreal, where I am still working today. Ironically, thirty-three years later I find myself back at the same point. We have just founded the International Institute of Stress, and I have to cope with the same problems of organization with which I was confronted in 1945.

When I arrived, the University of Montreal had just moved into its magnificent new campus, but virtually no research was being conducted in any of the standard departments at that time. Aware that they could not initiate meaningful research in all specialties at once, the university administration decided to create at least one research institute with top facilities.

Imagine the terror when I arrived at the new institute, fresh from my position at McGill, importing along with my other valuables 2,000 white rats! The university had no rat colony, and several administrators and students would have had no regret if that void had not been filled. People kept asking me in frenzied horror, "What if the rats somehow get loose and start to proliferate?"

My main professorial assignment at that time was teaching endocrinology, but I soon realized that there was no really up-to-date text, in either French or English. To fill this gap I wrote the *Textbook of Endocrinology,* under the imprint of "ACTA Endocrinologica, Université de Montréal, Montréal, Canada" – this was designed as the first step in establishing a university press. I wrote the book mainly for my own students, but I chose to do it in English in the hope that it might also be used by English-language universities. As research funds were scarce, I donated all royalties to the university, to help research and postgraduate teaching at our institute. Much to my surprise (and perhaps largely owing to the complimentary foreword written by Professor Bernardo A. Houssay, who happened to obtain the Nobel Prize the year the book came out), it had such an unexpected international success that five printings became necessary in 1947 and 1948 with a second edition of two printings in 1949. After that, the school refused to handle the book any longer for the most unusual reason-it was too successful! Since the university did not have the facilities for distributing the volume and its several translations throughout the world, I had to establish a publishing company of my own: ACTA Inc., Medical Publishers. Under these conditions I decided to cash in on the royalties myself since I had to look after all the expenses and organization required to put out this and all my subsequent monographs. Although I conducted the affairs of ACTA profitably, it took up too much of my time. Later I entrusted well-established publishers with the complicated business aspects of bringing the products of my urge to write before the world.

My work on stress gradually progressed from a strictly medical to a behavioral orientation. In 1956 I wrote *The Stress of Life,* convinced that the theory of stress should be explained to the general public. I am very proud of the vitality of this book which, after some twenty years, is still on the list of recommended readings in most medical and many secondary schools throughout the world. In view of the continued demand for it, I wrote a completely updated edition in 1976.

When I originally wrote the book, I included as an afterthought some proposals for a code of behavior which I thought might help others cope with stress as I had learned to. Much to my surprise, these philosophical "musings" prompted more response than the strictly scientific aspects of the book. It seemed that people were searching, not only to understand stress but even more to eliminate its ill effects by appropriate behavior.

CHAPTER NINE

The Mastery of Stress

The term "stress" has been used so loosely and applied to so many areas that it is perhaps easiest to understand what stress is *not*. Contrary to widespread public opinion, stress is not synonymous with nervous depression, tension, fatigue or discouragement. The only way to characterize stress is to call it a nonspecific response of the body to any demand. Under given circumstances, stress may cause exhaustion, a nervous breakdown, a cardiac accident, asthma or muscular fatigue. Still, these disturbances are not stress, but rather its diverse effects upon certain individuals.

You *should not and cannot avoid stress*, because to eliminate it completely would mean to destroy life itself. If you make no more demands upon your body, you are dead. Whatever we do – run up a flight of stairs, play tennis, worry or fight starvation – demands are made upon us. A lash of the whip and a passionate kiss can be equally stressful! Although one causes distress and the other eustress, both make certain common demands, necessitating adaptation to a change in our normal resting equilibrium. Even while we sleep, the heart must continue to beat, we must move the muscles that help the lungs to breathe, we continue to digest last night's meal, and even the brain does not cease to function as we dream. Consequently, it would be quite unthinkable that anyone could, or would even want to, avoid stress. However, the more we learn about conditioning and about the ways to deal with the stress of life, the more we can enjoy eustress, which is the spice of our existence. It gives us the only outlet we have to express our talents and energies, to pursue happiness.

Every one of us must learn to recognize what for him is "overstress" (hyperstress), when he has exceeded the limits of his adaptability; or "understress" (hypostress), when he suffers from lack of self-realization (physical immobility, boredom, sensory deprivation). Being overwrought is just as bad as being frustrated by the inability to express ourselves and find free outlets for our innate muscular or mental energy.

The way I see it, the stress of life has four basic variations, although in their most characteristic nonspecific manifestations they all depend upon the same central phenomenon. This might be illustrated as follows:

$$\begin{array}{c c c} & \text{Overstress} & \\ & \text{(hyperstress)} & \\ & | & \\ \text{Good stress} \quad\underline{\hspace{2cm}} & \text{STRESS} & \underline{\hspace{2cm}}\quad \text{Bad stress} \\ \text{(eustress)} & | & \text{(distress)} \\ & \text{Understress} & \\ & \text{(hypostress)} & \end{array}$$

Our goal, then, is to strike a balance between the equally destructive forces of hypo- and hyperstress, to find as much eustress as possible and minimize distress.

In the course of human history a multitude of recommendations have been made to find peace and happiness. The most popular among these included a rigid enforcement of the country's laws, a rigorous adherence to the commands and teachings of some purportedly infallible leader (sage, prophet or divinity), and the promotion of progress in science, technology or politics. Yet history has continued to demonstrate the fragility of all these guidelines.

With the ease of communications today, we are constantly bombarded by new methods of "coping with life." Journalists, sociologists and psychologists tell us that, as the population grows and the pace of life quickens, the world is becoming an increasingly frustrating place. Whether this is truer now than in the past, we would certainly all like to rid our lives of the bad effects of stress and enjoy as much eustress as possible. To meet this longing, new techniques spring up daily, all claiming to "reduce stress." Among these, some are worth taking seriously, others are nothing but fads. Because the field of stress research is so vast, I cannot claim to be an expert on every technique that attempts to provide means to reduce distress, but I do have some opinions based on our own research, and on self-observation.

It is usually not enough to say, "Relax and refrain from strenuous activities." Some people find sufficient diversion in leisure activities to keep their own stress level at a desirable point. But many of us have an irresistible drive to seek stress, in the form of challenge, competition and the like, even when we are supposed to be playing. It is a common experience for a person under pressure to get the feeling of merely wasting time when indulging in leisure activities. Not everyone knows how to play or how to enjoy the passive experiences of music, spectator sports or reading. When the pent-up energy of highly motivated people has no outlet for the type of work that they consider eustressful play, they turn to drugs, violence and other destructive activities. But there are alternatives, some good, some not so good.

Smoking, alcohol, tranquilizers and eating all help to relieve distress in those who suffer from nervous excitation. The trouble here is that these remedies tend to become problems themselves through their habit-forming properties.

The most diverse kinds of therapy are used to decrease the effects of distress. These include exercise, psychotherapy, physiotherapy, acupuncture and moxibustion, chiropractic, electroshock, sauna, hot and cold baths, balneotherapy, shortwave therapy – the list goes on and on!

In recent years, some of the Eastern methods of stress reduction have become very popular. Ginseng or eleutherococcus (extracted from Asiatic plants and long used in Eastern medicine) has received a great deal of attention. There are many clinical and a few experimental observations that suggest these preparations might exert a nonspecific antistress effect. Meanwhile, the results obtained in our own labs have been inconclusive.

Other procedures of Eastern origin that have taken hold, especially in North America, include Zen Buddhism, Hare Krishna, Yoga and – most popular of all – Transcendental Meditation (TM) and its variant, the "relaxation response." I am often associated with the TM movement having frequently lectured on stress both to TM teachers and to potential students. TM purports to relieve the bad effects of stress, and what I have tried to do is merely explain what stress *is*.   However, a misconception has grown that I am an expert in TM; I have tried to clarify this by admitting that I have never taken a course in TM, I am not a meditator and I have never conducted research on the effects of this technique.

I have spoken with Maharishi about the underlying principles and have written introductions and epilogues to several books on the subject, again limiting my remarks to the explanation of stress in the medical sense of the word without claiming to be an expert on the effects of the method.   I would like to take the course if I ever have the time, because I have met many practitioners who attest to its usefulness.   Of course, I would like to understand the underlying biological mechanisms through which it exerts its curative actions; but if something is proven to be helpful by experience, that's good enough for me.   After all, no one knows how aspirin really works, yet it has helped relieve pain in millions of people and no physician considers it unethical to employ this drug.

A modified version of this technique is advocated by Dr. Herbert Benson of Harvard, who calls his variant the "relaxation° response."   Like TM, this is a mental technique of deep relaxation which helps you clarify your thoughts.   Benson's method differs from TM in that it demysticizes the ceremonies behind meditating; he refuses to attach any importance to ceremonies, mantras and the like, and he comes up with a system that can be learned by anyone without the costly instruction involved in TM.

These schools of thought, and others like Jacobson's "progressive relaxation technique," claim results that are quite impressive.   Like those previously mentioned, the latter appears to produce some measurable objective physiological changes in the body, opposite to those considered to be characteristic of excessive stress.   Most of these techniques simply help us withdraw from our everyday preoccupations through physical and mental relaxation (whether or not accompanied by prayers, rituals and ceremonies).   In any event, the subjective feeling of relaxation produced is claimed to be more complete than that of a good night's sleep. If this is true I support them, but I think we need more evidence before we can objectively choose among these techniques. In my opinion, we cannot deny the value of such procedures simply because we do not know enough about them. After all, there is no logical relationship between religion and music or certain ceremonies either, yet all religions have (often quite independently of each other) developed rituals which include music, ceremonies and wearing certain vestments, all of which may largely help through subconscious mechanisms that are not explicable in modern scientific terms.

I mentioned earlier the differences between eustress, distress, hyperstress and hypostress. All of these have certain characteristics in common and are ramifications of the general stress concept. Hyperstress may be due to an excess of eustress (for we cannot tolerate excessively prolonged ecstasy or orgies) or to an excess of distress (for we cannot long withstand intensely unpleasant things). The various types of relaxation techniques seem to be able to combat hyperstress of either sort.

Relaxation therapy could not have any value in combating hypostress. In fact, exaggerating the time spent daily on TM or other methods has been said to cause disturbances similar to those of sensory deprivation (a form of hypostress). But in the rat race of modern life, hyperstress is the greater problem. Therefore, it seems to me, these techniques can be very useful to many people.

Most of these methods teach us – some more effectively than others – how to deal with "the cruel world." To my mind, however, our goal should not be merely to master techniques for shutting out the reality but to devise a better lifestyle. That is why my principal object is to perfect the behavioral code of altruistic egoism, which is in harmony with the laws of Nature.

We have tranquilizers that can reduce anxiety and tension, and we know of a variety of specific drugs that combat stress-induced high blood pressure, peptic ulcers, headaches and many other disturbances usually caused by stress in predisposed individuals; but all of these drugs are of limited efficiency and have some undesirable side-effects. Perhaps, eventually, pharmacology will give us a perfect remedy in the form of some totally innocuous pill or elixir which will protect the body and mind against all the bad effects of stress. Perhaps. Meanwhile, anybody can find help by following a code of behavior which is based on natural laws.   This has already been tried by many people wishing to establish a state of emotional equilibrium and well-being in the face of adversity.

To a large extent, the damage caused by stress can only be combated by the physician – for example, through the administration of syntoxic or catatoxic hormones – when Nature makes a mistake and does not respond to the challenge appropriately. Here again, contrary to widespread public opinion, Nature does not always know what is best for you (incidentally, neither does father nor mother!).   It is this misconception (not to say superstition) that leads so many people to pay large sums of money in order to obtain a diet consisting only of "natural foods." Poison mushrooms are very natural, but few people would consider them particularly healthy. It is not by instinct but through experience, intellect and investigation that we have learned to distinguish them from the edible kinds.   Similarly, pasteurized milk, cooked pork and many other artificially manipulated foods are preferable to the untreated, naturally available varieties. Furthermore, most of the lifesaving drugs are artificial and yet very useful in maintaining health. Our mental reactions to threatening stress situations are often, but not always, excellently guided by natural instinct.   Here research and logic must help us to develop a more satisfying code of behavior than that which we would follow if guided merely by natural impulses.

Once we really understand stress, each of us will be his own best physician, for no one can appreciate our mental needs better than we ourselves.   Everyone must learn to measure the stress level at which he personally functions best and then not go either above or below that. By careful self-observation we can gradually develop an instinctive feeling telling us that we are running above or below the stress level that corresponds to our own nature. In practice, no refined chemical tests can do more for us. I know when I have just "had enough of it," and then I stop. I don't need any complex scientific machinery for this.

Judging what is best for us personally is a matter of training through experience, which everybody has to acquire for himself.

But in this task we can be greatly aided by a thorough knowledge of the basic natural laws that have been clarified through research on stress. You must learn to balance the pleasures and stimulation of social engagements, trips and successful work against your requirements for peace, solitude and serenity. Everybody will arrive at this aim in a somewhat different manner, always characteristic of his own individuality. Some understand their inner needs through meditation and silence; others may only find their own stress level through danger signs such as insomnia, irritability, indigestion, headaches or depression. First of all, we must learn to analyze and be honest with ourselves. Then, step by step, an intelligent person will usually succeed in developing his own techniques, limiting his unnecessary telephone calls, his participation in social life, committee meetings, civic activities, etc., which he has blindly undertaken because "they were expected of him." This will leave much more time to do other things at which he is really good and which may be more useful both to himself and to society. Don't accept social obligations that people try to impose upon you if you dislike them. "Worthy causes" are not natural obligations and will only bore you, so disregard them. Do what you like and respect, without worrying about criticism, scandal or even all the money that you lose by deviating from generally accepted standards.

If you read the daily papers or watch news programs on television that do not interest you, just give that up and turn your attention to other things that you find more edifying. Don't allow the verbal terrorism of others to give you guilt feelings. Instead, save your energy for activities that are really meaningful.

"Even if you have the misfortune of having badly chosen your wife, at least choose your occupation wisely, because you will spend much more time with it than with her." I do not remember the author of this advice but, in any event, I fully agree with him—and by "occupation" I don't mean only your job, but whatever you decide to do throughout each day.

You must satisfy yourself first of all. Pleasure will come only from what you have done to earn it. As much as possible, try to awaken the creativity that may lie buried in your subconscious mind. Whatever steps you must take to exteriorize your talents, the accomplishment of this is the basic prerequisite for your development and satisfaction. It really doesn't matter whether you are a scientist, gardener, poet, musician, athlete or even a beachcomber; the essential thing is that you unfold your personality as far as you can, and thereby achieve happiness.

You should try very honestly to establish what you consider a noble aim in life, a goal worthy of your efforts, a pursuit which gives you maximal satisfaction. This is not always easy. You must be extremely sincere with yourself; you have to remember to choose only what *you* really want to do, not what your parents, friends, neighbors, teachers or preachers have virtually brainwashed you to do. To establish this is of the utmost importance because it helps you avoid some of the major frustrations in life, which are the principal sources of distress.

After that you must fight hard to attain your goal, but always stay within the limits of your capacity to withstand stress. We must learn how to face life gracefully from what we have established about the actions of syntoxic and catatoxic hormones. We need to know how to accept defeat when it is not worthwhile to win, or when the goal we have set for ourselves turns out to be unattainable; but we must also fight stubbornly until death if under given conditions, without defense, death would be inevitable anyway.

Each time you are the victim of some family disagreement or a disappointing experience at work, examine carefully whether it is really worth your while to defend your point of view. If not, just ignore the friction or, if necessary, cut your ties with the offender; if the goal is important, fight with all your strength. After the combat is over, whether you win or lose, return to solitude, breathe calmly, relax your muscles and empty your mind and body of all the aftermaths of the struggle, gradually returning to your normal pace of life. I once summarized these thoughts in a jingle that first appeared in *The Stress of Life.* It has now been reprinted on cards for distribution to student groups, tourists and other visitors to our Institute:

> "𝔉ight for 𝔭our highest
> 𝔄ttainable aim
> 𝔅ut do not put up
> ℜesistance in 𝔳ain."

Fifty years of research in laboratories and clinics have convinced me that the physiological mechanisms of adaptation to the stress of life are essentially the same on the cellular and molecular level as they are with regard to interpersonal and international relationships.

To my mind, the general syndrome of adaptation to the demands of life, which I have already outlined, is at the root of the great tensions characteristic of our time that manifest themselves in the relations between individuals and nations. Perhaps humanity's greatest problem today is determining how to face interpersonal and international stress situations as well as those created by changes in our inanimate environment.

Frustration and indecision are the most harmful psychogenic stressors, because neither uninhibited successful work nor even final and hopeless defeat (which can be solved by resignation to fate) is as demanding as the friction from unresolved contradictory efforts. We must learn to cope with the problems and demands which confront us daily in the twentieth century. That is why I have spent so much time and energy on efforts to apply the results of laboratory and clinical research to the formulation of natural directives for everyday behavior.

I start with the principle that man needs more natural ideals than those that guide his conduct at present. Consequently, I feel that the rules we must follow have to be based on the laws of Nature. We are part of Nature and therefore cannot disregard her laws with impunity. The beauty of this code is its perfect compatibility with any religion, political system or philosophy; yet, at the same time, it is quite independent of these.

My training and experience as a scientist do not qualify me to analyze the nature or purpose of the Creator, but only the mechanism of His creation. I feel more competent to act as a simple mechanic of the human machine than as a sage or prophet with the divine inspiration to reveal by whom and for what purpose it was created. In fact, when you come to think of it, attributes that various religions have ascribed to divinity are identical to those of Nature. *God has always existed and will always exist. His laws can never lose their validity and must necessarily be obeyed or you will suffer punishment. If you follow them, you will get recompensed.* Are these not the characteristics of Nature itself? Perhaps the concept of a divinity, a God, has always existed because it is the only one man can accept, and in this sense He is a personified interpretation of Nature. In another way, which brings religion and science equally close together, one might say that God (whatever your God might be) has created Nature in His own image and, hence, the laws of God are the laws of Nature.

From the purely biological point of view, we are machines. I am very interested in learning more about how these machines function or should function. I have spent most of my life studying the physiological aspects of resistance and adaptation to demands, but I now wish to give my principal attention to the ethics, the rules of behavior which can improve mental well-being. This is particularly important for our species because of the disproportionately well-developed central nervous system of man. Many of the diseases of our bodies are actually due to psychic malfunction, particularly to the habit of following ethical codes which are inappropriate for us. To my mind, the resulting frustrations are the primary causes of psychosomatic diseases.

As a result of these convictions, I am even more interested in behavior than in the genetic code which in chemical language contains the recipe for all our inherited characteristics. I can do nothing about my genetic code but – at least to some extent – I can modify my code of behavior. We know that the constituent elements of the genetic code are the same for every individual, yet billions of combinations are possible, each unique. It is an undeniable fact that every human being is unique. This is so by virtue of his soul, according to theologians; because of his mind, according to philosophers; and because of his chromosomes, skin, voice, odor, fingerprints and the structure of his proteins, according to scientists. Although every person is so different, there are common laws governing all of us, irrespective of individual variations in detail. In general, we might agree that we all share the aspiration to make life better, happier and more stable in the face of aggression by other people, disease or the ravages of old age.

I do not believe it possible to formulate a code of behavior that would be equally suitable for all of us. Even if certain parts of our machine are subject to the same rules — like those regulating energy consumption, muscular activity and digestion — people are too different in the details of their inherited or acquired characteristics to outline a magic formula that would be ideal for each one.

I feel that one of the wisest and most generally applicable behavioral laws ever formulated is the one expressed by variants of the "golden rule" in many religions: "Love thy neighbor as thyself." However, I simply cannot believe that anyone can have an equal interest in the well-being of his neighbor as in his own. Even among the most devotedly religious of my acquaintances, I know of no one who, if faced with very difficult choices about the promotion of his own good or that of others, could honestly say, "May God's will prevail."

Only a short time ago I tested this on a particularly devout friend of mine who had contradicted me on this point. As she is a mother who really adores her only son, I asked her to imagine the following situation: during a revolution, an enemy is killed by one of two sharpshooters, one of whom happens to be her son. Both suspects are captured; but as it is impossible to establish which of them is the killer, the enemy commander decides to shoot only one as an example to the population. To prove his own lack of prejudice he asks my friend, the mother of one suspect, to decide which one should be shot. I told her, "I respect your religious feelings, but be honest and tell me, would you be able to say 'May God's will prevail'?" She thought about this for a while, and then replied, in a voice full of emotion, "I must admit I could never pass up an opportunity to save my son's life." Because of the deep religious devotion and obvious honesty of the mother, this incident made a profound impression upon me, and I liked her even more for being so frank. Of course she had to think first of her own and her son's happiness, because that is how the Creator — be He a divinity or a law of Nature — has made us. We cannot help it. The big fish must eat the little fish to survive. No one can blame him for it because that is how he was created; the fish did not make himself that way.

I also feel that "Love thy neighbor as thyself" is unrealistic as a guideline for life because love on command is not possible. You can die on command on the battlefield. You can make great sacrifices for a relative because you feel a moral obligation to do so; but for you to really love someone, it is up to the other person to make himself lovable.

In questioning the "golden rule" I am only trying to substantiate the spirit of the Biblical command on the basis of purely scientific facts. I do not think I could improve upon its essence. My only criticism concerns language — I object merely to its wording as a command. However, I realize that in Biblical times a divine command was the only way to get the law accepted by people who had no way of knowing about stress, catatoxic and syntoxic hormones and attitudes, or the maintenance of homeostasis — the innate desire to protect the steady state, the safety, of our body.

When the Bible speaks of love, it does not merely mean love between wife and husband or parent and child. It has a much broader significance and includes all positive feelings such as respect, gratitude, admiration and goodwill — in essence, the concept of being or making yourself desirable.

In order to retain the wisdom of the old precept and yet make it acceptable in this age of science, we must translate it into today's language of biology. The idea of loving on command is impossible to obey in practice. Still it can become a scientifically defendable basic rule of motivation to earn love as a valuable capital for our own good.

After all, the Bible had to be translated from the original Hebrew into modern languages to make it generally understandable to the present population of the world. Even the ancient English formulation had to be modernized. Why not adjust the time-honored dictum to the rational and objectively demonstrable philosophy of modern science by saying: "*Earn* thy neighbor's love"?

My skepticism about the applicability of the "golden rule" led me to the formulation of my code of behavior, which I labeled altruistic egoism.

In naming my code of behavior, I wished to distinguish between egoism which is, according to *Webster's New World Dictionary,* "the doctrine that self-interest is the proper goal of all human actions," and egotism — "constant, excessive reference to oneself, self-conceit, selfishness." The possible confusion is understandable; I myself failed to make the proper distinction in *Stress Without Distress*. As explained by *Webster's:* "Egotism and egoism are sometimes used interchangeably, but egotism is generally considered the more opprobrious term."

The concept of altruistic egoism appears paradoxical because it is difficult to conceive of someone who is both an altruist and an egoist at the same time. Yet the underlying idea is very simple: you can be *effectively* selfish, giving free expression to your particular talents, and still maintain peace of mind. Altruistic egoism lets us give vent to our natural human egoistic tendencies without producing guilt feelings — for who would condemn him whose egoism expresses itself in the insatiable desire to be useful to others and thereby earn their love?

To fully understand the enormous biological force that can be derived from such a philosophy, it helps to remember what we have learned from Claude Bernard on the importance of the fixity of the *milieu intérieur* — that is, everything comprised within our skin surface, the totality of our person. If someone is exposed to cold, he shivers to produce heat and reestablish the fixity of his *milieu intérieur* — that is, his "homeostasis." When a person is given an inherently poisonous substance, he will try to destroy and get rid of it by means of catatoxic responses. If he overreacts to unimportant irritants, he will have to produce syntoxic hormones to diminish the excessive and useless defense reactions that are actually the immediate cause of his suffering. In both cases he will have to maintain the *status quo,* the internal equilibrium, in order to assure his own well-being.

To illustrate the practical applicability of altruistic egoism, take the following example:

Twenty-four passengers arrive at a little airport. All of them need to get to the same hotel, but there are only six taxis. One of three things can happen. The most aggressive egoists could run for the taxis and jump into them, leaving the other eighteen stranded and bitter with resentment. The pure altruist could yield precedence to all others and remain behind waiting indefinitely for a new taxi to arrive. The third possibility is that one person, over-coming his shyness, takes the initiative to suggest that, since there are only six taxis, the passengers should split up into six groups of four persons and everyone will get a ride. The twenty-four passengers do not act this way by either pure altruism or egoism but by altruistic egoism, because what is good for any one of them is also good for all others.

The passenger who proposed the generally satisfactory solu-tion was an altruistic egoist, yet his conduct was in perfect agree-ment with the Biblical teaching, because he did unto others what he wanted them to do unto him. Instead of creating resentment, he earned gratitude and friendly feelings. In daily life you will encounter many situations where an altruistic-egoistic solution is much more difficult to find, yet it is the only acceptable one.

Of course, you may say that all this is well known anyway. Most people agree that you should "live and let live," that an honest man sells his wares at a profit but also looks out for the interests of his clients. These recommendations are perfectly justified but they are based on beliefs and not on objective scien-tific data. They work for those who believe in them and only as long as they believe in them. Sooner or later, when the guide-lines do not suit somebody, he would conclude, "Well, why should I miss some exceptional opportunities to profit at other peoples' expense? What I am about to do is not really cheating and, if it is, who is going to find out? This time we must strike for more money, we must go to war because the provocation was too great and we are sure to win." If you look at any of these situations with the equanimity of scientific analysis and centuries of experience, any deviation from the code of altruistic egoism turned out to be harmful in the end. The few exceptions that I have been able to identify are so rare and so unpredictable that it is better to stick to the code than to gamble with self-authorized exceptions. In any event, it is extremely dangerous to prescribe changes to accepted procedures when deciding on important issues applicable to yourself. As my father said on my graduation, "Your job is to treat others but 'Never be your own doctor.' It is too tempting to see things the way you would like them to be."

I greatly appreciate people who can be in equilibrium and at peace with themselves and with the society in which they live. The man who has succeeded in earning his neighbor's love, gratitude and respect, whether through such a simple suggestion as the above mentioned taxi problem at the airport or a more complex variant of it, will have a feeling of security, usefulness and satisfaction.   Such a person will be protected by his code of behavior. This, I believe, is an ideal state for anyone, whether an artist, scientist, technician, housewife or unskilled laborer. Anyone can earn respect and goodwill and have a feeling of fulfillment and satisfaction, as long as he achieves something useful to the community.

At first the concept of altruistic egoism strikes some people as a repulsive bargain, in conflict with many religious ideals and based on the most selfish of needs. The impression is often left that my code is just another way of saying, "I'll scratch your back if you'll scratch mine." That is not at all what I wish to convey. My code has no strings attached. I offer figuratively to "scratch your back" without asking for anything in return. The value of this system rests purely on the statistical probability that if you have been unconditionally useful to many, in the long run some of the recipients of your goodwill will want to help you out. I try to be useful to people, convinced that, even if I never ask for reciprocity, some will eventually turn around and help me, trusting that in the future I might help them out again. And even if no one does, I have lost nothing.

Executives of large enterprises, generals, movie stars, scientists and multimillionaires can all be very successful in their own fields and yet complete failures as regards their personal happiness. From my point of view, such a person should not be envied, because real success depends not only upon public acclaim but much more upon an inner satisfaction and a sense of fulfillment.

It is also possible for someone to achieve success as an altruist by being useful to others while neglecting himself. Even if such attitudes are admirable in a sense, they cannot be considered as fulfilling the characteristics of complete success.

To adjust to the world you must establish an equilibrium with it. You must be able to say, "My ideal is to stay at my natural

level of accomplishment and behave as appropriately as I can."
This is the way I try to stay in balance with my surroundings,
both animate and inanimate. I need not have feelings of guilt
and shame nor any inferiority complexes about my behavior,
because I know I can do no more.

When I was a student at the school of the Benedictine Fathers
in Komárom, I suffered terribly because I could not accept the
idea of washing off my sins by beating my chest, repeating that I
was a miserable sinner and saying *"mea culpa, mea culpa."* I did
not feel like a miserable sinner. I knew I had my faults, but I
tried my best, making every effort to correct them; this gave me
more satisfaction than merely admitting my deficiencies.

Altruistic egoism rids you of such guilt feelings about your
natural egoism, for what you really want is to be useful to others.
If you act according to a code based only on solid and eternal
biological laws and independent of all prejudices and traditions
(without being in conflict with any creeds), you become free from
preconceived ideas that are incompatible with Nature. It is biologically justifiable to seek happiness in an atmosphere of serenity,
by contributing to the maintenance of society through your own
usefulness to others.

I know of no other philosophy that would better ensure our
security and satisfaction. All the traditional motives for the assurance of our survival and happiness — such as power, material wealth
or blind loyalty to an allegedly infallible leader — can suddenly lose
their value with changing circumstances. You may be rich today
and poor tomorrow. Only the goodwill of your neighbor remains
an asset, as long as you live and act so as to deserve it. In following
this code of life, I may say that I am a capitalist, not because I want
to accumulate a fortune of money or power but because I wish to
hoard a kind of wealth that is much more efficacious and durable.

I try to accumulate the goodwill and gratitude of others, and
especially self-respect, through the respect and love of others. If I
succeed in this I can become invulnerable, even if I have no riches
or strength, because no one will gain anything by attacking me,
and someone may even profit from having me around.

Let us not forget that, despite all of his armies and political
influence, Hitler was not as strong and secure as Einstein. The

Führer was forced to witness his destructive effect on his beloved Germany and finally had to commit suicide under the most humiliating circumstances. Einstein, though banished from his country, found numerous friends outside, all of whom were only too eager to assimilate him into their groups and provide him with facilities for a fruitful life. Actually, to a large extent, it is he who, through the atomic war, beat the *Führer* on the battlefield. Unless a person who practices altruistic egoism efficiently is killed outright (and even Hitler did not dare to kill Einstein), he will always have acquired enough friends to survive. Hence, the philosophy of life which frankly admits to doing things for one's own good yet sees the advantage in being useful to others is to my mind most acceptable, both biologically and morally.

I believe that a large part — if not the major part — of all violence, revolts, wars, alcoholism, drug addiction and other deviations in the contemporary behavior of the masses (especially of our youth) is due to a loss of the stabilizing support of constructive goals. People today cannot find suitable substitutes for the traditional aims; they used to, but can no longer, believe in such values as unquestioning, total loyalty to their religious ideals, rulers or political parties, the sanctity of the family or even the alleged security offered by accumulating a large amount of money.

Teilhard de Chardin said, "The future is in the hands of those who will have been able to give tomorrow's generation valid reasons to live and hope." The horror of not having any aim in life that we can confidently lean upon was more poetically expressed by Montaigne and earlier by Seneca in the statement: "No wind blows in favor of the ship that has no port of destination." A large portion of our youth has no final aim. They try to escape from life by any desperate spastic effort, because they no longer know where they really want to go.

I believe that science has destroyed the credibility of the strongest traditional aims by showing that most of them do not stand up to the rigid exigencies of scientific proof. All were based on absolute faith in an allegedly infallible authority which only too often proved to be fallible or even nonexistent.

In drawing up a balance sheet of the past, I am convinced that a scientifically acceptable code of ethics, a new philosophy of behavior, could do much more good to humanity in general than any discovery that a scientist could make. Moral principles continuously push man to perfect himself. However, in the domain of science, moral obligations are difficult to accept. If men of science attempt to be correctly understood, it is important for them at the outset to make a clear-cut distinction between science and morals.

Science has no "moral values" in the usual sense of the word. Nature does not wish; she merely acts. That does not mean that individual scientists cannot be guided by morality and strictly adhere to certain ethical or even religious codes. There are Catholic, Jewish, Mohammedan or Buddhist scientists with personal ethics or religious convictions, but these are totally unrelated to their science. The only truly biological moral laws are those designed to assure survival, preferably in a secure, happy state.

From the point of view of the natural sciences, the concepts of "good" and "bad" are difficult to define. Living beings can be "good" or "bad" only in relation to something or a wish for something. In biological morals there must be a fixed point of reference.

According to the eudemonist system of ethics, the moral value of actions is considered in terms of their ability to produce personal happiness but, despite the goals promulgated by virtually all ancient schools of philosophy – stoics, epicureans, the disciples of Plato – all have failed to achieve a happy life.

Later, in different forms and with some important modifications, Jeremy Bentham, James Mill and others tried at least to define the nature of happiness. Although we all want it, it is singularly difficult to define this state with any degree of precision. Mill believed that you should not look for personal pleasure by consciously seeking self-satisfaction, but rather trust that it will be given to you automatically if you do things that are inherently good. But again, "good" for whom, and what is "good"? You cannot learn a code of behavior or a language by using mere logic and intelligence; what you need is experience. If you live according to your philosophy, eventually the feeling will become reflex, unconscious and instinctive.

I am convinced that it is the same with happiness. Consider the pleasure it gives you to kiss someone you deeply love. If you have experienced the pleasure of a passionate embrace, you need no explanation; if you haven't, no one can help you by verbal descriptions.

If a man is a great patriot, no one has to tell him that he should do good for his country; if he is religious he feels the obligation to follow or even teach his faith. Whether a man is good or bad is a question that lies beyond the domain of science. Immunological defense reactions, although good for me, are bad for the microbes that feed on my body. These considerations must be taken into account if we wish to develop a philosophy of life, a code of behavior in harmony with the laws of Nature. I am always coming back to this aspect of my considerations, which I regard as the most important one. We must have a code composed of moral and ethical concepts that can be followed because they correspond to our nature and not exclusively because we believe them to be commanded by some infallible authority.

Everyone must decide for himself just what his aims in life should be, and I leave it up to philosophers, theologians and others to debate the ultimate purpose of man's existence. I see my own goal as the development and application of the code of behavior and motivation that I find best for myself. Because of the public acceptance I have met in explaining altruistic egoism, I continue to believe that it is a sound set of guidelines by which to live, and therefore feel it my "duty" to teach the code to those who want to listen. However, this is not a duty in the usual sense of the word, for it is not an obligation imposed upon me by someone else; it is one that makes me happy. As Nietzsche said:

> I slept and I dreamed that life is pleasure;
> I woke and I saw that it is duty;
> I worked and I realized that duty is pleasure.

The basic principles of altruistic egoism can be summarized by two simple words: *be necessary!* The trouble is that the scientific justification of the code cannot be explained in so few words; you have to live it to understand it completely. It has always been most frustrating to me when interviewers from the media have asked me to sum it up in a few sentences. Hundreds of people have tried to present my code in newspaper articles, on radio or television, but always only in an extremely abridged form, apologizing that they could not get more space or time from their superiors. I have suggested many times that it would be better to present my work only once or twice, but allowing for a more meaningful, extensive discussion. When I have hesitated to present forty years of medical research in such a condensed form, they have argued that the media can give only the essence in a nutshell. This has often led to misunderstandings, because the interviewers have felt that I either underestimate their ability to understand a succinct résumé or that I do not want to be troubled with teaching the masses.

Of course, this is not true. My code of behavior is useless if it cannot be assimilated by the population at large; it is not meant only for an intellectual aristocracy. That is precisely why I feel frustrated by the impossibility of satisfying the requests.

Recently this difficulty reached a climax, when I was asked to explain stress in five minutes on an American national hook-up television program. Not anxious to do so, I went through the usual arguments with the woman who was to interview me. As she was obviously offended by my reluctance, it suddenly occurred to me to explain my exasperation by example, and the following conversation ensued:

"Do you speak French?" I asked.

"No," she said.

"You see, we speak French at home and I teach in French at the university. But assuming I were the best teacher of this language and you the most gifted student, do you think I could teach you French in five minutes?"

"Evidently not," she answered, with a glimpse of understanding.

"Well, in France even the village idiot can speak French, but he certainly didn't learn it in five minutes."

There are things we can learn without any higher education or intelligence but they take time and experience to learn. This is certainly true when it comes to a philosophy of life.

It is only fair to say that many people apply my code to their own existence before ever having heard anyone speak about it or even realizing that this is what they do. Science has shown that people do many things well before they know why they do them.   When we are hungry, we eat; when our muscles become sluggish from sitting too long in the same position, we move about to relax them.   It it not necessary to understand the biochemistry of digestion or muscular contraction in order to act properly under such conditions.   But understanding the mechanism helps to strengthen our faith and enables us to improve our performance.   If a slot machine gets stuck, it is sometimes enough to give it a kick, but it is safer to call a mechanic who can repair it on the basis of his understanding.

Altruistic egoism has always been my unconscious guideline, although it took me a lifetime to formulate my concept of motivation in scientific terms and to illustrate it with examples of laws regulating tissue reactions in biology and particularly in medicine.   I first tried to analyze my code scientifically because of a deep desire to help my children overcome the difficulty of readjusting their motivation in our age of changing value systems, permissiveness, student unrest and continual strikes.

Unfortunately, a code of behavior, unless followed instinctively or taught at an early age, is not easily accepted.   In all honesty I must admit that I have not been uniformly successful with my efforts to help adults who already have deeply ingrained codes of their own.   Although I have not always achieved my goal with those in my immediate surroundings, I seem to have succeeded much better with scientists and laymen who have read my writings or listened to my lectures.   As the old saying goes, no one is a prophet in his own country.

Even if I cannot explain stress withing the space limits of an autobiography, I can try to summarize the code in a few easily remembered points.   When I wrote the first edition of *The Stress of Life* I was very proud to have converted thirty long years of research into a mere 300 pages; but when I took it to my publisher he informed me that the material was too long.   "Well, perhaps it isn't worth publishing," I suggested.   "No, no," he replied, "this is good, but you have to make a summary for people to read.   We have to publish the whole book, because if your peers don't have the factual material on which to accept it, nobody will listen to you." Undaunted, I returned to my office and turned out a ten-page summary. The editor looked at this and said, "Well, doctor, this is a little better, but you still have to cut it down." I didn't see how I could possibly describe the stress concept in fewer words, but he insisted on a summary of the summary. It was then that I thought up my jingle about not putting up resistance in vain.

Now I can do even better, if pressed, to condense the thoughts behind altruistic egoism. As I said, the entire philosophy boils down to two words: *be necessary!* But if asked to pick out the basic points for a "recipe against distress," I would reiterate:

Stress cannot be avoided. It is the body's response to any demand, and without making demands on any of our capacities, we would be dead. Our goal should be to live in the manner that gives us the most eustress (which is pleasant) and the least distress (which is detrimental).

We must each of us find our own stress level, and live neither more nor less intensely than Nature has intended.

We must have a goal, a "port of destination" that we ourselves, and not only society, consider worthy of our efforts.

We cannot avoid being egoists, because all living creatures are made to look out for themselves and for their own species first. This does not imply that we should be reckless egoists, caring nothing about the interests of others, for that would be unacceptable, not only on moral grounds, but because it is disadvantageous. We could not live in constant fear of retaliation from those we have wounded, nor could we tolerate the traumatic guilt complexes resulting from such behavior.

We must be altruists, not only because our creeds and education command us to do so, but because altruism has great value in terms of biological survival. Man is a social being who depends upon his environment; often he can earn the indispensable support of his surroundings only by offering his support in return. However, absolute altruism is contrary to man's nature, and would only encourage parasitic behavior where each person would rely solely on the assistance of others.

It is possible to marry these two apparently contradictory concepts through the code of "altruistic egoism," in which each member of society works for his own good but adjusts his aims to be maximally useful to others, thereby assuring his own security.

Bringing our own modern concepts to the ancient wisdom of the Bible, we can learn to *"earn* thy neighbor's love," each of us finding a way to protect our own interests by *being necessary and useful* to our fellow-men.

Even those who accept the value of my code as a means of facing the adversities inflicted by psychological reactions often doubt that it can be applied to extreme situations — for instance, coping with incurable disease or advanced age. Yet from my own experience, I believe that altruistic egoism can be just as useful in dealing with life's worst crises as in handling everyday problems.

When I was fifty years old, I began to develop an osteoarthritis, a deformation of the hip joint that was so painful that even large doses of strong painkillers had little effect. Eventually I could move about only with the help of two crutches and was confined to a wheelchair. Needless to say, I was greatly disturbed at the prospect of having to give up all my activities.

My surgeon, Dr. F. E. Stinchfield, recommended an operation which at the time was very dangerous: he would expose and remove all the bony irregularities, covering the joint surface with a metallic cap. Afraid of becoming nothing more than a burden to my family and myself, I agreed to the surgery.

As a result of the operation I developed a severely bleeding stress ulcer, much to the merriment of all the interns and residents of the hospital who came to see Selye suffering from "Selye's ulcer." Nevertheless, I continued to perform a daily regimen of exercises to maintain the motility of the painful artificial hip. Eventually I recovered and was able to return to my routine, proud to have licked the disease.

The operation had been performed in New York, and I had spent a long time recuperating there. I was full of restless energy and anxious to get right back to work. As soon as I landed at Montreal's Dorval airport, I phoned the institute to announce that I was back and on my way to the university. Upon my arrival I found two of my assistants waiting on the ground floor to help me into the elevator with my crutches. I flatly refused their aid, protesting that I had been taught in the hospital how to climb stairs on crutches and needed to practice. I went up four flights under my own steam, much to the terror of the escorts who insisted on following me. When I finally reached the institute I greeted everyone with a radiant smile of triumph!

That same day I wanted to spend some time in the sun, as I try to do whenever possible. During the summer the sun comes in at such a straight angle from above that I had to lie on the window sill to get its rays. This didn't bother me, even with my artificial hip, but everyone around me worried that my handicap would make it more likely than ever that I would finally fall off the seventh-floor ledge.

The staff was relieved when I eventually eased myself down from the window. But a few minutes later I informed them that, these barriers crossed, I now wanted to see if I could drive using only my good left leg. After quite a struggle to get into the car with my crutches and ride around the parking area, I looked up to the seventh floor to find the entire staff leaning out of the windows, nervously watching my performance. Although I had managed to circle around the courtyard, my circles were a little uncertain and square. The second time everything went perfectly, and I continued to drive myself to and from the university throughout my time on crutches.

I was really desperate when, a few years later, it became apparent that an osteoarthritis had attacked my other hip too. Still determined not become an invalid, I once more agreed to undergo surgery. This time a somewhat improved technique was used: the head of my hipbone was completely sawed off along with the socket from my pelvis. The surgeon replaced them with plastic objects, permanently inserted in my bones like fillings in a tooth. I went through the prolonged painful exercise period a second time, calling upon all my motivation to get me through the difficult time. Finally I was ready to get back to work, able to move about unaided. By now, the technique of this operation has improved so much that those who have undergone it in recent years will no longer be able to understand how difficult it was to face similar situations when the procedure was just in its developing stage.

Several years went by with few problems until, once again, I found myself needing surgery. This turned out to be a much more dangerous situation. An egg-shaped tumor had developed under the skin of my thigh, and it was diagnosed as a histiocytic reticulosarcoma, one of the most vicious cancers known to man. I had it removed immediately by a Montreal surgeon, Dr. J. E. Tabah, and his team. After the operation they severely irradiated the surrounding area with a cobalt bomb. I insisted on knowing my chances for a lasting recovery. Dr. Tabah spoke frankly, admitting that this type of cancer spreads rapidly and almost always kills within a year, except in the extremely rare cases when, purely by chance, the surgeon succeeds in removing all the cancer cells.

I refused to retreat from life in desperation and, although I knew it would take tremendous self-discipline, I was determined to continue living and working without worrying about the end. It's difficult to live normally when you are treated like a man condemned to die, so I told no one outside my immediate family about my predicament. In a sense, I refused to believe in my fate; I suppressed any thoughts of my presumably imminent death, and apparently even my closest friends and associates failed to notice any difference in my behavior. I rewrote my will, including several suggestions for the continuation of my work by my colleagues; and having taken care of that business, I promptly forced myself to disregard the whole calamity.

I immersed myself in my work, summoning all my strength to get on with living and avoid brooding. A year went by, then two, and it turned out that I was that fortunate exception. Now, years after the discovery of my cancer, I know the danger, though slight, still exists. My artificial hips could break down, my cancer could regain its vitality. In any case, I shall eventually die of old age. But nothing could ever deprive me of those years during which my code has allowed me to enjoy a life so full of pleasure and satisfaction. I may say that, apart from a few bad moments, I have lived happily through my seventy-one years.

I can never be sure if I handled my troubles in the best possible way; certainly my approach would not work for everyone. Sometimes the prolonged distress of knowing that you or someone you love will inevitably die causes irreparable psychological damage. Perhaps it is best to leave the incurable patient and his family blissfully ignorant. But in my case, I derive a great deal of satisfaction from knowing that even when I believed I was going to die I still lived up to my highest ideals.

I recently had another chance to act as a human guinea pig and put my code to the test. I had to undergo an emergency prostatectomy, requiring three days of pretreatment in the hospital. However, I had committed myself to a lecture before an important audience at one of Montreal's largest hotels and, as the sponsors had gone to a lot of trouble publicizing my address, I did not have the heart to call it off, even though the event fell on the third day of the pretreatment. I convinced my physicians to give me a four-hour leave from the hospital, allowing me to attend the scheduled cocktail party and dinner and present my address without disturbing the plans. The doctors warned me that I would not be able to lecture anyway, under such conditions, but I argued that I could.

Aided by altruistic egoism, I took up the challenge and reacted quite calmly and syntoxically. During the dinner, several of the guests asked me the meaning of the small wristband I had hoped to hide from view, but I answered that I would tell them only after the address. I spoke for over an hour in the same leisurely manner as usual. Being perfectly resigned to the inevitable events of the next day, I did not get excited or worried, because I did not want to "fight in vain."

The lecture was very well received, and after considerable applause and a standing ovation, the chairman gave me a gift and expressed his gratitude. Before the crowd dispersed I held up my hands and asked them to remain for one last remark. I then explained that the wristband was my identification as a resident patient at Hôtel Dieu Hospital, and that the following morning my surgeon, Dr. Jean Charbonneau, would be performing a major operation on me. In fact, I told them a car was waiting to take me back for some final preoperative treatment that same night. Because I was so relaxed myself, I had not wanted to make the audience feel ill at ease, but now that it was all over, I wished to tell them what was in store for me to illustrate the practicality of my code.

The applause was perhaps the warmest I have ever received; some of the women even had tears in their eyes as I quickly walked through the crowd to my car. And, you see, this really was not a major sacrifice for me, as I enjoyed every minute of it. As I have often said, "It is not what happens to you, but the way you take it." It gave me such satisfaction to know that, even under these difficult conditions, I knew how to take it. The operation went well, and I am now pleased as punch to be able to discuss it in retrospect, having managed once more to meet the stress of life, deriving only eustress and not distress.

My philosophy keeps me from fearing any other catastrophes which might spoil the enjoyment of my remaining years. During this time I shall pursue at my stress level the goals that *I* consider worthwhile and which correspond to *my* nature, without making any compromises to the prejudices of society and the behavior that is expected of me.

With my parents, about 1909. On the back of this postcard, my mother wrote to my grandmother, "As usual, little Hans did not keep quiet even for the minute it takes to expose such a photo. I had to give him a piece of chocolate to tranquilize him."

A few months later, sightseeing with my mother (*right*) and grandmother. The broad-brimmed hat, long hair and skirt worn by little boys at the time made it difficult to distinguish them from little girls. At least they did not make me wear such a bush of magnificent ostrich feathers as those on Mother's hat, which melt imperceptibly into the background shrubbery.

With my first intimate
friend, "Quack."

My father when he was about 52 years old.

My grandparents' summer home in Dornbach, a suburb of Vienna. I am the smallest speck on the top-floor balcony.

Here I am in Austrian *Lederhosen* on the grounds of the same summer residence with Madame Totier (*center*) and three chambermaids, about 1915.

By 1916, the purely French son of Madame Totier (*left*) had become so well-assimilated into his new culture that he too sported the Austrian folk costume, while I struck the swaggering pose of an obviously immodest adolescent.

Formal portrait just after exchanging "marriage vows" and swearing eternal love to my cousin Annemarie, who possessively places her chubby hand on "her man." My hair has been clipped short and she wears a floral decoration for the occasion.

My uncle Bruno, Annemarie's father, in the full regalia of an Austrian dueling fraternity.

College of the Benedictine Fathers in Komárom, where I received most of my early education. This was a gigantic edifice as compared to the little houses seen in the background and the one in front with the gas lamp.

Uncle Bruno in Austrian uniform, just before leaving for the front, proudly displaying his wife, Mellie, and Annemarie, and also one of the most modern automobiles of that period.

At a costume ball at my parents' house in Komárom.

Around the time when, as a second-year medical student at the University of Prague, I first though about "the syndrome of just being sick." My unfortunate love affair with Kweechka the pony had long been forgotten and I was still a passionate horseman.

My Czechoslovak passport, bearing the Canadian immigration stamp.

At my first wedding. On the left is my best man, Dr. J. S. L. Browne; on the right, the maid of honor, a friend of Penna's.

Cathy obviously sharing her mother's pleasure in music.

A few years later, the perfect lady.

As Assistant Professor of Biochemistry at McGill.

My second wife, Gabrielle, soon after our wedding.

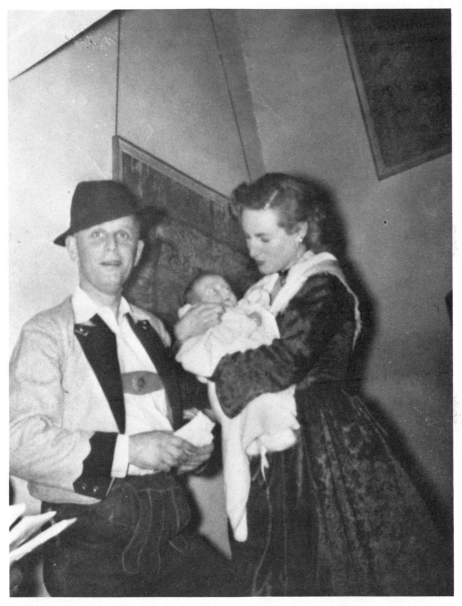

With our infant Marie at another costume ball, this time in our home in Montreal. My second wife and I are dressed in Austrian peasant costumes— mine is the one I wore as a university student during summer holidays, hers is an old family heirloom she inherited from my mother.

The family grows up.

The hour set aside daily before going to sleep for drawing pictures, mostly of animals God forgot to create. *From left to right*: Michel, Marie, André and Jean.

A daddy obviously proud of his daughter.

Surveying the completely destroyed wing of my library after 1962 fire.

Acting as bartender at a reception given in our home for one of the institute's "Claude Bernard Visiting Professors." During the more formal parts of these events, the bar is hidden behind sliding mirrors in the dining room.

I know just how I'm going to get out of this one on the radio!

世 利 得 範 洲

DIRECTOR & PROFESSOR

INSTITUTE OF EXPERIMENTAL
MEDICINE AND SURGERY
UNIVERSITY OF MONTREAL

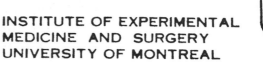

Official calling card (*left*), given to me so that I might introduce myself to the people I meet in Japan. Stamp (*right*) to make imprints of my name in Japanese, instead of an official signature which would take me a long time to master!

With my second wife on a lecture tour in Japan. I've given up both the crutches and the cigar since then.

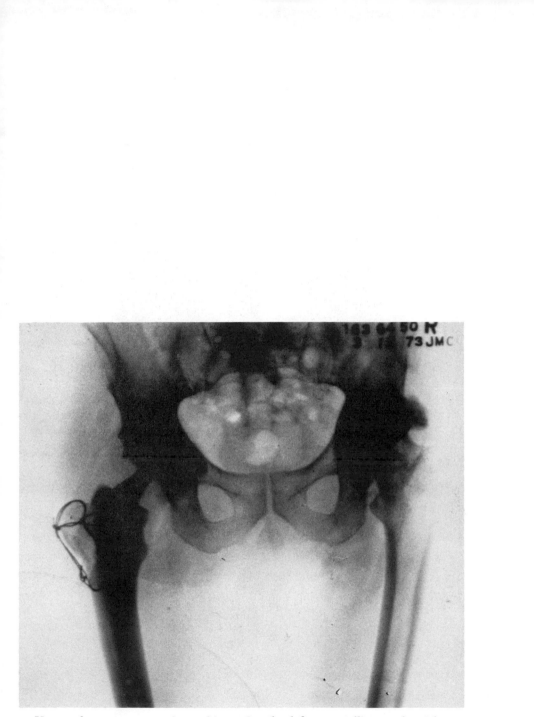

X-ray of my two nonexistent hips. On the left, a metallic; on the right, a plastic substitute.

My investiture in 1968 by the Governor General as Companion of the Order
of Canada.

At the bookstore of the Academy of Sciences in Budapest a crowd formed inside and far along the street to have me sign copies of the Hungarian translation of *The Stress of Life,* which is now into its seventh printing there.

The corner of my office where this book and most of my previous writings were dictated. The many volumes in the background are the manuscripts of my encyclopedia, *Stress in Health and Disease.* I sit in my typical working position, my feet resting on a dictionary and a specially constructed movable desk on my lap, allowing complete relaxation at work.

Getting ready for my bike exercises at 5:00 A.M. before going to work.

Enjoying the California sunshine during a break at a congress—undisturbed!

Ophthalmological examination of one of my patients. (Photo © by Karsh, Ottawa)

The present, while I was thinking about ways to write this revised edition of my autobiography. (Photo © Laszlo, Montreal)

With Louise Selye just after having our bilingual plaque placed on the wall of the Downtown Center of the International Institute of Stress. (Photo © Laszlo, Montreal)

"Selling" the Code

A scientific fact should speak for itself and be accepted on merit, not on the eloquence of its discoverer. Yet many theories and facts of considerable value have been buried in some unknown journal for decades, only to be rediscovered later by another scientist who does not even realize that his findings "were already known." But known to whom? Known to a scientist long since dead, who did not have the ability to make his findings generally available and accepted for practical exploitation? If so, the only thing the "rediscoverer" has added is salesmanship; sometimes it takes just that to make science useful. This is even more true of teaching, for a good teacher must be a bit of an actor and even an evangelist who has, and can impart to others, the enthusiasm necessary for learning.

Whether salesmanship and oratory are objectionable depends upon what you are trying to sell. People justly condemn those who do not believe in their products or ideas and still try to promote public acceptance, but you cannot teach students anything unless you honestly believe in its value and are enthusiastic about it. Great and successful innovators – philosophers, founders of religions, generals, scientists, statesmen – are not only zealous and honestly convinced that their efforts are worthwhile, they are also skillful organizers of "a sales force" of disciples, apostles and followers who help them disseminate their ideas and ideals.

I have found that the best way for me to reach the largest possible audience is through books and personal appearances. I especially like doing television interviews and radio broadcasts, as these allow me to communicate with a broad range of people. Judging from the response so far, my attempts have been successful, yet I wish I had time to do more.

What I would like to see is a coordination of other means of spreading the code of altruistic egoism. Novels or films could more vivdly present the applications of the code to daily problems, showing the impracticality of pure altruism and pure egoism as opposed to altruistic egoism. Educators might introduce the code to young students. Stress affects and interests everyone; I know that a good writer, photographer or painter could explore artistic methods of disseminating the philosophy. I even think that a motion picture could translate into theatrical language the inefficiency of crass egoism and absolute altruism as compared to the very satisfying combination of the two in a person who is an altruistic egoist. This might have even more meaning for the enormous crowds that frequent cinemas and appreciate such things best if translated into the terms of daily family life. All I can do is suggest these possibilities; my direct contribution is limited to outlining the scientific basis of my philosophy and teaching it by logic.

In order to share my code with the largest number of people, I now devote a great deal of my time to lecturing all over the globe. I have given up undergraduate teaching, but I continue to take my "professorial" duties very seriously because my philosophy of altruistic egoism has convinced me that this is how I can both be useful and earn the greatest amount of goodwill and gratitude.

My travels have been a source of both eustress and distress. The following itinerary prepared by my lecture coordinator shows that I am constantly on the go. This agenda is not even complete since unexpected engagements always come up, filling in the few empty days. Then again, even when a day is solidly booked with lectures and public appearances, I can never know in advance whether additional appointments have been made for me by those in charge of organizing the lecture. Thus, I can get to New York with a vague idea of my timetable, but I will find out upon arriving that I have been scheduled for additional television appearances or press conferences. Such a hectic agenda would distress many people, but I look at this as the best way of spreading my code.

September 2, Montreal Radio interview: CBC

September 9, Montreal Radio interview: Radio Canada

September 22, Montreal Radio interview: CKAC

September 24-26, Heidelberg, Germany Inauguration of new stress clinic, Klinikum der Universität Heidelberg

September 26, Paris British film crew will meet you at airport: briefing in taxi, filming in hotel room of documentary on smoking and health

September 26-28, Paris Address at the Sorbonne and meetings with R. Mallet, Chancellor of all the Parisian universities and Rector of the Sorbonne. Return after last morning meeting to the United States and stay overnight in Chicago 28th

September 29, East Stroudsburg, Pa. Address at East Stroudsburg State College in connection with Bicentennial celebration

October 3, Victoriaville, Que. Festival Positif '76. Your theme: "Gardez à l'esprit les aspects plaisants de la vie"

October 5, Aurora, Ill. District Two Illinois Nurses' Association. Your address: "Physiological responses to stress"

October 6-7, Ottawa Canadian Dept. of Health and Welfare, conference on "Health Promotion through Designed Environment." Your presentation: "Stress – its relationship to man and his environment"

October 13, Montreal Radio interview: CJAD, John Hardy Talk Show

October 17, Montreal Radio interview: Radio Canada. To be broadcast throughout francophone world in five episodes

October 17, Montreal Place des Arts: Jubilee meeting commemorating 40th anniversary of stress concept. 2500 tickets sold at $10 apiece. Keynote speech and satellite communication with Paris, R. Mallet

October 20, Montreal TV taping in your office: Télé-Metropole, "Citoyens du Monde"

October 21, Montreal Queen Elizabeth Hotel: Institute of Electrical and Electronics Engineers Inc., Canadian Communications and Power Conference. Keynote address, dinner

October 27-29, Hollywood, Fla. Pan American Medical Association, Golden Anniversary Congress. Presentation of paper. Banquet and presentation of plaque in your honor

October 29, New York Kittay Foundation Prize for Psychiatry: to be presented to you and Dr. James Olds

October 30, New York Meeting with publishers

November 1, Montreal Concordia University, Loyola Campus: Stress Week. Keynote address (public): "Stress without distress"

November 10, Toronto Canadian Chiropractic Convention. Keynote address to medical and paramedical professionals

November 12-13, Banff, Alberta Conference on "The Middle School Years," sponsored by Univ. of Alberta. Your presentation: "Stress and the middle school years"

November 13, Rockville Center, N.Y. Mercy Hospital Conference on Death and Bereavement. Keynote speech.

What is unique in this schedule is that I never relax by sightseeing. I plan to attend whatever conference is set up, often going directly from one city to the next in one day; I do not like to waste time between engagements. If I am invited to speak in one European city, and another event comes up for two days later in another city nearby, I often refuse if I can find no way to put my time to use between the lectures. I can find more beauty looking through a microscope and seeing the wonders of Nature's minute structure unadulterated than I could ever find in looking at the architecture or artwork of a foreign country. The shape of a delicately branched nerve cell, for example, offers not only understanding but also infinite beauty.

Because the demands on my time for lectures have become so numerous, I employ a lecture coordinator especially to organize my speaking engagements. She prepares my agenda, makes sure that my various appointments do not overlap and arranges for the necessary audio-visual materials.

This lecture coordinator also handles my honoraria. I know that, like sex in Victorian England, fees are not something that we talk about out in the open. But I feel justified in insisting on comparatively large honoraria for lectures. I receive an unusual number of invitations each year, some from very worthy organizations, others from groups that have no serious interest in stress, and the demand for a substantial honorarium weeds out most of the latter. The Society for the Protection of American Coyotes may think it would sound nice to have a professional scientist address their annual meeting, but when they hear about the honorarium, they quickly rethink their needs. That way both my time and their money are saved.

I have also found that when a group must try hard to raise funds, they will generally attempt to put together a more meaningful program. If much is at stake, they seem to put a greater effort into the preparations. Often this means opening the meeting up to the public, and I like this, for I prefer to speak to as many people as possible at one time.

It seems that a standard honorarium also helps to protect me against the criticism of doing favors for one cause rather than another. It's surprising how many groups feel that it is my duty to speak to them: "But we're a Hungarian group!" "But we're Austrians!" "But we're all French-speaking!" "But we're English-Canadians and you spoke for the French!" "But we're also Toyota fans!" Everyone seems to have a special reason why I'm really just "one of them" and why I should be morally obligated to address their organization.

Nevertheless, being involved in collecting lecture fees was always embarrassing for me. Now that we have incorporated the new nonprofit International Institute of Stress, the situation is different and I have no reason to feel awkward about accepting money, because checks are made payable directly to that organization for research on stress. Furthermore, neither I nor any member of my family is paid by institute funds, although this is perhaps not entirely true, since at the institute we manage to maintain a spirit which makes me feel that all the employees are members of my one great "family."

As you can see, I care little for material wealth. When I was at McGill and during my early days at the University of Montreal I quite happily donated the proceeds of my lectures to the university. I am even willing to give my personal fortune to the new institute if there is no other way to keep it alive. But I am not a true altruist, nor do I wish to be. My acceptance of honoraria is but one practical application of my code of altruistic egoism. I am happy to give what I can to a group or society if they in turn give me what I need — a chance to spread the code to a large audience and the funds to enable me to carry on my work.

When I am unable to attend a congress, usually because of timing, I am glad to suggest one of my present or former co-workers as a replacement. But I try to accept personally as many engagements as is physically possible. To do so, it is imperative that I have a well-arranged timetable with alternative solutions in case of plane delays, bad weather, transit strikes and so on.

A couple of unfortunate experiences taught me never to check my luggage when traveling by plane, since it can so easily go astray with all my slides inside. Virtually all my lectures are based on medical observations which depend entirely on photographic illustrations of our findings. Many years ago, I started out on a very complicated lecture tour to forty-six cities throughout Europe, stopping first in London, England. Upon my arrival at Heathrow Airport, my luggage could not be found. I was about to cancel the entire tour when a British colleague told me that he had prepared, for his own use, slides of my most important experiments from my first monograph on stress. They were of poor quality, being copies of printed black-and-white photographs, and far inferior to my carefully selected, beautiful color slides. Nevertheless, they did tide me over until my luggage was eventually located in London, Ontario. It was at that time that I decided never to part with my slides or indispensable personal articles.

Consequently I obtained a miniaturized shaving brush along with the thinnest possible pyjamas, underwear and suits (even a dress suit), so that I now travel all over the world with nothing but a handbag that I can take into the cabin with me. I try to foresee all other eventualities that may cause distress during such complicated trips. I come armed with earplugs in case of a noisy party in my hotel, and with emergency rations in case I get on connecting flights where no meals are served and I have no time to eat in between. I also bring duplicates of my travel plans, carrying one in my pocket, the other in my bag; and two pairs of eyeglasses, should one get lost, which happens quite often.

Still, it is impossible to account for everything that can happen, and often the results have been quite embarrassing or amusing. I recall one well-meaning chairman of a South American congress who wanted to please me with a flowery expression of gratitude after my speech.   He began, in his halting English, "I have had de greatest deaficulty to convince de governors to build dis enormous auditorium; dey said dat in dis city such a beek hall would never be fool, so I played trick on dem and invited Professor Selye; I knew he could fool any auditorium and, you see, he did."

A Finnish colleague introduced me by expounding enthusiastically on my particular lecturing style, ending up by saying, ". . . and now, you will hear a lecture in the inimitable style that has come to be identified throughout the world with the name of Dr. Silly!"

My travels have made me especially sensitive to these linguistic problems that arise when people try to communicate in a language other than their own.   I once attended a congress on the island of St. Martin, which is part French and part Dutch.   I went with three Americans to buy an alarm clock because I had forgotten my own and had to wake up early to prepare for a lecture.   We stopped at a local store where the native cashier handed me a receipt for my money, saying, "With this you can get your clock in Paqueechink."   None of us understood what she meant, thinking this must be another shop, or even another town.   I had to ask her to repeat her instructions three times.   Not wanting to offend her, we turned to seek information elsewhere, roaming through the large department store until we finally came upon a counter marked PACKAGING.

I also have vibrant memories of a certain Japanese chairman who, having translated every word of his prepared text with the aid of a dictionary, continued to refer to the members of our institute as "Professor Selye and his honorable accomplices."   And there was the young professor, excited after speaking about my achievements in the field of stress research and mentioning Selye and stress innumerable times, who finally gave me the floor with a flourish: ". . . and now, I present Dr. Stress."   (Some people even do that on purpose to please me by identifying the child with its proud father!)

In a 1972 speech, I encountered so many of the horrors that can spoil a lecture that the *Chicago Tribune* appropriately titled their editorial report on my ordeal as a "Speaker's Nightmare."

My plane was delayed so I arrived late for my speech, keeping several hundred people waiting. As soon as I had begun to talk, music trickled out of the public address system, which was somehow connected with others, and no one could fix it. I continued, asking for the first slide to be shown, and the slide came out backwards on a screen that was too small, cutting off half the picture. The microphone suddenly emitted a piercing shriek. As if that weren't enough, the audience was then treated to the sound effects of a boisterous cocktail party in the adjoining room, complete with giggling women, tinkling ice cubes and risqué jokes. It is always a speaker's dream to "bring down the house," and this time, I literally did just that — suddenly the huge floor-to-ceiling room dividers came down with a crash! As the papers reported, "The stress expert kept his cool," but I must admit I had just about reached my limit!

No matter how carefully the preparations are made, there is always the chance of an odd turn of events. At a huge medical congress in Berlin, I was to deliver the keynote address. I had carefully checked all the equipment beforehand, and after a few words of introduction, I asked for my first slide. It turned out that while I was being presented to the audience, someone had torn the electrical wire of the projector. I really could not imagine how I would speak about anatomical and histological changes without slides. My predicament was comparable to that of an explorer of some hitherto undescribed tropical country who is faced with the problem of illustrating the scenery, plants and animals using only words. It would mean little to speak of having seen "a huge lion," desperately emphasizing that "it was really enormous, you can't imagine how big it was and it looked so menacing when it let out a fear-inspiring roar."

I was temporarily at a loss; the audience was not only growing restless but they were evidently feeling sorry for me. However, with the despair of the moment, and realizing it was now impossible to give my carefully planned lecture on the pathology of stress, I heeded Dale Carnegie's advice, "If you get a lemon, then make lemonade." I told them that I would at least demonstrate my own resistance to distress if they would accept a change of title. I spoke of scientific creativity, a subject that interested me enough to write a book about it *(From Dream to Discovery)*. The extemporaneous address was a howling success, but I am sure the standing ovation I received was due more to my leisurely manner of avoiding embarrassment to the organizers than to the lecture itself.

I never use a manuscript for my address, because I prefer to adjust my words to the audience's reactions. This lends to my speeches an air of spontaneity which is not quite accurate, as I come armed with years of scientific experience and the tricks of the trade of lecturing. Nevertheless, I have been told that my lectures and media appearances come off as remarkably casual. Perhaps this is because I honestly have never experienced stage fright, whether I have had to speak to two or 2,000 people. I feel no different chatting with someone in my office than standing on a podium looking into a sea of unknown faces. I like to create a close rapport with my audience, and to do this I studiously avoid mannerisms that might lend that air of solemnity normally associated with the pulpit or lectern. Leaning against a blackboard or perching on the edge of a table suffices to abolish the air of academic formality. In fact, by now, I have found that lecturing in an armchair with no table or lectern between me and my audience gives a "fireside chat" atmosphere which suits my style perfectly. I also try to project a relaxed tone of voice, one that invites the audience to listen and question. It is not that I am pretending to be interested in their response; I really enjoy and learn from the feedback. I am not imagining myself alone with one person instead of a mass of people, and I'm not trying to calm a pounding heart or "butterflies" in the stomach. I simply do not feel any reason *not* to have confidence in my ability to discuss stress and avoid talking about anything else.

Stress enters into every kind of human activity, and I have managed to come in contact not only with many interesting scientific colleagues, but also with outstanding statesmen, artists, philosophers and other celebrities. I have been asked to speak about stress to air traffic controllers, environmentalists, biochemists, sociologists, surgeons, dentists, business executives, bacteriologists, bankers . . . the list is endless. A short time ago I served as a visiting professor of psychiatry at Harvard University's

Massachusetts General Hospital. This appointment was certainly not due to my profound knowledge of psychiatry — I am convinced that I would fail even the simplest examination on this subject. I admitted this when I was invited; however, my hosts disarmingly assured me that they were well aware of this but that I would only be expected to discuss the psychosomatic aspects of our research and its impact on the development of mental disease. Evaluating its strictly psychiatric implications would be left up to them.

Even if such events sometimes leave me feeling that I am stepping outside my field of competence, I am happy to have these contacts and consider them a marginal benefit of my scientific work. For example, a short time ago I was invited to participate in a taping for a BBC series called "The Age of Uncertainty," hosted by economist John Kenneth Galbraith. The discussion, I was told, would center around overpopulation, economic stability, nuclear power and American politics — all in relation to the rise of industrial society.

The guest list was impressive: Henry Kissinger (at that time Secretary of State), historian Arthur Schlesinger, Jr., newspaper publisher Katharine Graham and editor Thomas Winship, ex-Prime Ministers Edward Heath of Britain and Kukrit Pramoj of Thailand, Russian Academician Gyorgy Arbatov, economist Ralph Dahrendorf, British M.P. Shirley Williams and labor union leader Jack Jones. The taping would be done during an informal weekend meeting at Galbraith's farm in Vermont.

I was torn between feeling out of place among such notables and curiosity about the event but finally decided to attend. Although it was a fascinating experience to meet and talk with these eminent people during meals and walks through the countryside, I continued to feel that I could contribute little on the subjects raised. I managed to squeeze in some discussion of my pet topic of stress in the taped interviews, under the heading of keeping the human environment "livable, pleasant and safe," but the vast scope of the project necessarily limited the amount of time devoted to psychosocial factors.

Yet if I sometimes seem reticent about expressing opinions, because the questions I am asked are beyond my field of competence, people are often offended and I have been accused of conceit, indifference or even snobbery. I have tried to limit my participation to those areas where I feel I can contribute knowledgeably. Nevertheless, I am sometimes confronted with questions to which my response can only be "Why do they ask *me* . . .?"

As my face often appears on television or in newspapers, and because I travel so often, I also get to meet many lay people from all walks of life. This can be quite gratifying. Sometimes strangers will approach me merely to express gratitude for the help that my medical or behavioral research has given them. Other encounters are less rewarding to my "healing-oriented" mind: requests for autographs "for their children," congratulations on my latest book, expressions of pleasure to have met me. With time, these tend to become quite monotonous, but I suppose they are all part of "being in the public eye." It would not be honest to deny that I do like to feel useful and, particularly, to know that I have so many friends and well-wishers among people I have never met.

I am also frequently recognized because of my characteristic profile. This is the least offensive adjective I can think of as being applicable to my face. Some people say that it resembles that of my compatriot, the Canadian moose, because I lost the tip of my nose in an explosion in the chemistry lab during my early student days. Whenever I am recognized in airports, restaurants or on the street, I am flattered, but also a little disturbed that I can never be alone. My time is taken up by well-meaning "fans" who make complimentary remarks or by potential patients in search of a free consultation, so I am never sure I will be able to read, think or speak to a friend uninterrupted.

A few years ago I became so tired of being recognized that I bought a wig and a pair of large dark glasses to hide my identity on trips. The wig was just as white as my own natural hair, but it was curly and thick, reaching well below the customary nudity of my forehead. In addition, the adopted hair was very long, and bushy sideburns covered most of my cheek. Looking into a mirror, even I could not recognize myself. For two weeks nobody stopped me in public places and I felt secure that probably people could really not spot me, but it is possible that they just understood my desire to be left alone.

Then, when I was returning by plane to Montreal after an international stress congress in Paris, the gentleman seated on my left suddenly exclaimed, "Oh! Dr. Selye! I don't know what it is about you but you certainly seem to have changed." Well, what could I do? I admitted defeat and took off my expensive hairpiece, never to wear it again.

After the failure of such efforts to get peace for reading, rest or thought, I turned to my always-helpful counselor, Nature. How do animals get rid of unwanted intruders without using brutal physical force? There is the inkfish, who merely squirts a cloud of black fluid in which he disappears; but this trick is not particularly applicable to my problem when someone sits next to me at an airport or on a plane. Nor am I equipped with the mechanism of the skunk, who defends himself by letting out a repulsive, odoriferous secretion when he wants to be left alone. But, taking a tip from the skunk, I suddenly thought of garlic! I now always travel with a few bulbs of garlic in my pocket. In their natural dry envelope they emit no smell at all, but when cornered I peel one and slowly masticate it as if it were chewing gum. I happen to like garlic, so this does not bother me, but sooner or later my neighbor deserts me. There are regulations about not smoking in certain sections of a plane or in public places, but no provisions have been made about munching garlic wherever you want to and exhaling its perfume with sadistic satisfaction and a charming smile in the direction of your aggressor, especially if you explain that this is very good for your health.

On the other hand, there are certain advantages to being recognized, and there have been moments when I wished my face were better known. There was the time I stood in line to register at the Gordon Conference in New London, New Hampshire, with my wife and four children after a six-hour drive. As I looked very tired and was to address the conference in a few hours, a colleague next to me suggested I go up to the head of the line and identify myself to get faster service. Thereupon a bystander related the story of a famous American actor waiting in line to get into a theatre who was told by his wife, "You don't have to stand here, just tell them who you are." The actor replied, "Honey, if you have to tell them who you are — you ain't."

Sometimes my ambivalent relationship with fame presents both sides at once. There are always moments on trips to foreign universities when people come up and ask me to "just say a few words," possibly the hardest request for anyone to fulfill. It is not easy to come up at a moment's notice with an inspiring thought that will long be remembered. I recall that, while visiting a university in Chile, I was ushered into an auditorium full of medical students taking an exam. Beaming, my guide turned to me and said, "They're just writing about Selye's stress syndrome. Won't you say a few inspiring words? They would always remember this day." Here were these students, probably anxious to get on with their writing uninterrupted. What could I possibly say to them? When this happens I usually manage to make a few unpretentious remarks, but I still feel rather uncomfortable. I am always reminded of the ancient Christian who saved his life in the Roman arena by warning the lion that he would be expected to say a few impromptu words after the meal. I got out of this jam by giving them a brief summary of how I would write this exam, which was most welcome at this time.

Whatever the hazards of public exposure, personal appearances are the most effective means of spreading my code. Still, I know that like so many other things in life, a code of ethics and behavior cannot simply be acquired; it must be lived. Only after long periods of experimentation under the guidance of a teacher or parent does a code become a natural, instinctively followed set of principles.

I sometimes ask myself whether I have always managed to follow my own doctrine to perfection. I must admit that this is not the case. I feel I am doing fairly well at it, but still have not overcome all the hurdles. After all, the designer of a racing car is not necessarily its best driver.

If any member of a group — a family, a research team, an association or a commercial organization — is an absolute egoist or an absolute altruist, and consistently rewards and praises such one-sided behavior, it becomes very difficult to convince other members of the group to embrace altruistic egoism. If one lazy egoist gets away with this behavior because another absolute altruist blindly encourages him, giving him all he wants, the example of his success can do so much harm that no amount of education in altruistic egoism could compensate for the damage done. It is the same when, to achieve conformity within society, altruists encourage altruism or egoists promote egoism.

During a recent public address I was approached by a woman from the audience who explained that she was trying without success to apply my code of altruistic egoism to her life. It seems that her husband had a drinking problem which he refused to acknowledge, but which caused him to miss work, forget obligations and generally ignore the world outside his bottle. Perhaps he felt guilty over his own lack of accomplishment; but at any rate, whatever she or their children tried to achieve, he constantly ridiculed. He encouraged the children to skip school by readily giving them false certificates to convince the teachers that they were sick. He laughed when they ignored their mother's requests to study, thus reinforcing their disrespect of all her avowed values.

I wish I could have advised her, but I must admit my code is useless in such extreme cases. When someone is more frequently exposed to a destructive principle than to a constructive one and the former is presented more attractively, the latter will almost inevitably lose out, whatever its inherent merit. In this instance, the mother had two points against her. First, the husband was home more than she, as he no longer worked steadily while she was forced to do so. Second, what he proposed to the children seemed like more fun than the traditional rules of attending school and working hard. It might be that as they grew older and more aware, the children would see the real harm their father had caused them; but in the meantime the damage of his purely egoistic behavior was hard to combat.

There are two basic threats to the theory of altruistic egoism. One is the "saboteur," the other the "crocodile." In the above-mentioned example, the husband was a saboteur, and no matter how hard his wife tried, she could not counteract his influence upon their children. If a group of young boys are stealing from a store and one of them begins to protest that he really isn't sure they are doing the right thing, it's obvious that his friends will not suddenly "see the error of their ways" and return the merchandise. Instead, they will ridicule him as a simple-minded, unimaginative "goody-goody."

On the other hand, there are people who do not consciously try to destroy the good influences of others, but who are simply unable to respond in a constructive manner. Like the crocodile, they do not seem to have the brain structures necessary for attitudes other than fear, rage and aggression. In such cases, when no acts of altruism seem to work, it is a perfect waste of time to try altruistic egoism; we need to be capable of normal interactions. Fortunately, the true crocodile type is rare; and if you meet one, it is not your code that is to blame, for no philosophy of conduct is applicable in all situations, especially when manifestly abnormal personalities are involved. I know that my efforts have often been blocked through such sabotage and I can only hope that others may succeed better. Yet there will always be people blind to any kind of truth or beauty.

Through teaching or example you can improve whatever innate gifts you have; but you could never get a crocodile to lick your hand lovingly, any more than you could teach a wild leopard not to kill. My only consolation in this respect is that I have at least outlined a code which has stood the test many times, and which seems to benefit many people, and that I also manage to put my code to good use in my own everyday life.

CHAPTER ELEVEN

Life at Work

Inscribed over the entrance to our institute are these words, which I formulated to help newcomers to find guidelines toward successful research:

> Neither the prestige of your subject and
> The power of your instruments
> Nor the extent of your learnedness and
> The precision of your planning
> Can substitute for
> The originality of your approach and
> The keenness of your observation

In my work at the institute I always try to apply the goals I espouse through my code of behavior. On the whole, I find this very helpful in my interpersonal relationships. I demand a lot of my employees, but I am willing to give just as much. I know I am hard to get along with, and I admit this without any feelings of guilt or inferiority because I am convinced that I have helped many of my co-workers. Quite a few took my authoritarian demands for hard work and self-discipline very badly, but many of them came back years later merely to express their gratitude for my tough training that eventually proved to be most helpful to them. Others have understood from the start that I really wanted to help them, and have stayed with me for one to three decades. Some have continued to volunteer their help when needed even though, for personal reasons, they left the institute years ago. These people realized that there are no shortcuts in our profession; to work overtime on Saturdays, Sundays and other holidays is part of the game. Without even giving a thought to these sacrifices, we must accept them as the necessary limitations in the scientist's "private life."

I have always looked upon science in this light and tried to motivate my associates by explaining to them the efficiency of work thus conducted and the great personal satisfaction that can be derived from it. Besides, the *esprit de corps,* the sense of pride and honor of those who work together as a single group on something they believe in, has proven to be of extraordinary value. This applies not only to scientists but also to armies, missionary communities, ship crews, and particularly to group work in all major cataclysms such as wars, epidemics, earthquakes or fires. I remember that after the discovery of penicillin, the urgent need for it among our troops had a remarkable effect upon the efficient cooperation of scientists in all allied countries. Activity was stimulated, progress accelerated incredibly with regard to the chemical purification, the establishment of the structure formula, and the large-scale industrial synthesis of this powerful antibiotic.

This *esprit de corps* is also absolutely essential for the steady efforts of our own group to clarify the stress concept and make it available to medicine. I purposely tried to convince myself that the results of our investigations were anticipated impatiently and with considerable interest by physicians and patients throughout the world. I think it helped.

I am deeply impressed by the ability of Napoleon to inspire this feeling of cohesion in his armies, thereby keeping them functional even after defeat. By using this technique in our institute I have managed to induce my colleagues and the technical and secretarial staff to make extraordinary efforts to ensure the success of our work. Few other types of social organization could have accomplished this. You can be fully effective only if you really have faith in the value of what you do.

It has often been remarked that my code is fine for myself and for other scientists, or for artists and philosophers who can take pride in their profession, but what about people who do not have the privilege of higher education or special talents? How can the taxi driver, the person employed to press a button and photostat letters all day, or the garbage man take pride in his work? I strongly object to this criticism because I feel that mine is not a code limited to the intellectual aristocracy but a biological code applicable to everyone.

Although I don't like intrusions when I'm busy or if I'm preoccupied with a scientific problem, during my free time I like nothing more than approaching the "man on the street" to see how my code works on a practical level. A year ago, I set out to visit the ailing father of one of my former students. The elderly man lived on a remote sidestreet in the Bronx. I gave the address to a taxi driver, who managed to find the place despite the fact that even the street name was misspelled on my note. When we arrived, he announced, "Well, sir, this wasn't easy! There ain't no other driver in this city who could've got ya here. Nowadays they give licenses to anybody, but I think if ya drive a cab in Noo York ya oughta know the city proper. Otherwise ya just spoil the reputation of all us guys who make a living by getting ya where ya wanna go. Ya can be damn sure that if it's in Noo York, I'll find it for ya."

At the institute we used to have a Xerox man called "Uncle Bill." He was with us for fifteen years until he retired, and everybody liked him, even if he was sometimes grumpy. He once told me; "I used to be a streetcar driver when I was younger. Then they threw me out when they brought in the Metro system so I learned how to drive buses and, let me tell you, I did it real good. Everyone was satisfied, but then they decided to replace all us old guys with younger people and I got fired again. So when I saw your ad, where it said that even old and crippled folks could apply, I came here and you told me that all you had was this Xerox job and it ain't very interesting. But I didn't mind as long as I could be useful. Now all the doctors and secretaries come to me, not only with easy stuff but even with pictures that are difficult to Xerox, because they know damned well that if anybody can do it, Uncle Bill can. It kinda makes a guy feel good. It's nice to know that whatever happens that forces you out of one job, you can get another, and that people appreciate what you do."

I even have personal experience with the problems of garbage collectors. In reply to my question of why he selected this type of job, our garbage man — who is especially efficient — once answered, "I like it. I don't want to be where people look down on me because I don't have no schooling or fancy skills. I don't want to brag, but the supervisor himself told me I'm the best damned garbage collector in Montreal. I get more work done than any of the other guys and there has never been a complaint about me from the people I serve."

Apart from my immediate family, the best subjects I have for verification of how my code works in practice are my associates at the institute. I believe that the changes in our value system have done a great deal of harm to social relationships in many enterprises because they tend to encourage continuous insistence on one's own rights. This leads to our drawing up battle lines between management and workers and even among individual employee groups.

The development of a fighting stance between employee and employer further adds to the loss of personal warmth among the people who work together. It happened that a rather incompetent employee begged me to write him a letter of recommendation without mentioning that he had been fired for incompetence. In doing so, I did not discuss his professional qualifications and mentioned only whatever advantages I could find in his character or social behavior. Later he threatened me with a lawsuit for my having "unjustly discharged" him while admitting his high qualifications in writing. This has repeated itself at various times with other employees and, as a result, I have had to learn to be more careful.

When a secretary did something well during the first weeks of her trial period, I sent her memos about it as encouragement. Later this woman was judged too aggressive and unacceptable by her own colleagues, and she had to be discharged. With that, she showed our personnel administrator a collection of all the favorable memos (not mentioning the unfavorable ones) and threatened to take action through her union for unjustified dismissal.

Naturally, the more an employee searches regulations and contracts to find passages which may justify a diminution of his responsibilities or an augmentation of his rights, the less the employer feels any desire to help him on his own initiative, motivated merely by human kindness toward a person he can consider as a friend. Nowadays, employers are increasingly less inclined to worry about personal problems of their employees, and the relationship between them is at best limited to the rigid observance of the rights of both parties. Neither asks himself anymore what he could do for the other but what is the least he must do without inviting trouble. Such attitudes are hardly conducive to the creation of a friendly, pleasant atmosphere and a warm relationship among people who work together.

If a working relationship must end for one reason or another, I try to ensure that it ends pleasantly on all sides, but if not, I refuse to give in to any form of coercion or blackmail. The most extreme case of this in my experience was that of Mr. X, a six-foot-four giant who was employed in our editorial department but never did any work. After many warnings that went ignored, he was notified that his services were no longer required.

He entered my office while I was eating lunch and announced that he wanted to talk to me. I asked him if it could wait until I had finished my meal but he answered aggressively that it could not, that he would speak to me now. So what could I do? I listened. Mr. X said that he would not be fired under any circumstances and had taken precautions against such an event, as he had felt it coming for a long time. He showed me that he had installed a tape recorder on a shelf just above my chair and had taped every word uttered over the weekends, including some disobliging remarks about several people in high positions. Then he threatened me. "Unless you keep me on the payroll for as long as *I* want to stay, I'll send transcripts of these conversations to the top officials of this university and to every member of your family!"

I replied that I would not be blackmailed, but he only smiled, saying, "Well, I've foreseen this, too. I have connections with the underworld, and unless you do as I say, I'll have you beaten up until there'll be nothing left of you but a bag of skin filled with blood and broken bones." This was not a pleasant prospect, and the way he looked — towering and menacing, and probably under the influence of some drug — it didn't sound like an empty threat. Still, I calmly told him, "Go ahead, I just won't be blackmailed."

With that he lifted me up and threw me on the sofa, hollering that he would start getting me "tenderized" if I wouldn't give in.

"Go ahead," I countered. Then the giant's deeply tanned skin became ashen gray, and he slumped down on the sofa, turned to me limply and said, "Well, I have to hand it to you. You do have courage."

But as he went slinking out of the office he warned me that although it was too dangerous to do so right in the university because someone might hear my screams, some day soon he would carry out his plan to have his friends "teach me a lesson." After he left I phoned the Royal Canadian Mounted Police, and for some time after that there were police cruisers circling my house. Luckily his threats were empty because no one ever touched me, especially after Mr. X received a visit from the RCMP, who informed him that he might want to reconsider his plans. I don't believe that he ever intended to take such violent action, only that he desperately wanted to be back on the payroll.

This was certainly the worst incident of its kind, but I have been threatened more than a few times, and never regretted having refused to give in to blackmail. Even if it was sometimes tempting to do small favors under pressure or to spend minor amounts of money to avoid major trouble, I knew that once you have given in, you have provided the blackmailer with an open invitation to repeat his demands over and over because, in submitting once, you have admitted your guilt. Actually, in the case of Mr. X, there was very little he could have put on tape. I see few people on the weekends and, even assuming that on the spur of the moment I might have said I thought the Minister of Health was an ass or I suspected a technician of having sex in his lab on my time — so what?

With all my research and philosophizing, it is only fair to admit that I do not succeed in every case but, as time goes on, I feel that I win more often than I lose in my efforts to approximate an optimal interpersonal relationship. One such example involved a young Czech doctor, Pavel Rohan, who copied down the following transcript as a souvenir. He had recently joined our institute to continue his post-graduate studies, and whenever I tried to discuss his experiments, he would become completely inarticulate. I pointed this out and he blurted, "Well, I know, but sometimes I suddenly hate you so much that I become speechless."

At first this remark took me aback, but then I replied, "Unfortunately, this is entirely mutual, but the delightful thing about it is that we can admit all this without in the least endangering the cordiality of our friendship."

Over the years I have developed many techniques which help me to concentrate on the essentials at work. When I want solitude I lock myself in my office, disconnect the telephone and switch on a red light placed on my door at eye level above a sign that says "Please do not disturb." Occasionally we must overcome our "good manners" to gain a stretch of time for quiet thought or meditative relaxation.

If the red light is not turned on, staff members are encouraged to enter my office without knocking. After entering, the employee whispers his name. If he needs to speak with me, he waits until I respond; if he only wants to retrieve something from my office or make an entry in my calendar, he does so without explanation. In this way my thoughts are not interrupted every time anyone needs something.

I like to do everything right away, as soon as the idea hits me. My guideline is to do everything instantly if possible, even if it could be left until later, because this way I avoid overcrowding my memory reservoir. This is the opposite of the "mañana" philosophy. If I am engaged in a conversation with someone in my office and I suddenly remember something I should have said to my secretary, I tell her on the intercom system immediately so I can get it off my mind. Even if this interrupts my conversation for a minute, I am assured that my idea will not be forgotten. For the same reason (and because I have found that even secretaries can forget), I keep a notebook filled with every detail that must be left until later. This diminishes the "information pollution" which, with the explosion of scientific literature and the increasing demands of personal communications with people interested in stress, has brought me close to the limits of my tolerance.

If a co-worker must know about one of my phone conversations, he picks up an extension line in my secretary's office so I will not have to explain the same thing again later. This also guarantees that my associate gets every shading of the discussion. Of course, this is done only with the knowledge and consent of the persons involved.

Another characteristic of my life at work is that whenever I must explain something I like to proceed systematically, covering all pertinent points in a logical order. Therefore, it is disturbing to me if people interrupt me while I speak. Often this happens through an attempt to anticipate the next point:

I: "Here are three books. Let's put the first on shelf A, the second on shelf B . . ."
He: "And the third on shelf C?"

Actually, I was about to say that the third book should go on shelf Y; the point of the conversation was that they should *not* be placed on successive shelves.

A variant of this is:

I: "Let's put this book on shelf A, the second on B . . ."
He: "Where shall we put the third book?"

Obviously, I would have come to this point myself!

Rather than be annoyed by such disturbances, I try to avoid situations that I know will distress me. In doing so, I have perfected a technique known as "Operation Nightingale" to get away elegantly from a boring visitor with whom I should like to interrupt conversation, without possibly giving offense. This procedure goes as follows:

I call my secretary on the intercom and ask her whether she has finished typing the manuscript for Dr. Nightingale. Of course, this is a secret code message because we do not have any Dr. Nightingale at our institute. Two minutes after I have asked this question she automatically rushes into my office in great excitement and says, "Sorry to interrupt you but they called from the dean's office. They want you immediately in connection with some unexpected emergency which could not be settled in your absence." In this manner I can get out of the interview without being rude, and it is impossible for the visitor to detect any connection between my question about a manuscript and the emergency that has arisen.

I can divulge this technique without giving offense because, in order to be able to talk about this rather typical escape route of mine, I have replaced the names by completely different ones — but I will naturally not reveal the modification now in use!

As in most offices, my phone calls are screened to minimize unnecessary conversations. Every once in a while this can cause some confusion. For example, in 1946, my wife was not at all happy when she asked for me on the phone and a new secretary politely gave the standard answer: "Please put your problem in the form of a letter because Dr. Selye is too busy to accept phone calls. Of course, if it is something personal, just mark your letter 'confidential' and it will not be opened by the office staff."

Whenever I permit myself such retreats, I realize that the world does continue to spin without me after all! In fact, colleagues and other staff members learn to make their own decisions and take responsibility for their actions. Still, I am offended when I find someone not doing his job. Partially, I am ashamed at being so petty to care and so indiscreet to watch what others are doing. But also if I work hard on my part of our team effort, it annoys me to see others take their duties lightly, especially when they profess to care so much about the work.

Until my days became too crowded with lectures and conferences about stress, I always personally surveyed the behavior of our laboratory animals and made myself responsible for all autopsies and microscopic investigations. Such active participation in the labs made me rather obnoxious to my co-workers and graduate students, because I quickly developed a habit of never believing any written report or tabulation without repeating the work myself or having it done again before my eyes. Often this proved to be an unnecessary precaution; but quite frequently I did detect severe errors in technique or evaluation, in which cases my co-workers were always grateful.

Whenever I could not look after every detail, I would use spot tests, verifying one or another operation with special care. My assistants began to say that I am endowed by heaven (or perhaps by hell!) with what they called "lathotropism," a very disconcerting quality. From "lathos," meaning mistake, and "tropism," attraction toward. This term reflects a peculiar instinct I have that guides me directly toward an error. It's likely that, merely by glancing at a page, I can pick out the only three errors of typing, or that among the hundreds of rat cages in our labs, I will spot the only one with the water bottle empty.

However, this quality is not foolproof, and once I really chose the wrong time to be suspicious. A group of graduate students were conducting a series of tests in which the rats had to be injected at scheduled intervals around the clock. With my usual "I'm-from-Missouri" attitude, I doubted that the students were actually visiting the lab in the early morning hours; on the few occasions that I checked at 6:00 A.M., they had been late. So one evening before leaving the institute I entered the lab and hung up a sarcastic note: "Ha Ha! I was here and you weren't," assuming that the student would, following my suspicions, fail to show up for the 6:00 A.M. injection.

As luck would have it, the next morning I had trouble with my car and arrived at work at 6:30, behind my usual routine. When I came to my office I found a label on the door saying: "Ha Ha! *I* was here and *you* weren't!" I have not lived this down yet, nearly fifteen years later, because the student in question, Dr. Beatriz Tuchweber, received her Ph.D. at the institute and stayed on, having now reached the rank of associate professor at the University of Montreal.

Fortunately, my criticism is not always so far off the mark, and sometimes it manages to do some good. If I correct someone but notice that the conversation becomes tinged with emotion and leads nowhere, I walk out. I think this is the most tactful way to settle differences of opinion which can no longer be resolved by logical argument.

However, if I can avoid the problem by a demonstration, I do not discuss, I demonstrate. For example, if a technician tells me that some surgical operation cannot be performed and I am unable to convince her of the contrary, I roll up my sleeves and perform the operation. This inevitably stops the argument. I know I am asking for much, but mediocrity has no place in our group because I strongly believe in the inherent value of excellence.

I am sure many readers will consider it pettiness to enumerate such things or even to have these thoughts, but I am convinced they were necessary in order for me to do what I did in the time I had available. Perhaps this is due to a flaw in my character or vision, but as I am supposed to write an honest autobiography, I feel that I have to declare the code by which I have lived. In fact, I shall even give you a code of maxims which I have formulated over the years and which have been in operation both at the University of Montreal and, with minor modifications, at our institute. Many of my colleagues may consider them useful guides worth being photocopied and handed out to the entire personnel.

MAXIMS OF THE INSTITUTE

(Follow these rules and live happily ever after.)

1. *If at all possible, do it now.* A given job takes the same time now or later. Even if it is disagreeable or difficult, you gain nothing by postponing it; you only prolong the worry and remorse for keeping duties pending.

2. *If not possible now, "follow-up."* Note the next step on your calendar and persist to the end. This is never impossible because (*A*) if you decline my instructions, you have no responsibility, because the task of finding someone who *can* follow them reverts to me; (*B*) if you accept and succeed, the task is accomplished; (*C*) if you accept, thinking you can complete the task, but later find you can't, report back to me immediately — thus, responsibility again reverts to me. Of course, this rule is applicable not only in relation to people who work for me directly but to anyone in the institute dealing with people who report to him or to her.

Naturally, the more a person can accomplish the better, but no one will be blamed unless the employee deserts the job by inertia, without turning it over to someone who can do it or gives proof that it cannot be done.

3. *Never do yourself what a less qualified person could accomplish.* It is a mere waste of talent to perform tasks that could be turned over to a less highly qualified co-worker. Delegate authority whenever possible, but remember that if you accepted the job, you remain responsible, even for having chosen a substitute, and it is up to you to judge how much personal supervision is needed. This is advantageous for the senior, because only by turning over some of his duties to subordinates can he advance still further. It is also advantageous for the junior, because gradually he advances

to a higher post.   It is also economic for the institute, because every task is performed by the least highly paid person capable of accomplishing the objective.

Hence, never grudge the time it takes to train someone else for a job that he could learn.

4. *Site visits.*   All senior administrative personnel should learn as much as possible about the work done by others and the facilities (offices, labs, instruments, materials) at their disposal. Technical competence in various departments is not necessary for administration.   It is indispensable, however, to know what a job consists of (the time it takes, the fatigue it causes, the competence it requires) for anyone who has a voice in overall organization, promotions, discharges, interrelations between departments, improvement of working conditions, etc.   To administer, say, a histology laboratory, it is not necessary to understand histology. It is essential, however, to know how many hours are needed for embedding, sectioning, etc., how much intelligence and technical skill is required for these manipulations and how feasible it would be to replace an absent member (e.g., because of sickness or vacation) by someone from another laboratory.

5. *Flexibility of structure.*   The institute must constantly readjust its activities in conformity with its changing research and teaching topics; hence, it is impossible to assure permanent employment of all members unless they can be exchanged between departments.   If there is little work in one or the other sector, it should be possible to transfer at least some of its employees to another department of the institute where the staff is overworked. To arrange such transfers, the administrative staff must have become acquainted with the essential prerequisites of each section through site visits.

6. *Explain by example, not by argument.*   Since the administrative staff is usually less qualified in special techniques (chemistry, histology, documentation) than is the subordinate staff performing this work, arguments about inefficiency are rarely fruitful.   Usually, you can convince only by example.   If you find that the typist makes too many errors, or is too slow in preparing a complex table, she may not accept your judgment.   But she will always be convinced if you show her on one sample that

the same task can be performed more efficiently by yourself, or if you can't do it, by someone else.   Such conviction by example usually also has teaching value by revealing why the job was not efficiently performed and how improvements could be made.

7. *Keep a reserve list of agenda.*   You can largely avoid overworking one section of the institute while another has nothing to do if you keep lists of relatively non-urgent agenda to be performed whenever time permits.   Often there suddenly is no work for one individual or group; if that happens while the supervisor is very busy, he cannot be expected to find occupations at a moment's notice unless he has prepared a waiting list of them.

8. *Don't touch what is going well.*   It is dangerous to try to improve procedures which are satisfactory.   There are always lots of things that are going badly or not going at all; think of these first.

9. *Give responsibility to the person who wants it.*   There are people who work very conscientiously from 9:00 to 5:00, but their interests are entirely outside the institute.   Do not despise them just because their attitude toward work is not the same as yours.   There are enough people who enjoy the challenge of growing responsibilities, perfection and maximal accomplishment. It has happened to us repeatedly that employees came to us from other departments of the University simply because they were bored.   Some people just prefer to work for a living than to obtain the same income as a handout through unemployment relief. On the other hand, it also happens that people leave us because they are overworked.   Enthusiastic leadership and ambition are indispensable, but we also need people willing to be led and to perform the many monotonous chores of the institute conscientiously.   Many of these are tasks which the more highly motivated would soon want to abandon.

By contrast, those who accept the largest number of the most complicated tasks also deserve the most assistance and the greatest consideration.   If a high level performer complains about minor negligences, it is tempting to accuse him of making a mountain out of a molehill.   Do not forget that importance and magnitude are always relative concepts.   It would be exaggerated to complain about a single grain of sand on the floor, but the same grain in a chronometer assumes an altogether different importance.

10. *Smooth transfer of duties.*   Before accepting responsibilities for any task previously performed by someone else, insist on a complete explanation by your predecessor.   If you feel that the task has been badly done and cannot be carried on efficiently as it stands, write a memo to administration specifying areas in which you cannot assume immediate responsibility for past errors.   Similarly, when you transfer to a job (e.g., because of advancement to a higher position or resignation from the institute), it is an elementary rule of proper behavior to train a competent successor.   Efficiency in assumption and transfer of duties will be conscientiously emphasized in all our letters of recommendation.

It is considered especially unfair to accept promotion to the post of a predecessor and then blame him for any weakness in the system which he built up but you are using (e.g., when someone accepts responsibility for a filing system, he cannot claim credit when it works and blame his predecessor when it doesn't).   He should not take on the job before being reasonably sure he can do it.

11. *Never overrule the decisions of a chief.*   Once a person has been placed in charge of a task, do not impose your views upon him.   You may express your own opinion but the decision must remain his.   Otherwise, he can never have the authority to assume full responsibility and relieve you of it.   The only way to solve the problem of a chief who consistently makes erroneous decisions is to replace him.

12. *Stop arguing as soon as your interlocutor has fully understood your point.*   In any worthwhile argument, defend your point of view frankly and persistently but only until you are convinced that your interlocutor has fully grasped your meaning even though he still disagrees.   Never try to convince by emotional restatement of your viewpoint; this only leads to tension and a fruitless waste of time.   Having silenced your opponent does not necessarily mean that you have convinced him.   More likely, it means that he agrees to obey.

13. *Do one thing at a time, but many things concurrently.*   This appears to be a paradox and it takes some experience to follow both, apparently contradictory, instructions.   Finish one thing at a time, for if you fight on too many fronts simultaneously,

you spread your energy so thin that nothing worthwhile will be completely terminated. This leads to a continuous feeling of inadequacy which is most depressing. On the other hand, when a complex job requires numerous distinct activities, do not give yourself the excuse that it is not worthwhile to start with step 3 if, for unavoidable reasons, steps 1 and 2 are not yet feasible. If you have to write a complex scientific paper, you first have to possess all the experimental evidence. However, if one or two experiments cannot yet be completed for lack of materials, that does not prevent you from gathering the entire pertinent literature, formulating a suitable title and making an outline of the publication's structure.   Indeed, the introduction, discussion and summary can often be prepared in rough form and tables made for all terminated experiments if you add the last data and make minor changes in interpretation following completion of all pertinent experiments.   The same is true for virtually all other activities in the institute.   The art is to develop the discipline necessary to stay with an important problem until it is solved without being deviated from the main line by parallel activities.

14. *Never follow a "great idea" after the bottom has dropped out of it.* After you have made an apparently important observation, first try to confirm it beyond any possible doubt. If the facts fail to support your original concept, the plan is dead; don't follow it just because it seemed to be so promising and you have already invested so much time in plans to develop it. Yet, before dropping it completely, re-examine the possibilities of the original observation when interpreted in a totally different way.

For example, you find that an ovarian extract causes thymus atrophy. You are greatly excited about the possibility of a new thymolytic hormone. You make extensive plans about the way to identify, purify and apply the new principle. You subsequently find that extracts of many other organs and numerous toxic chemicals exert the same thymolytic effect. Do not rationalize all these observations in the light of your original concept, trying to prove that everything acts through your supposed new ovarian hormone. Realize that the bottom fell out of your original dream; there remains no reason to concentrate on the ovary. However, the first observation was correct. Examine its possibilities as a key to totally unrelated and hitherto unsuspected manifestations of life. This is how the concept of stress began to take shape.

It seems to me that any normally motivated person should want to progress at work. But there are three ways of going about it: by merit and by being useful; by changing employment until you find the best paid and least onerous job; or by joining a pressure group.

In my experience, those who follow the first method usually develop a justified feeling of job security, both in themselves and in their employers. Those who choose the second route spend most of their time studying the classified ads or asking around for job openings. This involves almost as much effort and ingenuity as the achievement of progress through merit in their present job, but the feeling of insecurity and the constant change of environment tend to create dissatisfied, neurotic personalities. A few more dollars or an occasional extra holiday hardly seem worth this sacrifice. Those who follow the third method are, to my mind, the most insecure. They do not feel necessary and do not trust their inherent usefulness as individuals; therefore, they have to join pressure groups in which the mere strength in numbers gives some power to each individual of the group.

The real nomads of society keep looking for a better place all their lives. They never know the pleasure of security and of being affectionately accepted as useful, loyal and respectable permanent members of a group they can call their own.

I recently wrote an encyclopedia of stress entitled *Stress in Health and Disease,* which is based on my forty years of experience and the enormous amount of information gathered by our documentation service. The importance of such a treatise, and the great attention to detail which I have placed in its construction, explain my uncompromising attitude toward fundamental research and its evaluation. This attitude unfortunately makes me lose some of my useful co-workers, but those who remain form an efficient and happy group.

Still, I have had very serious disappointments, mostly among those who swore that they trusted me and believed in the value of my work, so I could count on their help whatever happened. After I reached the official age of retirement and both my future and theirs were in jeopardy, I needed their loyalty most for professional and personal — I would almost say sentimental —reasons. I never asked anyone to take a loyalty oath; these people offered its equivalent on their own initiatives. However, I don't hate those who left me because for some biological (not moral) reasons, I am unable to hate in the usual sense of the word. I continue to act, and honestly feel, friendly toward them but I try to limit my personal contacts with them as much as possible without giving offense, because this is my only way of protecting myself against being hurt again.

When I think of these occasional disappointments I am reminded of a story my grandmother used to tell me and my cousin, Annemarie Byloff, the daughter of my mother's brother Bruno and my closest childhood friend. I can't say whether certain memorable experiences played an important role in forming my character or whether, on the other hand, I remember various apparently insignificant events because they resonated with my developing personality. In any case, I have vivid recollections of some of Grandma's tales (to which both of us listened with fascinated attention), and I'm sure that a few of them greatly influenced my own way of looking at life. One of our favorites was the story of a little girl who loved a beautiful doll. She had seen the lovely toy in the window of an extremely expensive shop on the Ringstrasse, in the most elegant shopping district of Vienna. She would gaze at the doll in speechless admiration for hours and her rather poor parents had the greatest difficulty in tearing her away. It was quite beyond their humble means to purchase such a fine toy.

Two years passed, and the girl would still stare longingly at the window whenever she walked by. Finally her parents could resist her pleas no more, so they bought the doll for their daughter, who immediately became deeply attached to it. She would make dresses for the doll, comb its shiny blond hair carefully, and treat it as tenderly as if it were a real child. For her the toy was the embodiment of perfection. Then one day it slipped out of her hands onto the concrete floor and broke into smithereens, revealing that there was nothing inside but sawdust.

Whenever my grandmother would reach this part of the story, Annemarie would begin to cry. We would demand to hear the tale again and again, and she would always weep bitterly at the end. It moved me very deeply too, enough to remember the story after more than sixty-five years. To me, it remains a symbol of those people who seem so wonderful on superficial acquaintance but turn out to have nothing of substance when you actually come to know them.

I have had occasion to think of this story many times during my career because, as my assistants often pointed out, I have always been tempted to consider every new member of our institute as the most promising and original candidate to make a great scientist. (Henceforth, I shall use "he" instead of the cumbersome "he or she" to designate both sexes of our species whenever the remark is obviously applicable to either sex.) I would shower him with favors, often finding out later that much of his enthusiasm was only superficial, that he really did not love or understand Nature as much as it had first appeared but merely wanted to become famous quickly.

Upon discovering this, I would suddenly lose interest in them. Although I had spent much time and attention on their training in the beginning, as soon as I found out that there was nothing inside but sawdust, I would "put them in the icebox." This is an expression coined by my colleagues for my peculiar habit of not wishing to fire people until I could find some kind of acceptable job for them elsewhere. However, when it became obvious that there was nothing to be gained from it, I did not want to lose time by training them further, so I would simply ignore their presence, letting them do what they pleased. Apparently, being "put in the icebox" was considered the worst punishment possible, far more traumatic than severe reproach and criticism, because I only attempt to correct those people I think are worth educating. If I found someone to be filled with sawdust, I never lost my temper or raised my voice in anger; I simply wouldn't bother with him. This again was a reflection of one of my mottoes, for I would "fight for my highest attainable aim, but never put up resistance in vain."

During my long life, I have had many adversaries, both among professional scientists and among co-workers and social acquaintances, and I must admit I avoided the company of many of them for a variety of reasons. Those on my staff whom I disliked did not stay long, perhaps because they did not like my ways either, or because I pointed out that I wanted "to run a happy ship" and they would have more of a future elsewhere. Among those who remained either on the research staff or in various administrative, editorial and secretarial positions, there were many whom I liked and continue to like intensely. It would be odious to mention them by name because they are too numerous to be listed and those not included might feel slighted. But as one example, Mr. Kai Nielsen was the first and only member of my "staff" during the early experiments on stress at McGill; he remained with me for thirty-five years until his retirement in 1970 and came to master a great many complex laboratory techniques. We were about the same age when he joined me as an untrained laboratory assistant. He helped me by holding the rats steady for injection. But more importantly he steadied me – during those busy days when my theories were so viciously attacked – with the stabilizing effect of his always friendly, even-minded Danish personality. I am not particularly gregarious but there were and are many associates in both my private and professional life whom I manifestly like very much, mainly because they are trustworthy, warm-hearted and pleased to be useful.

Achievement is more important to me than academic quali- fications. Pasteur, one of the greatest doctors of all times, had no M.D., but this did not make him any less of an eminent physician. I care more about the kind of work a person is capable of doing than about his formal preparation for the job. We once had a domestic servant whom I kept surprising in the act of reading my textbooks in the kitchen. I quickly fired her but rehired her the same day at a higher salary as a technician in the institute. Even without formal schooling she showed enough originality and interest to perform her job admirably.

Of course, sometimes my indifference to formal job prerequi- sites must give way to stronger forces and, unfortunately, from time to time I have had to turn down the applications of people I really would have loved to see work with our group, merely because it was just legally impossible to accept them. For ex- ample, I have often received applications from highly qualified people who were approaching or had reached the official retirement age of our university. I have had to refuse them, accepting instead inexperienced and much less qualified people just because they were younger.

I vivdly remember an incident some fifteen years ago that made a deep impression on me. It did not influence my work or way of life and might be considered as incidental, except for the symbolic value I attached to it. For me it exemplified one of the most regrettable features of our social system.

We needed a moderately qualified junior technical assistant for our pharmacy, for whom the budget provided only a modest salary. After a stream of candidates had come and gone in response to a newspaper ad, a perfectly charming and suitable girl was introduced to our administrator. She seemed to be very pleased with the salary offered and when she was later brought into my office, I approved her appointment immediately after a brief conversation.

An hour later I asked the administrator when the new girl would be starting and was told she had already left. She had seemed highly motivated and entirely capable of performing the job, and everyone had been impressed with her; it was agreed that she would begin the next day. Then she had been asked to fill in a formal questionnaire and, in doing so, she had exclaimed how lucky she was to have found such a perfect job: "You know," she had remarked, "it's really a coincidence that you needed me for the pharmacy, as I'm a graduate pharmacist! I arrived from Haiti six months ago but no one would hire me, although I finally would have accepted any work, no matter what the salary. Every time they'd see I'm black, they'd turn down my application. I'd just about given up hope of ever using my degree!"

In a burst of enthusiasm at finally having conquered one barrier, the poor girl had just set up another for herself. Had she not mentioned her diploma, everyone would have been satisfied, but our funds were minimal and we simply could not afford to meet the salary required for a graduate pharmacist in compliance with the demands of the university's unions.

Racial prejudice was never as strong in Canada as it used to be in certain parts of the United States, for example; yet it had been sufficiently widespread at the time to exclude this girl from every possible source of income.

After accumulating three earned and twenty honorary degrees, it's easy for me to realize how little formal diplomas actually mean. Some of my most useful co-workers engaged in highly complicated work have no official degree whatsoever, and not one of the two dozen people handling my complex stress library is actually trained as a librarian.

One of the best librarians we ever had was previously a novelist in Hungary; but as his English and French were not good enough for him to continue his literary work here, he had become a filing clerk in an office when I discovered him. Eventually he not only became director of our library service but we even co-authored a book describing our special system for the codification and retrieval of scientific literature. Assistants like these have convinced me that it is only a matter of recognizing and promoting talent and motivation that counts, and not what diplomas a person has.

Of course, you do have to get your training somewhere, somehow; the point is that school is not necessarily the best place, nor is an official certificate a guarantee of competence. I once worked with a former elevator boy who later became head of our histology division. I have also cooperated with an inmate in a penitentiary, a physician who was serving time for murder. He claimed to be innocent, but whatever his moral foibles might have been, he managed to do excellent translations of scientific texts.

People who care about what they do please and help me far more than those who work only for their salary or out of a sense of duty. Those who really show an interest in their work also enjoy it much more than those who merely come equipped with diplomas that officially qualify them to do research.

I have great respect for the British system of aristocracy, which has managed to maintain itself better than most others because it is not exclusively inbred but still largely assimilative. It permits a commoner to become a Peer of the Realm for outstanding accomplishment in the service of his country, sometimes with striking disregard for the exact type of contribution he has made—whether in science, on the battlefield or in business.

Isaac D'Israeli, the son of a Jew expelled from Spain during the Inquisition, produced many outstanding literary works. His son, Benjamin Disraeli, Earl of Beaconsfield, was likewise an outstanding man of letters, but his chief contribution to Britain was in his statesmanship, which was instrumental in building the Empire. It was this achievement that earned him the personal affection of Queen Victoria, for whom he secured the title "Empress of India." At the historic Berlin Congress even Bismarck was greatly impressed by the vision and firmness of the "old Jew" who undoubtedly added much to the prestige of British aristocracy. Likewise, strictly by merit, Nelson became a viscount through his victory over Napoleon, and Beaverbrook, a journalist, was rewarded with the title of baron for his achievements as a newspaper magnate.

But aristocracy by merit is not exclusively a British monopoly. Napoleon, who was of common origins himself, became Emperor of France through his military and political accomplishments and went on to build up a powerful new aristocracy of merit, based on his famous principle that every common soldier potentially carries his marshal's staff in his rucksack and would acquire the right to use it whenever he had shown his capability to do so. Even in the present French army, a soldier does not necessarily have to attend St. Cyr or any other highly reputed officer's school to become a general. In the Austro-Hungarian monarchy, on the other hand, a soldier could never rise above the rank of noncommissioned officer unless he were a "gentleman" by breeding and had attended the imperial cadets' school.

I don't really believe in "certified competence." It has been said of François-Joseph Lefebvre, who because of outstanding accomplishments was made Marshal of France and Duke of Danzig by Napoleon, that when he and his wife were invited to a reception at the Imperial Court, his wife was worried about the prospect of mixing with the ancient Bourbon aristocracy. "François," she said, "imagine! We will have to mix with all those *real* aristocrats, all of whom have innumerable distinguished ancestors. I used to be a laundress! Neither of us has any ancestors to brag about." Upon this, her husband reassured her with the statement that would become so famous: "Catherine, we may have no ancestors but we are far superior; we *are* ancestors."

I have always believed and have always told my students that your highest rank is your name. In the end it makes little difference what official ranks, degrees and decorations you have, but people will remember what you have done with your talents. According to Thomas L. Masson, a friend once said to Cato the Elder, "It's a scandal that no statue has been erected for you in Rome! I'm going to form a committee." To which Cato replied, "No. I would rather have people ask, 'Why isn't there a statue for Cato?' than 'Why is there one?'" I admit that this anecdote has often helped me to overcome the disappointment of not having obtained some official recognition, award or medal for certain accomplishments.

Still, for very personal reasons, I am especially proud of having been made a Companion of the Order of Canada. This decoration, the highest of our country, represents to me my real certificate of naturalization, an official acceptance, and reinforces my feeling of being a part of Canadian life. As a citizen by choice, and not by birth, this recognition has helped me to consider myself fully adopted by Canada.

Another type of honor had special significance for me personally. On a lecture trip to Brazil many years ago, I learned from a man who lived in a small village outside Rio de Janeiro that he had baptized his son Edouardo Hans Selye de Oliveira Gonzales. As a memento, he brought me a photograph album illustrating the baptismal ceremonies for my namesake. Very few people know about this event and it certainly is not likely to bring me any international glory, but I derived great satisfaction from the fact that someone whom I had never met and who lives so far from my country would appreciate my work sufficiently to name his son after me.

A totally different kind of distinction, and one that I was very happy and surprised to receive, came to me from Lieutenant Colonel Donald Robinson, Chief Historian of the U.S. Armed Forces on General Eisenhower's staff, who included my biography in his bestseller, *The Hundred Most Important People in the World Today*, along with chapters on such eminent people as Stalin, Churchill, Pope Pius XII and Nehru. In this case I have no remorse about false modesty because I really did not feel I was one of the hundred most important people in the world.   But if I can ever really get the stress concept to be a generally accepted, stabilizing influence on human society, then perhaps my work may equal that of some others mentioned in this volume, even if my role eventually turns out to have been a very small one in the future of stress research.

The approval of others, as expressed by honors of all kinds, is an important incentive for most, if not for all, of us — it certainly has been for me.   But I have never allowed this thirst for approval to become the ultimate aim of my life.   No true scientist would want to win a coveted distinction at the price of becoming a petty politician whose energy is so consumed by string-pulling that he has none left for research.

Besides, I am aware that there can be only one president of a society, one chairman in a department, and to always strive to be top dog would be futile.   Moreover, anyone who is not content with being just a valuable member, though not necessarily the recognized leader, can console himself by knowing that he is the best, even if others do not see him that way.   This attitude can do him much good, and others are not hurt as long as he makes no case of it.   No one can always be the "fairest in the land"; yet we can believe we are if it makes us feel better.   This harmless game of pretending has the added advantage of protecting us from often cruel reality, where our true abilities must be put to the test, and where we sometimes fail.

Another of my grandmother's stories is pertinent to the idea of putting greatness to the test.   Her tale was based on a poem entitled *Die Glocke* (The Bell), by the eighteenth-century German poet, Friedrich von Schiller.   My cousin Annemarie and I would continually beg her to repeat the story, because she told it in such a moving way, with her slow, soft Viennese accent.   Without Grandma's voice and facial expressions, it doesn't seem extraordinary in retrospect; in fact, I have often reread the original poem, but it does not convey the impression that seems to have left such unforgettable marks on my soul.   This is how she told it:

For generations, an old family of bellmakers had handed down the professional secrets that made them so successful. Finally they got an order for the biggest bell that had ever been

made in the region.   It was to be placed in the tower of a large
church high in the mountains, and when it rang it would attract
the faithful from far away.   The bellmakers put all their efforts
into the assignment, in which the entire family participated.
The craftsmen first made a hole for the mold, deep in the ground.
They put years of work into perfecting preliminary models, determining the best shape and alloy of metals and the precise temperature at which the melted alloy should be poured.   All went as
planned.   Finally they lifted the bell out of the ground and tested
it in the steeple of the church down in their valley.   The tone was
beautiful.   Its melody was sheer music.   Then the entire family
undertook the arduous task of transporting the heavy bell to the
top of the highest mountain.   They lifted it into the steeple of
the cathedral and, as they held their breath, the first note sounded
from the summit.

At this point in the story, Grandma would pause dramatically,
then, slowly and quietly, she would add: "Down in the valley
it had sounded strong and pure but, alas, once installed high in
the mountains its tone fell flat."

I recall this story when I see colleagues, influential and successful as the big chiefs of local clinics or laboratories, present their
work at large international congresses.   In their own little valleys
they sound beautiful, but not when they try to reach the mighty
peaks.   The test of real value comes, I believe, when a scientific
observation or concept is not only of provincial importance but
recognized all over the world.

Yet once a scientist or, for that matter, anyone in any field
reaches the heights and proves himself, why must he try to appear
modest?   I have met few scientists who are not interested in the
approval of their colleagues and do not care whether they get
credit for their discoveries.   Few of them pick up a book or
reprint on their own subject without immediately consulting
the author index to see if they have been quoted.   Why are most
of them so desperately ashamed of this?

I believe we have every right to be proud of something that
earns us respect and appreciation.   In my opinion – and I do not
say "in my humble opinion" – vanity becomes objectionable
only when pride in accomplishment turns into an indiscriminate

craving after fame for its own sake. No scientist worthy of the name measures his success by the number of people who acclaim him, but a truly dedicated scientist is entitled to enjoy success based upon the approval of his peers.

In the words of Charles Richet, "Modesty is a fault of which scientists are virtually free. And this is very fortunate. Where would we be if the scientist would begin to doubt his own intelligence? His timidity would paralyze all progress. He must have faith not only in science as such but in his own science. He must not believe himself infallible, but when he experiments or reasons he should have an intangible confidence in his intellectual strength." What the scientist really needs is a kind of megalomania tempered by humility. He must have enough self-confidence to reach for the stars and yet enough humility to realize, without disappointment, that he will never reach them.

I think that modesty is a second-rate virtue, a last resort for self-esteem. Winston Churchill allegedly said about Lord Attlee, who was much admired for his modesty, "Yes, but it is easy for him. He has so much to be modest about."

This reminds me of a similar remark made by one of my professors at McGill. In the days when there was still a great deal of opposition to my work on stress, I often used to eat my lunch in the cafeteria of the McGill-affiliated Royal Victoria Hospital. One day I sat with a group of interns, residents, senior physicians and even the chief of medicine, Professor J. C. Meakins, the author of one of the most popular textbooks in North American universities at the time. In the course of our conversation a junior intern began to make sarcastic remarks about my "triad of stress" and the entire General Adaptation Syndrome. "You know, Dr. Selye," he chided, "your findings and theories may be the most commonly discussed ideas in contemporary medicine —everyone speaks about stress in every connection — but your concept of nonspecificity is holding back progress. In the final analysis I'm convinced it will be said that your work held back medical progress by centuries!"

I was stunned by his remark, expressed with considerable emotion. But then Professor Meakins turned to the young man, who had never published a scientific paper, and said in his quiet, fatherly voice, "You know, George, you're safe.   No one will ever say that about your work."

Although I don't advocate modesty, I detest the other side of the coin, that obnoxious type of immodesty that consists of bragging about any of your accomplishments or humiliating others to make yourself appear more outstanding by comparison. As a child I learned the charming Austrian peasant saying, "Johnny-boy, don't stretch out so tall — you ain't that little." Only very small people depend upon unearned acclaim.

Often, discoveries made by others have been attributed to me. I have been given credit for the discovery of cortisone, merely because I happened to baptize the corticoids, a group to which this hormone belongs. I dislike being complimented for others' achievements and always try to explain the source of the misunderstanding.

I believe that what I *do* undertake is usually well done and I do not feel the need to benefit from another's accomplishments. Likewise, status symbols have little meaning to me. Whatever status I may have in society depends upon my scientific accomplishments and should not be influenced by external signs of importance.

For instance, I drive an inexpensive but excellent little Toyota (nicknamed "Geisha"), which perhaps looks somewhat odd in the main *Cour d'Honneur* (Court of Honor) of the university, where only the chief administrative officers and heads of departments are allowed to park.   My car is quite conspicuous by its inconspicuousness amidst the large, elegant models driven by the president, vice-presidents, deans and my senior colleagues.

Actually, I used to drive an old but still impressive Cadillac when I was named full professor, because I felt it would be undignified for a man in my august position to drive a less prestigious car. A few years later I bought a Mercury Cougar which was less impressive and, being new, was also cheaper to maintain. It was only after the stress concept had brought me twenty honorary doctorates and ninety medals that I felt sufficiently relieved of social obligations to buy my present inexpensive but dearly beloved "Geisha."   This car satisfies all my needs; it is easy to park and invariably starts on command, even when the temperature drops to thirty degrees below the freezing point during a really severe Canadian winter.

My tastes in other matters are also quite simple. I do not take lavish vacations in Florida or in any other warm climate, despite my great yearning for sun. Instead, whenever possible, I get some sunshine in a room that has been baptized "Little Florida," although it is officially designated as laboratory R-724. If there is some sunshine around noon I retire there, exposing my torso to the sun's rays. At the same time, I take my lunch and answer my correspondence on a dictaphone. During the summer months, the institute's roof becomes my "Florida." I try to spend a few hours a day basking in the sun, and I find that this does me more good than any medicine; my blood pressure is always several points lower after a relaxing sunbath.

Occasionally I receive graduate students and assistants in my little "Florida." Some of them find it a little bizarre to meet their director nude to the waist when they first see me in this condition. But after a while they get used to it and often join me to discuss scientific matters, likewise shedding as much of their wardrobe as is compatible with decency. In "Florida" we have the additional advantage of not being disturbed, for no one ever comes univited, and there are no telephones to bother us.

If during the day something extraordinarily funny happens or someone tells me a particularly amusing story, I virtually explode in raucous laughter, to a point where I can be heard throughout the corridors of our institute. I am told that my assistants characterize these outbursts by the statement, "There goes the chief, neighing again!"

My taste in music is far from being eclectic. I can become quite sentimental about Hungarian gypsy music but, on the other hand, I also enjoy Bach, Beethoven and Wagner. Still, I could not compare the joy I gain from any kind of music or other form of art with that which I derive from understanding. To learn something that is very new, to discover and unveil the art of Nature, the masterpieces of creation — that is my greatest source of mental satisfaction. I like to enjoy Nature raw, unadulterated (I am almost tempted to say "in the nude") by immediate contact with her, not through an interpreter.

Like my choice of an automobile, my preferences in food are quite commonplace, except perhaps for my fondness for horsemeat. During my childhood in Austria at the time of World War I, the only meat available to us was that of horses that had given their lives for the Fatherland on the Russian front. The meat was shipped back to us preserved in permanganate. It was actually spoiled meat, made innocuous only by the disinfectant, but we were so hungry that it tasted wonderful — except for the permanganate. Ever since that time I have retained a particular dislike for the purple color of this disinfectant.

I never had any of the common prejudices against extraordinary dishes such as horsemeat, frog's legs, snails, raw fish and bizarre sea food. I like to taste things that I have never eaten; and if it tastes good I enjoy it, no matter how it looks or smells.

My tastes in other things are also quite simple, except when lack of comfort would interfere with my work. Fashion and such matters are not important to me. My clothes are of the best quality, but I am not ashamed to say that I wear a thirty-year-old coat and shoes that must be about twenty years old. (Such endurance would probably be impossible today, given the quality of modern products.) Perhaps this goes back to my Viennese youth, for it was a common standard that one's *Lederhosen* must not look new, as wearing immaculate ones was a sign of the *nouveau riche.* As youngsters, we would make the leather look more worn out, purposely breaking them in by wallowing in the grass. I suppose this is somewhat like the stigma attached to new jeans today.

The Hungarian hussars had a similar antipathy for new clothes. In fact, it was quite common for an officer to select an orderly with the same shoe size as his own, merely so the servant could break in a new pair of boots. (Curiously, the hussars never extended this practice to "breaking in" their new fiancées.)

Some years ago the staff of the institute got together to buy me a birthday gift. After days of discussion they finally settled on what was then a new item in the fashion world — a luxurious and expensive Pierre Cardin shirt. They presented it to me at our daily tea break; and I was greatly pleased by the beauty of the shirt and even more by their gesture.

However, I could never understand the necessity of having sleeves and cuffs on shirts, so I proceeded to have the sleeves cut off for the sake of comfort. It took me some time to realize why everyone looked so puzzled and disappointed when I wore the shirt. With my simple tastes I didn't even realize what a revolting crime I had committed in mutilating a Pierre Cardin design.

Personal ownership was never important to me, especially after my parents' loss of all their possessions as a consequence of the first World War. If someone gave me a valuable Titian, I would be so afraid of having it stolen that I would not enjoy having it in my home. I never wish that I could own the beautiful objects of art in museums or galleries as I prefer to enjoy them without the responsibility of their custody.

On the other hand, I have spared no expense in furnishing, carpeting and soundproofing my office or obtaining the best available tools for my work, the most expensive of which is my carefully indexed documentation service on stress. But all this is purely for utilitarian motives. The furniture is comfortable and I have assumed the habit of leaning back in my cushioned swivel chair and placing my feet on the table in an attitude of complete relaxation. I am surrounded by wall shelves with books, statuettes, vases and pictures, all of which I like not for their value but for their meaning to me personally. Some of them are from former students, some were presented on the occasion of lectures I have given throughout the world, and others were the gifts of visiting investigators from different countries. For example, Pasteur Valéry Radot, knowing I am a great admirer of Louis Pasteur, brought me an excellent autographed portrait of his illustrious grandfather.

I am especially fond of an old Bull clock that is my only material heritage, as the few remaining worldly goods of my parents were destroyed in 1956, during the uprising against the communist government in Hungary. This clock has told me the time of day ever since my early childhood in Komárom. My mother had an extraordinary collection of more than one hundred antique clocks of all types and periods. It was part of the Selye daily routine for a watchmaker to make his rounds, checking that the clocks were all adjusted and functioning perfectly. I still remember the peculiar concert created when they all rang in chorus on the hour. Some of them even played melodies.

At any rate, I do not believe in making an office or laboratory into a museum, but I often enjoy having some beautiful objects around me that serve a utilitarian purpose, only because their presence enhances the quality of my work. After all, I spend most of my waking hours at the institute, and there is no reason to make any sharp distinction between the home and office atmospheres.

When I am away from the office I stick to the principle that I need only as much luxury as is necessary to work efficiently. I travel first-class, especially because my artificial hips can become extremely painful after a long, uncomfortable flight. And I like to stay in first-rate hotels, not because of the splendor offered but because I am most likely to have a relaxing night's sleep in a high-quality establishment. After all, I would not be much use giving advice on stress if I arrived for a lecture overstressed.

During the day I never read anything but scientific matter; but in bed, after glancing through the daily paper, I like to read novels, autobiographies or, once in a while, poetry. If I am tempted to "travel," I read foreign authors in the original text; this gives me the feeling of a complete change in atmosphere and culture. But no literary creation is as interesting as life itself, in and around me. Here everything is real, nothing could be imitation or false interpretation. I do not like authors to explain life to me, unless they express original ideas which had never occured to me before.

Speaking of reading in bed, I should perhaps confess one habit that is considered quite odd by those who know about it. I much prefer paperbacks printed on cheap paper to luxuriously bound hardcover volumes, which are not only more expensive but heavy and bulky. If the paperback happens to be too voluminous, I cut the book into two or three sections, stabilizing the pages with bands of tape. Then I often throw away the pages as I finish each one. After completing the volume, if I decide the book is worth keeping for my collection or giving as a present, the expense of a second copy is negligible. Of course, for important works that will be re-read or lent to others, I prefer the hardcover version.

I greatly appreciate humorous literature, but not slapstick. My tastes lie somewhere between dry British humor and French *esprit*. For example, I like the thought of Elbert Hubbard as quoted by Daninos: "Do not take life too seriously; you won't get out of it alive anyway."

At the present time I am in my "philosophical period." I have rediscovered the ancient sages. I am very much interested in the thoughts of Socrates and Plato. Their ideas have survived for centuries; we must take them into account and respect them in any effort to formulate a philosophy of life. I believe that you cannot speak about ethics, ethology, morals or behavior without knowing the great masters of thought. Up to now I have always written as a physician, histologist or biochemist; but I feel the time has come for me to explore another approach to the great problem of finding natural guidelines for behavior and improving our ability to adapt to change through contemplation and reasoning.

CHAPTER TWELVE

My "Private Life"

Mon métier et mon art c'est de vivre
(My work and my art is to live)
– Montaigne

As my life progresses, the distinction between work and leisure activities becomes more and more hazy, to the point where I wonder whether I have any private life – or, indeed, if perhaps all my life is private. To me, all things – my family, co-workers, thoughts and writings – are only different aspects of Nature. I experience my body, my mind, my actions and my surroundings as a coordinated whole, and can no longer say "this is my work, while this is my private life," for my life is my work.

I became especially aware of this after spending an evening at the luxurious home of a physician who had built up an extremely lucrative private practice in California. After dinner, we sat before the enormous scenic window of his living room and looked out into the darkness. He explained that he is fond of flowers, and that outside the window is a rose garden – which he then proceeded to illuminate in red, green, blue and every other shade of the spectrum by pressing different buttons on a control panel attached to his armchair. It was a rather expensive and complex installation often in need of repair, he said, but after a tiresome day in the office he enjoyed the totally different rewards of a personal private life at home. Among other things, he liked to relax by contemplating this display.

I am also fond of flowers, and I thought of how plain my single cactus looks by comparison. But then I wouldn't really enjoy Nature by pressing the buttons on that panel anyway;

after a few minutes, I am afraid, I would get bored. My "rose garden" is my research institute. It permits me to contemplate much more wondrous and varied aspects of Nature. In addition, it occasionally turns up a useful fruit. Besides — come to think of it — I can even brag that my playground is much more expensive than his and I don't have to pay for it from taxable income; it is given to me free and I am paid to play in it.

I have told this story often because it symbolizes how I feel about my work. Perhaps I was heavily influenced by my Catholic training, which taught me to follow God's command to Adam: "And in the sweat of your brow you will eat bread until you return to the ground" (Genesis 3:19).

This work ethic is basic to virtually all religions, perhaps because it is a biological necessity that man must work, irrespective of the results produced by his efforts. Being biological, this need to accomplish something is an innate part of our brains. We are built to do something; if nothing constructive presents itself, we turn to destructive actions as an outlet for our energy.

In the first printing of my book *From Dream to Discovery,* I tried to answer a question often asked of me — namely, to describe a typical day in my life. I picked at random January 26, 1963, and came up with the following description:

4:30 A.M. Becoming partially conscious. Thirty minutes of conversation (about calciphylaxis) between my conscious and unconscious self.

5:00 A.M. Return to complete consciousness. Explosive severance from bed. Exercise (chest expander, sit-ups, stationary bicycle). Shave. Ice-cold bath. Kiss wife and children good-by. (They all mutter incomprehensible sounds without regaining consciousness.) Make and eat breakfast in kitchen.

6:00 A.M. Limp two blocks through thick snow to garage and drive to institute. (Just remembered this is my birthday. The 56th!)

6:20 A.M. Two minutes of chummy grumbling (politics, weather) with night watchman in porter's lodge. Repair to office. Light first pipe.

6:30 A.M. Dictate on tape first rough text for forthcoming book *Mast Cells.*

8:30 A.M. Mrs. Staub, Chief of Secretariat, arrives — comfortingly radiating energy as usual — to discuss agenda for the day: proofreading a manuscript; organization of European lecture tour; correspondence; preparation of author index for mast cell book; checks to be made out for car repairs and children's schools.

8:40 A.M. Dictation for *Mast Cells.*

9:00 A.M. Noise in corridor; entire staff arrives. Mail brought in (opened) by Miss St. Aubin. She has already separated from my folder all items to be answered by mimeographed form letters (to patients who do not know that I don't practice, high school students who want impossible help with essays on stress, inventors who want to sell cancer cures), or by other members of the staff (administrator, librarian, grants officer, editorial secretaries, assistant in charge of postgraduate students, purchasing agent). As always, I answer my own personal and scientific mail immediately, although, as far as possible, merely by reference to previously prepared sample letters (acceptance or refusal of lecture invitations, arrangements for visits to our institute, etc.).

9:30 A.M. Lab rounds. For me, this is the most important part of the day. Assistants and I go through all labs to watch progress of experiments, particularly the clinical behavior of experimental animals, and to discuss possible need for changes in treatment.

10:30 A.M. Autopsy conference. Entire graduate staff gathers in autopsy room. To save time, the animals are already partly prepared for autopsy. (Each group is placed with its protocol; wherever comparatively inaccessible parts have to be examined, these are already partly dissected, etc.) Assisted by the chiefs of the two main laboratory units (Dr. Giulio Gabbiani, 7th floor; Dr. Beatriz Tuchweber, 8th floor), I perform all autopsies with binocular loupe and head lamp, pointing out interesting details to the others. Slides of instructive specimens from previous autopsies are exhibited for discussion at three microscopes in autopsy room. Last minute check of plans for all experiments to be started today. Discussion of two noteworthy papers on stress that recently came to the attention of staff members.   Consideration of qualifications of one Italian and one Indian physician who applied for postgraduate fellowships. (I wish people would not look over my shoulder when I'm making confidential entries in my notebook during autopsy conferences.   By now the staff is so international that I have to write Hungarian text in the Russian alphabet for privacy and this is difficult.)

12:15 P.M. Back to office for brief discussion with Mr. Mercier, institute administrator (on hiring of a new assistant librarian, structural changes in surgery, purchase of an ultra-violet lamp, raises in certain salaries).

12:30 P.M. It being a sunny day, I repair to "Florida" for lunch (pea soup, cold cuts, coffee, grapes) which I take basking in the sun (stripped to the waist, the rest of me being carefully wrapped in an electric blanket against the bitter cold).   After lunch, reading (still in glorious sun) of yesterday's (not so glorious) dictation on *Mast Cells*.

1:15 P.M. Back to office for cigar (Upmann's) and reading of Dr. René Veilleux's thesis on *La Réaction Anaphylactoïde Calcifiante*.

3:15 P.M. Join staff in solarium for tea and cookies, a tradition I enjoy because it allows members of all departments to mix freely.

3:30 P.M. Study of day's histology in my office.   Selection of some instructive slides for tomorrow's autopsy conference. Six representative slides are taken to illustrate points in a paper on calciphylaxis that I dictated yesterday.   Certain regions of microscopic slides are marked for photography (by Miss Barath) and their legends dictated at microscope. Other slides are sent (to Mr. Nielsen) for additional special stains.

6:00 P.M. Mrs. Staub comes in to report about phone calls, messages, and the day's secretarial work.   She delivers copy transcribed from my tapes.

6:15 P.M. Reading of copy just received.

6:40 P.M. Drive home.

6:55 P.M. Fifteen minutes of exercise on stationary bicycle while children report about school and play.

7:10 P.M. Dinner.   During soup and meat course we play "Geography."   (I mention the names of cities, children have to identify in which country they are.)   Again, Michel has trouble with Tegucigalpa!   Marie keeps the scores.   Jeanot, having most points, gets all the glory and the ten cents foreseen for the winner.   According to house rules, this game must stop when dessert is served to let Mommy talk.   Mommy talks.

7:40 P.M. We repair to bedroom for distribution of daily prizes: best report about school and play (ten cents), first place in "Geography" (ten cents), consolation prizes to the others (candy).   Drawing imaginary, improbable-looking animals.

8:00 P.M.   Kids out.   Reading *Il Gattopardo* by Lampedusa.

9:30 P.M.   Lights out.   Another fifteen minutes of half-conscious floating in the world of calciphylaxis. Then sleep . . . sleep . . .sleep . . .

Fifteen years later I still follow essentially the same routine, but with a different cast of characters.   Having become a little lazier, I now get up sometimes as late as 5:00 or even 5:30 A.M.   I pull my old stiff limbs out of bed with one sudden swing; otherwise I could never do it.   Weather permitting, I engage in fifteen minutes of vigorous exercise, riding my bicycle up and down the hills of the McGill campus; other days I go for a swim in the small plastic pool set up in our basement.   I then fix breakfast while listening to the morning news.

After jogging (as quickly as my hips permit) to the same garage where I have kept my car for the past thirty years, I drive to the university.   I take from my small refrigerator whatever is to be prepared for that day's lunch (main dish usually horsemeat and French-Canadian *fèves au lard,* baked beans with maple syrup but without lard because of my diet).

I feel rested, fresh and optimistic about everything in the morning, becoming increasingly tired and pessimistic as the day wears on, so I try to take care of the most important business early in the day.   Much of my time is spent in writing books or articles and giving television, radio and newspaper interviews, interspersed with receiving foreign visitors to the institute.

Lately, much of my office time is taken up in organizing our new International Institute of Stress. I always hated doing administrative work, but I find it stimulating when it relates to this institution, probably because it brings back to my mind those same emotions I faced years ago when I first helped set up the Institute of Experimental Medicine and Surgery. Once again I must seek financial backing, outline research programs, establish international connections for teaching and clinical applications, select an efficient staff and coordinate an extensive library. Meanwhile, at least, this necessarily cuts out all lab work and undergraduate teaching; but on the other hand it allows me to put to good use my traveling schedule, for I am constantly establishing new associations that might prove mutually beneficial for coordinating research on stress.

At 4:40 P.M., after the staff has gone, I take a look at the results of the day's work: transcriptions of my dictation, letters to sign, editorial suggestions to approve, budgetary questions. I go through as much material as possible, but after this my energy is exhausted. I leave my office every day at about 5:00 P.M. with unfailing regularity, rushing home in time to hear the 6:00 P.M. CBC news.

Once I get there I generally do sit-ups and some weight-lifting. I jump into my miniature pool for a quick swim in ice-cold water, then run up to take a hot bath.

Around 7:30 P.M., after dinner with Louise, I install myself comfortably in bed, unless we are visited by André, the only one of my children whom I still see regularly. André frequently talks about legal issues, which do not particularly interest me, but I get a great deal of pleasure from hearing his enthusiastic reactions to university life and his chosen profession. He is consumed by the same passion and persistence that I have for science. The conversation often turns to one of our favorite topics; namely, the fine points of expression in particular languages. André is concerned because he must plead in court using both French and English.

Eventually, I am left alone to read a little. I gradually become too tired to read anything heavy, having abandoned the newspaper for more serious reading, and I put my book aside to look at a few jokes out of *Ludas Matyi*, a Hungarian humor magazine I receive regularly and anonymously, thanks to some generous Hungarian benefactor. But after a couple of minutes I can hardly concentrate, even on this, so at 9:45 I turn out the light and let myself wander into that half-conscious world before sleep . . . sleep . . . sleep.

Even as a medical student during vacations at home, I used to get up between 5:00 and 6:00 in the morning and study all day in our garden, with only brief interruptions for exercise or meals until about 5:30 P.M. My mother warned me that if I continued to work at this pace it would get me nowhere because I would soon break down in a nervous collapse and exhaustion. I was told that I was a young man in a hurry. This was true; I was rushing to get a good start in life. Now that I am a little less young, I am called an old man in a hurry and this is dead right again, as I want to complete my work as far as the time remaining to me permits.

To conserve my time, I have even taken on the job of being my own barber. I still like to wear my hair very short in the back and on the sides, as was the custom in my student days. For the last twenty-five years I've managed to avoid barber shops by mastering the art of cutting my own locks, using a pair of electric clippers (employed for shearing our rats) and two mirrors. I perform this operation once or twice a month and my hair is always neat, although my secretary tells me that it is sometimes a little uneven for the first few days afterwards. I wonder how many hours I have saved by never having to go to the barber shop, wait for my turn and then undergo the complex ritual that has become customary at such occasions in order to justify the price.

I am always on guard lest time slip away, making me lose my chance to do everything I wish. Possibly this helps to explain why just about the only type of dream I seem to remember consists of different situations in which I missed my aim. I am late for the departure of a plane, a meeting or a public address. Sometimes I lose my way in a foreign city. It is always the same general problem, and when I realize that I have no chance left to accomplish what I want, I suddenly wake up in a sweat. Whenever this happens I tell myself, "Here you go again, dreaming that you're late." Perhaps this is what racehorses have nightmares about.

Incidentally, for those insomniacs looking for solace, I'm afraid I cannot offer much advice. Usually I readily fall asleep again, unless work during the preceding day has been particularly hard on me. If I do have difficulties falling asleep, I use a trick that perhaps I should not recommend become some people may become addicted to the habit and overdo it: I take a small gulp of whiskey. This has a tranquilizing effect on me.

I am often asked in what language I dream, as I speak so many in our institute and on lecture tours. When I was first questioned about this, I could not recall. But upon awakening one night in Moscow after speaking Russian all day I immediately made a great effort to remember the language I had used in my dream. In repeating the last sentence, I noticed it was in Russian, but in very bad Russian — full of grammatical errors. I am neither a professional linguist nor an interpreter of dreams, but it seems to me that I melt into my changing environments as far as language is concerned, even as regards my subconscious. Anyway, I learned that my Russian is even worse when allowed to flow freely than it is under conscious voluntary verification.

I am also asked how I spend my leisure time, my weekends. How did I spend last Sunday? I did what I have been doing virtually every "holiday," and what I will probably do for the rest of my life: work. I come to the institute on weekends, holidays, in good weather and bad. I have selected a kind of work which for me is play. It does not tire me. I get much more fun out of analyzing Nature — and particularly my pet child, stress — than from going fishing, playing golf or driving through the countryside. What I do is indispensable to me, and I actually find it relaxing. If I were prevented from working, that would be my greatest frustration. In the words of George Bernard Shaw: "Labor is doing what we must; leisure is doing what we like."

Someone recently told me a story about Thomas Edison. If the names were changed, this could also be my story. One summer evening, when Edison returned home tired form work, his wife said, "You have worked long enough without a rest. You can easily afford a nice vacation."

"But where will I go?" he asked.

"Decide where you would rather be than anywhere else on earth, and go there."

"Very well," promised Edison. "I will go tomorrow."

The next morning he went back to work in his lab.

I am reminded of my work even upon entering my home— which I have now transformed into the International Institute of Stress — a brick house opposite the McGill campus. Over the door is a symbol that looks to passers-by like a bit of chicken wire. I carved it by hanging out of the second-floor window while my wife held my feet. Endocrinologists recognize this symbol as the steroid nucleus, the basic structure characteristic of all the corticoids. When I bought the house in the early 1930s, few people expected these hormones to become as important as they have proved to be today, especially in relation to stress and the General Adaptation Syndrome, but I sensed that they would probably act as the most important guideline of my work. As the house had an empty coat of arms over its entrance and our family had no heraldic emblem, I decided to create my own. In retrospect it seems to have been well chosen, for steroids became the centerpiece of my activity. This coat of arms, though, is a symbol not only of steroids but of the fact that, quite literally, I always live my work — whether at home or in the office.

I have been praised and criticized for such single-mindedness. I know that the public — especially the American public — expects a scientist to be a "nice sociable guy," a good mixer who is just like anybody else. But I don't agree that this is desirable. In the words of Clifton Fadiman,

Scientists frequently are very approachable human beings as well as trained and often highly creative people. But do we want our scientists to waste their time in approachability? Do we really care that they have wholesome hobbies and the mandatory five healthy children? Are they not worth more to us if they're as crusty as Newton, as odd as Pascal, as remote a Willard Gibbs? Shouldn't they be let alone so that they can do their work instead of being compelled to placate us with that ole fishin' pole? I am not convinced that the common run of us really prefer geniality to genius.

I love what I do and I have an insatiable desire to learn all I can about the stress of life. This often makes me quite frustrated when I realize the enormity of the subject. Stress touches upon virtually every aspect of life and I certainly could not accumulate all the knowledge I would need to be familiar with every branch of the field. If I am so frustrated by my limitations in this particular field, I am even more overwhelmed when I think of the rest of the knowledge that I would like to accumulate. For instance, because of my devotion to work, I neglect reading about current events to the extent that I would desire. Sometimes I feel hopelessly incompetent in appraising the real issues behind the newspaper comments.

When, as a medical student, I first visited the library of our department of biochemistry, I found all the shelves of one huge wall completely filled with the innumerable volumes of Abderhalden's *Handbook of Biological Methods* and Beilstein's *Handbook of Organic Chemistry.* It took me a long time to recover from this sight. Never before had I so clearly realized my own limitations. Every volume that I happened to look up contained important information for one who, like myself, wanted to study biochemical problems. Yet I could see at a glance that even if I lived to be a hundred I could never master it all. I am reminded of this experience whenever I see the bewildered eyes of a graduate student on first entering my library, which now contains about a million entries on endocrinology and more than 150,000 on stress-related subjects only.

Many a talented young man must have been permanently frightened away from research as a result of such frustrating experiences. The only way I managed to overcome my feeling of inferiority was by telling myself, "If others can do it, I can do it." Actually, I had no basis for this "optimism by analogy," but it worked. It restored my self-confidence. In fact, I still use it whenever I realize my hopeless inadequacy for a task − which happens quite often.

Too many people work hard for some immediate objective which promises leisure to enjoy life tomorrow, but tomorrow never becomes today. There is always another objective which promises even more leisure in exchange for just a little more work. That is why so few people in the usual walks of life retain that wonderful gift which they all possessed as children: the ability to really enjoy themselves. But it hurts to be conscious of this defect, so adults dope themselves with more work (or alcohol) to divert attention from their loss. The inspired painter, poet, composer, astronomer or biologist never grows up in this respect; he does not lose the abstract treasures of his naïve innocence, no matter how poor or how old he may be. He retains the child-like ability to enjoy the impractical. And pleasures are always impractical; they can lead us to no reward. They are the reward.

The really acquisitive person is so busy reinvesting that he never learns how to cash in. "Realistic people" who pursue "practical aims" are rarely as realistic and practical, in the long run of life, as the dreamers who pursue only their dreams. True scientists — even when they become very old — retain a certain romanticism, a dreamy, imaginative habit of mind; they continue to dwell on the adventurous, the picturesque, the unusual; they never cease to be thrilled by the heroic grandeur and infallible consistency of the laws that govern the harmony of Nature in and around man.

Whenever I feel pregnant with a new idea, I suffer. Not being a woman, I cannot compare this feeling with real birth pangs, but I imagine it has much in common with them. It bears a definite element of frustration because there is something very desirable in you that must come out though you don't know how to push. For those who have not experienced the feeling, it is difficult to describe it other than by analogies from everyday life, and these necessarily sound ridiculous when used to characterize the birth of an idea. But when I discussed this sensation with other scientists, they immediately knew what I meant when I compared it to what we feel when we want to sneeze and cannot, or when a word is on the tip of our tongue and we are unable to utter it. Less conventionally, I could also compare this suffering to that of monumental gas pains — a very appropriate analogy, as the majority of all mental gestations produce nothing but gas. Unfortunately, before birth, the nature of the gestation product cannot be determined; as far as I can tell, the birth pangs that precede the delivery of valuable and worthless ideas are the same.

Intuitive flashes are usually followed by feelings of great happiness, exhilaration and relief. All the accumulated fatigue and frustration of the preceding periods of fact-gathering and incubation disappear at once. The resulting sensation of extreme well-being and energy gives me, at least temporarily, the impression of being up to any task that may present itself in the future. At the same time there comes the "eureka impulse," the desire to sally forth and tell everybody. It makes me very unhappy if there is no one around who would understand the meaning of my finding when I hit upon something that I think is really important. Even so, I have never given in to this impulse quite as much as did Archimedes who hurried out of his bathtub and into the streets unclad. But then, never having discovered anything as important as the law of specific gravity, I am not at all sure I could have resisted the degree of temptation to which he was exposed. It is pleasant and relaxing to give in to the "eureka impulse," but I have learned to keep it under reasonable control; the temptation is not strong enough to make me rush out with insufficient clothing in search of a public or rush into print with insufficient evidence.

When I do get an idea, I jot it down no matter where I am. I always keep a notebook and pen with me in case inspiration strikes when I am not at my desk. I also keep writing materials next to my bed so that I can hold onto those nocturnal ideas that seem so brilliant but vanish mysteriously, leaving no trace in the morning. Otto Loewi, one of the greatest medical scientists of our time, told me that he used to do the same thing, although not always with great success. In fact, he said, the idea for his most important experiment came to him one night when he awoke suddenly. Immediately realizing the transcendent value of his dream, he jotted down his thoughts. Unfortunately, the next morning he could not decipher his scribble. Try as he might, he could not remember what the hunch was, until the following night when he again awoke with the same flash of insight. This time he aroused himself sufficiently to take legible notes, and the next day he performed his famous experiment on the chemical transmission of nerve impulses, showing that if two isolated frog hearts connected only by artificial tubes are perfused with the same solution, stimulation of the nerve of one heart causes a change in cardiac rhythm which is transmitted to the other heart by the perfusing liquid.

Sir Frederick Banting related a similar incident about his work with diabetes. Soon after World War I, he set up medical practice in a small Canadian town. One evening he read an article on the degenerative changes that take place in the pancreas after blockage of its duct by concrements. He went to bed but could not sleep, because of the intriguing though vague impression that such degenerative changes might help the elucidation of the then mysterious part played by the pancreas in diabetes. It was not until about two o'clock in the morning that an idea suddenly crystallized in his mind. He immediately wrote it down in these words: "Ligate pancreatic ducts of dogs. Wait six to eight weeks for degeneration. Remove the residue and extract." This half-conscious thought led to Banting's most important contribution to medical history, the discovery of the antidiabetic hormone, insulin.

It often happens that our best ideas come when we are diverted from work. Einstein, Darwin and many others reported that inspiration struck them when they were sick in bed, eating a meal or pursuing some other unrelated activity. It seems that after I have saturated myself with the material necessary for the appraisal of a new correlation, I am invariably too close to some aspect of it to see things in their true perspective as part of a whole. Besides, in the lab or office, the visible aspects of my subject (chemicals, microscope, experimental animals, papers, books) focus attention too one-sidedly on details which interfere with the big intuitive leap necessary for making a great new correlation.

Sometimes it helps if I temporarily change the subject. When things begin to become routine or I feel I am getting into a rut with my thinking processes, I often put the subject aside and pick up something else for the time being. Frequently, the novelty of the new activity stimulates me to complete the original project. At other times I find it more helpful merely to get away by taking a walk, reading or sleeping.

After the idea is clearly formulated, I like to discuss it with my colleagues, for it helps my thoughts crystallize if I explain them. I try to distinguish between the actual errors I make and the misunderstandings caused by failure to describe the project or idea. I like to keep an open mind and take into account the objections of others, and in this way valid criticism can be very constructive.

I have had many periods of discouragement in the course of my life, from the beginning of my career when my professors and classmates refused to take seriously my theories on "the syndrome of just being sick" up to the present day. In fact, I might have the dubious honor of being one of the most frequently attacked medical research people of our time. My response to such attacks is very simple. I ask myself first of all: "Are you right or wrong?" If I feel I am right, I defend my point of view with boundless tenacity; if I am wrong, I admit it without hesitation. I never accept defeat simply because everyone appears to be against me.

One of the articles which pleased me most in 1975 was a broadside attack on my work on stress. It enumerated the most serious problems related to my work and bore the descriptive title "A Historical View of the Stress Field." The journal in which this review was published asked me to explain my attitude toward these criticisms and I answered them one by one. I have even ordered reprints from the journal in which the attack and my reply were published together. I know of no other instance in medical literature when an author paid money to obtain reprints of his adversary's arguments for distribution among scientists interested in his field.

However, this attack was well written and it contained most of the points on which my stress theory had been misunderstood by one person or another. Had I published a clarification of these issues on my own initiative in 1975, I would undoubtedly have been accused of seeking easy victories by demolishing opinions that are rarely in doubt anymore. I would have been a Don Quixote attacking scientific windmills. But such reviews help me to "clean out the weeds" that tend to creep into the interpretation of the stress concept, and it is important for me to go on doing this. On such a vast subject as stress, it is likely that one observation or another will cause confusion in the minds of those who cannot find time to survey the picture in its entirety. It is not easy to keep track of some 150,000 publications on stress. One researcher's conclusions may conflict with the data published elsewhere in an unrelated journal or in a language unfamiliar to him, but the contradiction could never be detected and rectified without an appropriate overview.

Although I welcome a good debate, I sometimes give too much vent to my compulsion to encourage criticism of my work. At a colloquium on stress arranged in London during the mid-fifties, when research in this field was particularly active throughout the world, I was asked to prepare a list of subjects for discussion. Thinking that it would be most instructive to review the weakest points in the stress concept, I carefully compiled a complete inventory of them. This list was circulated among the invited guests, but without mentioning that I had prepared it. The impression created was that the concept consisted only of de-batable points, and that the object of the colloquium was to annihilate me. Only when the discussion was well under way did I begin to realize this, and I experienced the rather uncomfortable feeling of having been unconsciously maneuvered into the position of an enforced public hara-kiri.

At this point, one of the participants got up and delivered a lengthy and biting oration on all the weak points in the stress theory, flaws to which, said he, my attention had been called "by those who had prepared the program." But he expressed particular concern over the hundreds, nay thousands, of publications that had encumbered the medical literature of all countries as a result of my description of the General Adaptation Syndrome. "Those of us," he exclaimed in a tone of desperation, "who are responsible for clinical work, cannot possibly keep up-to-date with this avalanche of stress literature! How can we be expected to teach the subject to our students?"

I was somewhat taken aback, having been unprepared to justify the excessive interest created by the stress concept. All I managed to say was that "I fully agree. Those of us who do not have the time to learn about stress should not be asked to teach the subject to students." It was immediately obvious from the reaction of my listeners that this recommendation struck them as being, on the whole, rather reasonable.

When criticism is just, I am not afraid to revise my thinking. As I mentioned earlier, I mistakenly used the term "egotism" instead of "egoism" when first describing my code in my book *Stress Without Distress*. Once the error was explained to me, I immediately began to use the correct phrasing. After reading the British edition of that book, Sir Hans Krebs (the Nobel laureate in chemistry) wrote to inform me that a remark that I attributed to Montaigne was, in truth, expressed in slightly different terms by Seneca some 1,500 years earlier: *Ignoranti quem portum petat nullus suus ventus est* (He who knows not his port of destination has no favorable wind). As this is one of my favorite quotes, I have again used it in this book, but this time, thanks to Sir Hans, with the earlier author cited.

But when criticism is not well founded I am quick to correct the errors lest misunderstandings grow. This often leads to humorous situations. I was once scheduled to lecture in Buenos Aires at a large stress symposium. I arrived late and, not wanting to disturb the speaker by making my way up to the podium, I slipped into the only vacant seat I could find, at the back of the gallery. The audience listened attentively as the speaker continued his emphatic discussion of the latest developments in stress research, sprinkling his address with erroneous quotations prefaced by "Selye said this" and "Selye said that."

At last I could no longer resist correcting him, and I spoke up from my place at the back of the hall. The speaker indignantly replied, "Well, I spent a year studying Selye's publications so I am quite sure, my dear sir, that I know his opinions." By then those who knew me personally were beginning to look restless so, having failed to convince him, I finally said, "But, I *am* Selye!" This brought forth gales of laughter from the audience and a small, embarrassed smile from the speaker. I hadn't wanted to be offensive but, after all, he was badly misrepresenting my work.

That experience reminded me of the story of two patients in an insane asylum. One committed all sorts of reprehensible, antisocial acts, excusing his behavior by saying, "But I am Christ and God my Father has commanded me to do this." Whereupon the second patient responded with great dignity and authority, "That simply is not true. I have never commanded you to do such things.

It is important in science not only to rectify errors but to keep an open mind when something unexpected results from investigations.

At one point in my research I was interested in finding out how stressful the injection of air into the chest cavity of rats would be, as this procedure was used in the clinical treatment of tuberculosis. While I was doing this, a group of Brazilian physicians visiting the institute were shown into my lab by one of my assistants. As I turned to greet them, the needle I was using slipped under the rat's skin. The air formed an egg-shaped connective tissue sac. When I saw this development, I thought, "Why not use air as a mold with which to force connective tissue to form a sac of predictable size and shape for the study of inflammation in a 'living test tube'?" Later, I developed this technique and it proved to be a very practical procedure, one which is now generally employed and known as the "granuloma pouch" technique.

Not all of my discoveries can be attributed to sheer chance. I do know that my development as a scientist is, in part, due to my admiration of many great thinkers whose carefully planned experiments set a fine example not only for me but for countless others. I am undoubtedly a hero-worshipper, but I cannot claim any great originality in the choice of my heroes. Einstein, for example, represents to me one of the highest summits that the human intellect can reach. I also admire Bertrand Russell as a philosopher. I do not have the competence to appreciate his mathematical genius, but as a person he always impressed me very much and he had a considerable influence upon my thinking.

In the field in which I am better prepared to appraise accomplishment, my special heroes are Claude Bernard, Louis Pasteur, Robert Koch and Paul Erlich. To these I might add a few others with whom I had or still have personal contacts: I. P. Pavlov, who described the conditioned reflexes; Walter Cannon, who gave us the "fight-or-flight" reaction, which greatly stimulated my own work; the two Canadians, Wilder Penfield, the eminent neurosurgeon, and Sir Frederick Banting, who guided my work in its early stages; Julius Axelrod and Earl Sutherland, both American scientists; and the distinguished Swedish physiologist Ulf von Euler, known for his research on adrenal medullary and sympathetic nervous hormones that participate in the stress reaction. The latter three scientists were my guests as visiting "Claude Bernard" professors at our institute and also discussed their life problems and motivations with some of my graduate students and colleagues at our home. (I take pride in mentioning that I recognized their greatness and invited them to address our group before each of them was awarded the Nobel Prize.)

Among the noted scientists who set a fine example for me, it was first of all Cannon who gave me the greatest stimulation and taught me more than any other person in my chosen field. My work on stress was primarily inspired by his discovery of the "emergency reaction." Although I was much younger than he and never studied under his direction, he treated me as a colleague. I repeatedly visited his laboratory and he came to see mine. He was the first to recognize the important part played by the adrenalins (epinephrine and norepinephrine) of the adrenal medulla during fight-or-flight reactions, and he showed particular interest in my approach to adaptation. It is perhaps ironic, and not without instructive value for future generations of scientists, that I could never convince him of some of the most basic tenets of my contribution to this field — namely, (1) that there is not merely an acute emergency response of the body but an entire General Adaptation Syndrome consisting of the alarm reaction followed by the stage of resistance and eventually by the stage of exhaustion; (2) the pituitary and adrenal cortex play a decisive role in this response; (3) the reaction is totally nonspecific and merely represents the body's reply to the common aspects of any kind of demand; and (4) the most diverse diseases can result from stress, depending upon the simultaneous influence of different conditioning agents.

Occasionally in my work on stress and the G.A.S., I stumbled upon unrelated findings that were of sufficient importance for me to give them my attention for a while. I have already mentioned the "granuloma pouch." Another discovery of this type was the steroid hormone anesthesia, which I described in great detail in *From Dream to Discovery*. When I first saw my rats immobilized by the injection of steroids, I was not quite sure if they actually were under anesthesia, merely paralyzed or in deep shock. I thought that Wilder Penfield would be the best authority to consult, as founding chief of the Montreal Neurological Institute.

I phoned him to ask whether I could demonstrate the steroid hormone anesthesia to him and he enthusiastically agreed to see me. I left my McGill lab, taking along a bottle of a progesterone solution (the only steroid yet tested for this effect) as well as a few rats, and rushed across the street to the Neurological Institute. There I injected my animals before Penfield's eyes. As predicted, they went to sleep within a few minutes without showing any signs characteristic of shock or paralysis, and Penfield assured me that they were actually anesthetized. Despite his high academic position and worldwide reputation, he discussed these matters (with me, a mere postgraduate fellow!) with a lack of formality and a youthful enthusiasm that impressed me greatly and reminded me of the way Cannon had spoken to me. Apparently, the real giants of science feel no need to emphasize their eminence by their interpersonal behavior.

I have spoken before about my admiration of greatness and excellence *per se*. One of my more personal heroes was Frank the racehorse. I do not mean a racehorse type of man but an actual animal. He had won many races, the last one at the age of twenty-two. This, for a horse, is really "golden age," and Frank's owner decided not to race him anymore. At his last race a farmer from northern Quebec who greatly admired the beauty and motivation of this beast bought him at a very modest price. Frank was obviously not a useful farm horse but only an extra mouth to feed on the pasture. Although the farmer was reputedly very stingy, he decided to purchase the animal simply because of his innate elegance and the elevating effect of his intense motivation to win. He let Frank graze on the pasture, hoping to increase the beauty of his farm by the presence of this splendid animal.

At first Frank had a little trouble getting used to retirement. He ran, but his soul was not in it for he no longer had a race to win, an aim to work for. Then one day the owner of a neighboring summer cottage put his eight-year-old daughter, Louise, on Frank's back, holding the horse carefully so she would not fall off. She had never learned how to ride and there was not even a saddle for her to hold onto. As soon as Frank felt the weight of the girl on his back, he tore himself free and started to race, much to the consternation of all those who stood around. Disappearing into the woods, Louise held on to his mane and did not fall off. Two hours later Frank came back with her and she was ecstatic. She was just a natural rider.

Louise's parents never wanted her to ride again, for they had nearly worried themselves to death during the two-hour outing. Louise cried bitterly, wanting to feel the ectasy of Frank's speed as often as possible.

Frank trotted over to the neighbors' cottage several times in the hope of being able to carry Louise, but to no avail. Yet, eventually the old horse found a way. He came to Louise's window around midnight when the family was asleep and started to whinny gently. Louise woke up, climbed through the window in her nightgown, right onto Frank's back, and off they went in a wild gallop through the woods. Every time they came to trees with branches just slightly above his own height, Frank carefully avoided them. Instinctively he side-stepped spots on the trails that might have been dangerous for his little rider. At two o'clock in the morning he returned to Louise's window, placing himself close enough for her to climb back in again.

This game repeated itself every day during four consecutive summers when the farmer's neighbors would again come out to their cottage to spend the holidays. The farmer told me that the horse always knew when Louise was in residence, because Frank never went to the window after she left with her parents but immediately returned for his nightly outings the very day they arrived. They made quite a picture – the little girl with her two blond pigtails and the tall dark-brown horse.

I would never have believed this story, except that both the farmer and the girl confirmed its truth. On the fifth year when Louise again returned for her summer vacation, she heard that Frank had died. He had continued to run until the last day and then went off to his stall by himself. In the morning the farmer found him dead but still standing on his feet. Apparently, as a result of his continuous intense muscular excercise, rigor mortis set in very rapidly, allowing him the glory of dying on his feet, of "dying with his boots on," so to speak.

When Louise heard of Frank's death, she disappeared into the woods to cry in solitude and when she came back she looked up at her mother with tears in her eyes and said, "Well, he was twenty-six years old and he had to die, but at least he died on his feet."

Frank's intense motivation, his pride in peak accomplishment and his altruistic egoism all gave him the irresistible desire to earn the love of his neighbor, Louise. Frank carried her for his own satisfaction; but while gaining an outlet for his instinct to run, he managed to do good for her. These are the same feelings that have motivated me throughout my career. Today this Louise is my wife and I am happy to act as her old racehorse. Frank was my brother in the animal world and his personality convinced me, better than any scientific discovery, that my code of behavior is based on the common laws of Nature that must regulate our conduct.

Although they inspire me purely on an intellectual level, I would certainly have welcomed a little practical advice from some of my human heroes, especially those involved in fields similar to my own. For anyone completely devoted to a cause, it is inevitably difficult to balance the demands of family life and the rigors of hard work. When you are truly in love with your career, a feeling of solitude and emotional isolation often results. It is especially difficult when one person in a married couple does not have the same technical training and instruction as the other. How can he or she share in the other's motivations, preoccupations and satisfactions? Of course, these dangers should be realized before marriage, and many people discuss this matter with a prospective spouse, so that both partners may weigh the disadvantages against the advantages of such a union.

At the outset, however, it is impossible for either partner to truly assess the enormous difficulties posed by the communication and sharing of feelings and experiences during a lifetime. Although specific examples may be shocking to people who have not met comparable conditions, let us take the case of Judy and George, who were desperately in love with each other at the respective ages of eighteen and twenty-two. They wanted to get married and honestly could swear an oath of loyalty in church before the representatives of their gods, promising to love and cherish each other for the rest of their lives. They did believe it and had every intention of doing so, but forty years later, Judy and George — still the same people, legally speaking, and still having the same age difference between them — were just not the same people they had been *biologically*.   Every cell in their bodies had changed. Their behavior had been greatly modified by the society they lived in and particularly by each other's developements; in such cases, it is entirely beyond the control of the people involved to go on really loving each other.   Of course, George can still look after Judy's welfare in every respect if he feels morally responsible for her, despite everything that has changed, but duty is not love.   For a marriage to be really successful, you must work for it and work for it all the time as long as it lasts.   Judy must remain lovable and must earn George's love.   She has to work for it, and the same is true for George; otherwise, the union has lost its original purpose.   It merely becomes obedience to a self-imposed command, a pact instead of an act of love.

A woman who marries a soldier, sailor or traveling salesman cannot appraise in advance just what it will mean to be left alone so often, perhaps with the responsibility of looking after young children.

To be the spouse of a very ambitious person with a highly complex career may be even more demanding, especially because there are very few interests the couple shares.   The manual worker, postman, clerk or businessman has many feelings to which his wife can more readily relate.   But, as the great French physiologist Charles Richet said: "Science demands much greater sacrifices. It does not permit any sharing.   It demands that certain men devote to it their whole existence, their whole intelligence, their whole labor."   Although the work of the scientist may not actually separate him from his spouse for long periods, he is still deprived of the pleasure of coming home in the evening and explaining to his life's companion the meaningfulness of the day's events; to understand his preoccupations, a lifelong specialization would be required, and that might change the very nature that originally attracted him to his wife.

In my case, when I return home in the evening, I would like to share my thoughts with my wife by speaking about the pharmacology of steroid hormones or some other topic of interest to me.   But what could she be expected to say about such things?

Unless you can maintain a strong, purely emotional attraction and look after each other's happiness in daily life, such marriages are doomed to fail.

When I was a young medical student, my great dream was to marry a girl with whom I could share all my concerns. I even coined an expression for it because I thought about it so often. I felt that the pleasures of physical intimacy were not reason enough to wed, that there should be a "kissing of the minds" to harmoniously complement emotional love and intellectual understanding. I did not realize then that among scientists this is exceedingly rare. Perhaps as a result of having to compete in a field hitherto dominated by men, or because the scientist's career is so exacting intellectually, it seems that some (not all) women scientists tend to become too masculine. The most feminine and lovable aspects of a woman's mind — warmth, charm and self-sacrificing empathy, the soft pliability that lends itself best to giving and receiving through caresses in every sense of the word— these perhaps do not mix with the harsh, single-minded discipline required to excel in science.

Yet this feat is not impossible. There have been women who achieved prominence in the sciences and nevertheless managed to maintain perfect emotional and intellectual intimacy with their equally eminent husbands. Among these enviable couples were Frédéric and Irène Joliot-Curie, her parents, Pierre and Marie Curie, and Carl Ferdinand Cori and his wife Gerty Theresa. However, I cannot claim to have known any of these couples sufficiently to be certain that I have interpreted their intimate personal relationships correctly. I spent several weeks with the Joliot-Curies, often eating lunch with them in Moscow where we were attending the Jubilee Meeting of the Soviet Academy. Carl Cori, like me, received his M.D. from the German University of Prague. I met him and his wife several times after they came to America. I knew Marie Curie as a medical student in Paris, where I attended her physics lectures out of sheer admiration, without really understanding much of what she said. I was fascinated by her precisely because she managed to remain so entirely feminine, despite her intense scientific activity and her advanced age. She always wore conservative but extremely elegant black dresses and expressed herself in a rigidly scientific yet caressing, soft language. After the lectures I would think up some questions to ask just for the chance to speak to her and see her up close. Although I was almost half a century younger than she and our fleeting contacts occurred nearly fifty years ago, in a respectful way I am still in love with her, or at least with the femininity she represented to me.

In each of these marriages, husband and wife gave manifest proof of their joint scientific talents by cooperating in work that earned them the Nobel Prize conjointly. From what I could discover, all were capable of truly sharing both their emotional and professional lives.

I know of only two marriages where the wife was a scientist and the husband was not. As far as I could tell, both of these were very solid unions. But in both cases the women, though successful, were not extremely motivated to achieve peak accomplishment, and the men were themselves quite active in their nonscientific careers. So in this respect I cannot make any well-founded useful generalizations.

Having been married thrice myself, once to a medical doctor and twice outside the profession, I am no longer sure if a "kissing of the minds" is ever possible, whether or not a man marries someone who shares his interest in science. I admit that I feel remorseful about not being as good a husband as I should have been to my first two wives and you may ask yourself why, when I asked both my former wives to marry me, I did not foresee the problems that would arise. Perhaps I should have, but I did not.

My first wife and I got married after a very brief courtship in my native Austria. In retrospect, I feel we rushed into marriage under very emotional, romantic circumstances. My second wife was my secretary and her truly unusual beauty may have blinded my reason and sense of fairness. After the breakdown of my first marriage, I again married rather rapidly on the rebound.

Before asking them to marry me, I admitted my monomania to both my wives and explained to them that, for me, science would always come first, much like an instinct that I could never overcome. However, I think that in both instances I did this mostly in a subconscious effort to wash my hands of the consequences.

I don't think either of them realized just how intense my mono-mania would be.

My first wife was protestant; hence, the church wedding — the only one of consequence in Quebec at that time — was easily annulled by the Archdiocese of New York. My second wife, a devout Roman Catholic, at first hesitated to marry a divorced man, but after I explained that actually, in a religious sense, I was never married because my first marriage was annulled by the Vatican, she was no longer worried.

When I considered these marriages, it always seemed to me that women are more adaptable to social change than men, but I underestimated the difficulties of adjusting to life with a "race horse." I thought my second wife, Gabrielle, could adjust to her new role without great difficulty, but looking back, I realize I may have overestimated her desire and her ability to readjust her social life to the professorial community to which I introduced her. Charmed by her aristocratic air, I believed — and hoped — it would not be such a difficult transition for her. After it became apparent that I was wrong, I went on living under conditions which were very difficult for me, in order to protect the children. Her whole philosophy of life was almost exactly the opposite of mine, but I did not want to break up this marriage until the children were all independent.

I certainly had no desire to melt into the high society of Pitts-burgh in which my first wife was raised. Despite her mother's influence, she did not like that kind of life either, so no great friction was caused by my feelings. Anyway, at the time of our marriage in 1936 we were young and deeply emotional and no obstacles seemed insurmountable.

I met my first wife at a music festival in Salzburg. She was visiting Austria with her mother and I think my Tyrolean costume, my familiarity with the local way of life and my respectable position on the teaching staff of a well-recognized Canadian uni-versity helped considerably in making me acceptable to both daughter and mother. I took my new friend for a brief visit to my parents in Komárom, where our graceful family home also had a reassuring effect. When I introduced her to my parents, I mentioned that she was from Pennsylvania. My mother exclaimed,

"Oh, Penna!" She had seen this abbreviation on a license plate from that state, and my new wife became known as "Penna" from then on.

Penna did not plan on going into medicine or science, as she was about to obtain her degree in music at the then-very-elegant Vassar College in New York state. But she sensed that she could never really marry me without marrying medicine as well, so immediately after our wedding she registered at McGill. She obtained her M.D. without any difficulty and wanted greatly to share my scientific interests; yet that "kissing of the minds" never occurred. I should have foreseen this also because, no matter how hard you try, you cannot become obsessed with science merely on the basis of marital love.

I'm afraid that our daughter, Catherine, suffered most, for she was torn by the influence of the two of us. Her early life in Montreal was spent constantly in my company, perhaps arousing her instinctive feelings for science. But after her first years she was brought up by her mother, who returned to her family and later remarried in Pittsburgh. Cathy took on the American nationality of her stepfather and, much to my disappointment, also his name. I consented, knowing it would make life easier for the child if she did not have to explain why her name was different from her mother's.

An adult now, she has her own life in New York City. She visits me in Montreal and I look her up whenever I can, which is far too rarely, but it was inevitable that we should drift apart. Still, we try to keep in touch, even though the peculiar circumstances of our lives made it impossible for us to become as close to each other as we might have wished.

Although she never showed any special interest in medicine, I see in her with great satisfaction some of my own dominant passions, especially a love of Nature that led to her decision to become a marine biologist. She is extremely skilled at underwater diving, and this natural talent helps her considerably in a career that she has practiced for some time, out of sheer preference, without any formal training. Eventually she decided to get a degree, but she is going about it in a leisurely manner, interrupting her studies with expeditions all over the world. I keep getting fascinating letters about the marine life of little islands in the Pacific whose very existence was unknown to me. She seems to have established excellent social relationships with the dolphins who, with their proverbial wisdom, have devised the oddest complicated water games which they have taught her to play by pushing her about as she swims among them.

Only a few days ago she unexpectedly wrote from a minute island near Guadalcanal where some friends of hers have set up a marine laboratory. Because of unusually strong winds and rain, she could not get into the water as planned, so to while away the time she climbed up a "vine tunnel" one hundred and fifty feet high. This, she explained, is formed by the roots of a fig tree which twine down and strangle a nearby tree, rotting the other's trunk and leaving a tunnel about two feet wide. I am likewise fascinated to read her colorful descriptions of the animals she has encountered on these journeys. She concludes her latest letter:

> I am writing you now by kerosene lamp in this grass house my friends have made up on stilts over the intertidal part of the beach. The bat (a family pet) is swooping around over my head and we are drinking warm beer as there is no electricity and therefore no refrigeration. Homemade bread, fresh oysters and lobster for dinner!
>
> Love, Cathy

There is no evident relationship between her letter and histology, the structure of steroid hormones or anything else I have dealt with in connection with stress research. Yet, given different circumstances of early childhood, I can quite imagine myself finding excitement in the same kind of life. It amuses me greatly to see that a love and admiration of Nature has sifted through five generations of Selyes to this girl, even though I have had no real family ties with her since she was five.

Some feel that the children, even more than the wife, benefit from public recognition of a man's achievements. It is true that they are often proud of their father's accomplishments, especially after they have grown up. Sometimes, however, children resent the distance created by the special interests and the position occupied by the man they know first of all as "daddy."

When my other daughter, Marie, was eight years old, she once came home from school deeply disturbed and in tears. She related how two of her teachers were talking about her undistinguished scholastic record and, unaware that she was listening to their conversation, one of them remarked, "Well, little Marie Selye is trying to do what she can but, as far as her academic accomplishments are concerned, she couldn't have inherited much from her father!" Marie obviously felt that I was responsible, since she told me, "You see, if you weren't so well known, nobody would have criticized my record in school." At times like these I asked myself in heartfelt despair, "Is it really up to the father not to distinguish himself in any way, to justify the weakness of his children?"

I remembered that I had been confronted with the same situation as a child. Because he ran the Selye Clinic, my father was something of a local celebrity in Komárom, and whenever I was introduced it was as "Dr. Selye's little boy, Hans." I resented not being appreciated for my own merit and wished I could be known as something other than "Hugo Selye's son."

But my reaction was completely different from my daughter's. It made me so mad to be a mere appendage to the family name that I decided quite consciously to assert myself as a person in my own right. I wouldn't say that this became my sole motivation, but it definitely gave me satisfaction when I was eventually introduced as "Hans Selye, the top student in his class at medical school," and later, as "Hans Selye, father of the stress concept."

Sometimes in presenting me a chairman may add, "His father was a well-known surgeon, and Dr. Selye represents the fourth generation of Selye physicians." This makes me proud today, for I no longer have to prove to myself that I can be successful on my own, but that was a very real need for a long time.

Having looked at the problem from both sides I can only conclude that it is not up to the father not to distinguish himself, but rather the responsibility of the child to overcome his weaknesses and achieve something independently. The determination to equal or even outdo a parent's reputation can and does act as a major stimulus for many children. Once again this demonstrates my firm belief that it's not what happens to you but how you take it that determines how well you cope with the stress of life.

I have already suggested that the "do-your-own-thing" attitude is the only intelligent one a person can take, and I have tried to adopt this with regard to my children. Despite my desire to have at least one child carry on the Selye tradition of becoming physicians, none of them did. The only one who really accepted the work ethic part of my philosophy is my son André. In fact, he even wanted to become a surgeon like his grandfather but an unfortunate accident prevented him from doing so.

When my children were young I used to take them to the institute on weekends where they would watch me work in the lab. I showed them how to dissect rats and, little by little, they became familiar with the basics of anatomy. Sometimes I could not do my work with four lively kids around, so I would send them down to the courtyard of the university to play for a while. One day André, then in the first year of elementary school, was having a whale of a time riding up and down the newly installed but not-yet-perfected escalator leading up to the principal building. He caught his right hand in a gap at the end of the escalator; all the skin and two of his fingers were cut off and the tendons were exposed to the dirty machine oil. He lay partly unconscious as I rushed down after being notified by the watchman.

Through my connections with some excellent plastic surgeons we immediately rushed him to an operating room and, although it was Sunday, I managed to assemble a team of top surgeons. At first we feared that the hand would have to be amputated but it was saved after a series of skin and tendon transplants from other parts of his body, a veritable triumph of modern surgery accomplished by Drs. Martin Entin and Hamilton Baxter. It was obvious that with his right hand badly damaged, André would never become a first-rate surgeon, so he went into another field. He is now in his last year at law school and doing well. I would have preferred him to be a scientist, or at least a practicing physician, because I hoped I could share my views about medical problems with him and be useful with professional advice. Still I feel that in his case, my educational efforts were not in vain.

Eventually my other children also found their place in life, though frankly not in the manner I would have liked. I might have been able to help them more had their problems arisen later, or had I developed my code of altruistic egoism sooner. But it was precisely their difficulties that stimulated me to develop a biologically justifiable motivation and philosophy of life. By that time they had already left home and were less readily influenced by their father's code than by the saboteurs of that code with whom they associated. Even so, perhaps it is not entirely wishful thinking when I say that maybe the sight of my happy state at seventy-one, despite all the adversities to which I have been exposed, will begin to raise my credibility with them. Perhaps someday they will still accept me as the well-meaning father figure I would like to be. If I manage to teach them to be as content as I am when they reach my age, I will be most satisfied.

From my account, the possibility of a happy family life may seem remote to young colleagues just starting their careers. It is not. I'm sure I would have profited greatly if early in my career I could have read a similarly frank disclosure. This confession has also been a kind of catharsis for me, and now that I have put all this on record I feel truly relieved.

CHAPTER THIRTEEN

Questions People Ask Me

I am reluctant to express authoritative opinions about religion, politics, philosophy and the like because I feel that these are outside the limits of my competence. But it seems that people want to understand the man behind the scientist. Consequently, in the following pages I have presented a series of answers to the questions I am most frequently asked.

In general, scientists try to be scrupulously honest with themselves regarding their work; they may not be quite so eager to examine the reasons for their behavior toward society. But no one can live at peace with himself unless he clearly sees and understands his own motives and opinions. I have examined my feelings on some of life's basic questions. They may not be popular, but if I discuss them here in spite of this, I don't think that anyone can rightfully criticize me for not being honest.

Science and Faith
Nature evidently includes man; he, like everything in the universe, acts according to certain laws which are governed by a Force. As a scientist, that is as far as I can go, for science is not concerned with faith but with knowledge. I try to acquire expertise in problems I can understand, or at least can directly experience. The supernatural is, by definition, beyond those limits, but even if it is inexplicable, I am guided by faith in some kind of Force that dominates the universe. Not knowing is very different from not believing.

I can conceive of a deity different from that envisioned by any traditional religion, be it occidental or oriental, without it having features incompatible with any of them. The scientist can make no categorical statement concerning the nature of the Creator; he must understand where the possibilities of science end and those of faith and philosophy begin. We cannot speak in scientific terms about that which goes beyond the powers of human intelligence; this would be like measuring distances in pounds. The difference between faith and science is a qualitative one. If I remain in the domain in which I have acquired some experience, I can say only that I firmly believe in the existence of a Creator, an all-powerful, infallible, eternal entity. The atheist attributes to Nature that which every religion credits to its particular God, and the convictions of science are based upon the laws of Nature.

Nature can do all that is feasible. She is eternal; when man will have disappeared from the world Nature will still be there. She is infallible. Water boils at 100°C (212°F) at sea level. This is a fact. One cannot argue about it.

The scientist is used to accepting only the intelligible or the measurable. Yet he may ask himself questions about the creative intelligence of the universe. On this point I share the opinion of André Gide, who allegedly stated that "it is a fertile talent of man to retain the ability of doubt." In fact, complacency of spirit provided by a feeling of certainty blocks all possibilities of new discoveries and hinders the invention of unpredictable but marvelous things. In other words, you can't teach one who thinks he already knows. It was Claude Bernard who said, "The great principle of experimentation is doubt, the philosophical doubt which leaves to the spirit the liberty of its initiative."

People usually think that, while their religions are built on faith, and poetry on dreams, the first prerequisite for research is pure intelligence. Yet it is indispensable that scientists engaged in basic research retain the capacity to dream their very own dreams. To make your dreams come true, you must first be a dreamer.

I have long pondered this point. At a certain time in my life, I reached a crossroad between well-established routes of investigation (supported by research foundations and bound to yield results) and unexplored new avenues which seemed very promising to me but offered no assurance of success. It was at that time that I was moved to write my one and only poem — unless it is a prayer — in which I tried to describe the scientist's need for faith in the following terms, outlined in *From Dream to Discovery:*

Almighty Drive who, through the ages,
Have kept men trying to master Nature by understanding,
Give me faith — for that is what I need most now.

This is a rare and solemn moment in my life:
I stumbled across what seems to be
A new path into the unknown.
A road that promises to lead me closer to You:
The law behind the unknown.

I think I have the instinctive feeling,
And patiently, through the years, I have acquired the kind
   of knowledge
Needed to explore Your laws.
But my faith was weakened by this apprenticeship.
No longer can it steer me steadily towards my goal.
For I have come to distrust faith and overvalue proof.
So, let reverence for the unfailing power of all Your
   known laws
Be the source of my faith in the worth of discovering the
   next commandment.

Sometimes I feel lonesome, uncertain on my new trail,
For where I go no one has been before
And there is no one with whom to share the things I see — or
   think I see.
Still, to succeed, I must convince others to follow me
   and help;
For I also need their faith in me to reinforce my own
Which has so little evidence to lean on now,
For now is the beginning.

A long and hazardous course lies between me and my goal,
How could I travel alone?
How could I force this fog of half-understanding,
That confuses my sense of direction?

The other shore is not in sight — alas, there may be none:
Yet I — like all those who, before me,
Have succumbed to the lure of the vast unknown —
Must take this risk in exchange
For each chance to experience the thrill of discovery.

And that thrill I need, or my mind will perish,
For — thanks to You — it was not built to stand
The stale security of well-charted shore waters.

I cannot know whether You listen,
But I do know that I must pray:

Almighty Drive who, through the ages,
Have kept men trying to master Nature by understanding,
Give me faith now — for that is what I need most.

Many people think that science is the cornerstone of intellectual
life. Probably most scientists would agree with this view. Theoretically, it is possible that eventually we shall understand all
the reactions in our body with the aid of computers or even more
sophisticated and efficacious instruments that might be discovered
in the future to help us solve millions of problems simultaneously.
In answer to a question about this, Einstein reputedly replied that
eventually it might be possible to express all natural phenomena
in mathematical terms, but this would not make any sense. What
would you gain from translating Beethoven's Ninth Symphony
into curves of air pressure variations affecting the eardrum? Yet,
according to Heisenberg's principle of indeterminacy in mechanics,
it is impossible to assert in terms of the conventional geometric
propositions of motion that a given particle (such as an electron)
is at any time at a specified point and moving at a specified velocity
in a predictable direction, because the more accurately either factor
can be measured, the less accurately the other can be ascertained.
This principle of indeterminacy casts some doubt even upon the
theoretical possibility of ever learning the evolution of all phenomena by a complete verification of the *status quo* at any one time.
    All this shows that science does not have an answer to every-
thing. If you hit upon a phenomenon that cannot be explained,

you must admit that two possibilities exist: either science will someday succeed in clarifying its mechanism and nature, or the matter is beyond the reach of science.

It is worth bearing in mind that it is impossible to imagine anything that has no previously experienced characteristics. Try to imagine a color, or mixture of colors, that you have never seen before and that does not appear in the spectrum. You need boundless creative imagination to approximate the complexities of the Great Unknown.

I have often asked myself why, in pictures and sculptures, God was always represented in an anthropomorphic form — that is to say, resembling a human being, an animal or at least something previously experienced. We go even further in the case of the Holy Spirit, which is pictured as a dove. In primitive religions the divinities and spirits, believed to represent and personify virtually any phenomenon or being, are likewise depicted as similar to man, animals, the sun, the moon, etc., because it is impossible to imagine a being or thing not composed of previously experienced characteristics. And yet, in certain religions, God is not seen in anthropomorphic terms; in fact, some specify that He created man in his own image, but not in the bodily sense of the term.

By now I have no difficulty in imagining the supreme Creator as having no form at all. Even though electricity is a great force, it has no shape. It is somewhat primitive to think that the all-powerful, great Creator must resemble something that we have already seen.

It is curious that certain black tribes depict God as similar to a white man, yet many statues of the Holy Virgin represent her as a black woman. It reveals a similar limitation of our imaginative powers that throughout the ages the governing spirits have always been created in the image of man or animals, merely because it is difficult to realize that a being may exist merely by virtue of its power without having any particular shape.

In my book *In Vivo*, I used an example of a being which I called Martius DNA-RNA, an extremely intelligent, nonhuman messenger who found his way from Mars to Earth and consisted of nothing but the ribonucleic acid derivatives (DNA and RNA) that constitute the genetic code necessary for the reproduction of its own kind by any living being. It was invisible but extremely powerful; I allowed my imagination to play with the way it might respond to life on our planet. In fact, I can quite easily imagine a divinity that has no body or substance and actually corresponds to the eternal, infallible laws of Nature that have created everything in the universe, laws that must be honored and could never be disobeyed. Aren't these the characteristics that every religion attributes to its God?

On twentieth-century man

I have often wondered if twentieth-century man is appreciably more intelligent than his predecessors of a few centuries ago. I do not think that intelligence as such has undergone any considerable development since Confucius, Socrates and Aristotle. On the other hand, twentieth-century man has learned a great many new facts, so that with essentially the same level of intellect he can accomplish much more than his predecessors.

It is wrong to believe that pure intellect is appreciably enhanced because humanism yields increasingly more territory to man's daily preoccupations with science and technology. One of the most eminent representatives of behaviorism, B. F. Skinner, explains many reactions in a very mechanical way, through the agency of external factors that modify our behavior. This sounds as though our mind and body were simply machines which can be programmed in a predictable way to respond with certain reaction forms. While this is undoubtedly true of some types of operational conditioning, it seems difficult to reduce all forms of complex human behavior to such simple mechanisms.

It would not be possible to analyze the justification of this type of psychology here, although it does have a highly reputable following. One thing is certain: the final aim of human life must be a humanistic one. It really does not matter whether the elements of our reaction forms are mere reflexes. The main point is to obtain objectives which humanists accept as having an inherent value. The reflexes of a painter or a musician are essential for his work; he could not express his art without them, but this fact does not minimize the value of his intelligence and creative spirit. The artist can undoubtedly create even if he does not constantly direct his actions by intellectual analysis, because most of his movements have become automatic.

Can we eliminate war?
Personally, I do not believe that this is very probable. In fact, I would have great difficulty in even imagining such a happy state. Yet I feel we must try everything in our power to diminish the aggressive tendencies of man.

Even if some biologists insist that wars have a beneficial effect in controlling overpopulation, even if martial glories have given great satisfaction to many warriors, there are certainly better ways to keep the population explosion under control or to give an outlet to man's desire to express his powers and talents.

Many men have marched bravely to the battlefield only to be maimed for life or even to die in the service of some "infallible" authority to whom they felt they must be absolutely loyal. The proverbial "war to end all wars," the patriotic, political, religious and other motives that at one time seem to have great value, invariably lose their credibility within some ten, hundred or thousand years.

Only the laws of Nature are eternal. That is why, of all the concepts I have formulated, I would consider that of altruistic egoism to be the most important and most useful to man. If you have understood and assimilated the idea of altruistic egoism based on knowledge, not on blind faith, you will have acquired the most powerful weapon with which to combat friction with individuals and groups. To appreciate fully the need for such an approach, just think of all the conflicts raging right now between Catholic and Protestant Irish people, blacks and whites in South Africa and Rhodesia, Israelis and Arabs, Moslems and Hindus, Flemish- and French-speaking Belgians, French- and English-speaking Canadians, capitalists and communists, and even within the three language groups of otherwise so peaceful Switzerland. The mere enumeration of all the present conflicts, often between quite closely related groups, would fill the rest of this book.

Péguy said: "War is based on competition and the feeling of inferiority." There is a way to circumvent this feeling, and I would like to take a positive view. Those who rely on pure altruism naturally consider themselves inferior; no one likes to feel he must depend on pity or charity. Absolute egoism, on the other hand, inevitably creates competitive strife; when someone tries to take from his neighbors for his personal advantage, a warlike state is bound to arise.

If, however, these two basic sentiments are combined and altruistic actions are turned to your own benefit, all these sources of friction are avoided. With altruistic egoism, rivalry can result only in the reinforcement of one person's desire to be useful to another, and this will be rewarded by the most powerful and lasting value that exists: the esteem and love of your neighbor.

It has become quite popular to explain war as a phenomenon due to innate human feelings of aggression, but to me this does not justify its existence. Man like any other living being has aggressive tendencies which, when kept within proper limits, serve a useful purpose in defending his life and, consequently, the life of his species.

Thanks to his highly developed brain, man also has greater control over his actions than any other living creature. To use this ability to its fullest capacity was one of my major objectives in formulating the code of altruistic egoism. Aggressiveness is innate, but it can be considerably enhanced through provocative behavior or suppressed through a system of ethics. If we succeed in explaining to individuals, and particularly to those in control of the behavior of large groups (nations, religious devotees, management, labor) that they can better satisfy egoistic impulses by earning the goodwill of others than by attacking them, we will have succeeded in controlling human aggression better than by any other means advanced so far.

Naturally, the degree of innate aggressiveness is of considerable importance. A crocodile would be much more difficult to control than a lamb and among human beings we find all transitions between the crocodile and lamb type. The question of basic capacities is common to all aspects of teaching. An Eskimo living in the Artic who has never heard of theoretical physics could not possibly become an expert in this field without proper education, but with a given amount of innate capacity for learning, he can be considerably influenced by external circumstances.

People who are fully occupied and satisfied with some constructive activity are certainly less likely to show aggressiveness than those who are bored, idle and discontent with the behavior of others.

"All men are created equal"

People sometimes ask me whether I think that all human beings are created equal and should have the same rights. I know that this contention is incorporated in the American constitution, but I believe that its usual simplistic interpretation is manifestly false. Some people are fat, others lean; some are intelligent, others stupid; Mr. X is weak and sickly, whereas Mr. Y enjoys an iron constitution.   Not even identical twins are completely equal, especially when they are raised under different circumstances. What Abraham Lincoln wanted to say in his historic speech was that all human beings should have the same chance to achieve happiness.   But it is ridiculous to question the fact that we are not only far from being born equal but, in practice, cannot even be given the same chances for accomplishment. The blind cannot be offered the right, nor do they want the opportunity, to become airplane pilots, any more than it would be worth the time and effort required to teach the feebleminded how to become theoretical physicists.

The same applies to the women's liberation movement.   A woman should have the same access to careers and the same possibilities for physical and mental development as a man. However, this is true only within certain limits imposed by Nature. As her body and mind are different from those of a man, she cannot use her possibilities in exactly the same manner. A woman should not be deprived of any rights just because she is female. I do not know of *many* women who want to be miners, garbage collectors or longshoremen (or even "longshorewomen"), but if there is a woman who wishes to perform one of these occupations and can meet the physical requirements, I see no reason to prevent her from fulfilling her ambition.

Still, I do find some of the linguistic arguments to be nonsensical and even harmful to the other legitimate causes of feminism because they expose the movement to ridicule. When I submitted the manuscript of one of my latest books to a publisher, his editor went as far as to advise me not to speak of "mankind" or even of "humanity" because the word "human" comes from "homo," the man! I find the kind of militancy that dictates such changes perfectly ridiculous! I really do not say this because of male chauvinism or any feelings of misogyny. On the contrary, among the staff at my institute there is a preponderance of women, and I am very satisfied with them. It is just the silliness of the argument that I object to. As Winston Churchill replied when his editor warned him never to end a sentence with a preposition, "This is a situation up with which I will not put."

From time to time, I am asked what role women have played in my personal life. I willingly admit that I have had, and at the age of seventy-one still have, unbelievable luck with women – I like them all! Unfortunately, this feeling is not always reciprocated. When I say that I like women, one must not necessarily see anything lecherous in this, but I must say that love has always played an important role in my life. For example . . .

No! That's enough! I made it clear in the beginning that I would "tell the truth and nothing but the truth but not *all* the truth" and, upon thinking it over, this is the moment when I should take advantage of that first warning.

In order not to irritate those with strong feminist feelings, I do try to avoid the words "man" or "he," substituting the much more cumbersome and often quaint expression "person," as in "persons have certain basic needs," but I cannot reconcile myself to using phrases like "he or she can reproduce his or her species"; in fact, neither of them could do so unaided.

I am strongly in favor of equality for women as far as Nature permits its implementation. Man cannot be given the right to give birth to a baby. Where is the concept of equality in all this? Men and women are not biologically equal and there is nothing we can, or even want to, do about it *(vive la difference!)*; but one sex should not be considered superior to the other. Of course, this means that for the same or equivalent accomplishments men and women should receive the same rewards.

For similar reasons, one cannot say that all races are "equal." Each of them has its good and bad characteristics and, like the two sexes, they should have the same rights — but only in proportion to what they really want and can do.

If we accepted egalitarian principles unconditionally, we would open the door to injustice because it would be left up to society— often through rigid laws — to establish who can do what. Not being equally constituted, however, each individual must be appraised on his own merits. Some people are willing to take the risks inherent in being independent — they like to be their own boss; others prefer to give up certain rights to benefit by the protection of a powerful group (family, labor union, political party, nation) and the security offered by being part of it. However, the more independent you are, the more you have to acquire the force of self-regulation and self-discipline. If you look around, you can readily see that in modern society not everybody has or even desires to use these qualities.

Throughout history, despite the moral justification and the fanatic fights about freeing the serfs or slaves, many of them did not actually want compulsory freedom because they preferred the security and protection offered by a kindhearted and strong master. It goes without saying that everyone should have the right to freedom; but this should include the right to renounce it if, under the circumstances, life would be better without freedom. The choice should depend not only on the serf, slave or servant but also on the master's willingness to accept his responsibilities in such a relationship of interdependence.

How effective is true "democracy"?
Many politicians use the term "democracy" as though it were a synonym of "good government." Even the most totalitarian and autocratic rulers or ruling parties present their ideas by distorting them to fit this label. So let us first understand what the term really means. According to *Webster's Dictionary,* democracy is "government in which the people hold the ruling power either directly or through elected representatives; rule by the ruled."

I support this ideal notion fully, but I ask myself whether such a system could ever exist. As far as I can see, democracy has never really materialized in any society, present or past. The people cannot rule directly because no individual constituting a society can effectively influence the behavior of all others. Nor can there by rule be truly elected representatives, because an entire nation can never unanimously agree on who their representatives ought to be. All governments are largely totalitarian, with power being concentrated in and subject to the will of one or a few persons. These may have obtained their supremacy either by the mere chance of heredity (as in autocratic monarchies with their hereditary monarchs and aristocrats), or through the clever political manipulation of the masses necessary to assure a majority of votes.

We need not discuss autocratic hereditary monarchies at length, as they are virtually extinct. There is little I can say in their favor except that, by inheriting power, the future ruler can be groomed from early infancy for his difficult responsibilities. Furthermore, once in power, he need not debase himself or spend a great deal of the nation's energy and money to campaign for a majority of votes in order to be re-elected. These two points are not to be underestimated, but the great drawback of hereditary power is its extraordinary risk. If the ruler is vicious or insane, there is nothing the masses can do except resort to "illegal" revolt or remove him through exile or assassination.

To my mind, elected government is not much better. Once in power, few politicians can resist the temptation to act just like hereditary rulers, except that they are not quite as free to perform arbitrary or even illegal acts. They hesitate to do so because they feel that at least in theory, they should conform to the will of the people. However, an elected official never actually assumes power by representing the majority; he only represents the majority of voters who have been convinced by clever campaigns to cast their ballots for him. The two are certainly not the same. The vast majority of the population is totally unprepared to appraise which candidate is best qualified and most highly motivated to do what is right for his constituency or what the individual voter actually expects.

Despite my lack of experience in this field and my awareness of the criticism that such remarks can bring me, I shall give free vent to my heretical attitudes about the democratic system: I believe that it is unjust to give an equal vote to every person.

To me, it does not seem right that lazy, good-for-nothing people, the most unscrupulous parasites who are a burden to society, should have as much to say about the management of the nation as those whose whole life is devoted to constructive work for the common good.

Moral considerations aside, it seems neither efficient nor in the best interests of the community to give the same voting power to an imbecile and an intellectual giant; nor should an introverted, uninformed recluse, living in solitude somewhere in the wilderness, have the same influence upon modern society as a highly competent sociologist or political scientist.

I am fully aware of the dangers of deciding who should have how many votes, but I think the solution to this problem would be a most worthwhile undertaking for experts in the social sciences. Mistakes would undoubtedly be made, but I see no reason why these should be any more frequent or perilous than those made by judges or surgeons appraising problems of equal, and sometimes greater, consequence. Errors of interpretation are unavoidable in any human act, but mistakes are less likely when a problem is dealt with by an expert in the matter rather than when left up to a mere counting of votes. To me, the latter is like appraising the strength of an army by the number of weapons possessed, without taking into account whether these are arrows or atomic bombs.

Einstein is reputed to have said that a scientific argument can never be decided democratically by a majority; because if among a hundred people ninety-nine say that a theory is false and one says it is correct, that one represents a majority if, in fact, his judgment reflects the truth.

Just as taxes are adjusted to income, so I think it would be more meaningful to give rewards for accomplishment in the form of votes, instead of medals, titles and other honors. It would not strike me as either unjust or inefficient if, in the selection of people for positions in command, a person who never accomplished anything and always lived a parasitic life would have no vote and an Einstein would have thousands.

This type of remuneration would be in excellent agreement with my general philosophy, based on the promotion of altruistic egoism which motivates you and helps you to *earn* your neighbor's love, trust, approval and appreciation.

On social insurance

I think it is highly desirable to provide security for those who suffer from things for which they bear no responsibility — for example, disease or the infirmities of old age. However, this assistance should be proportionate both to their previous accomplishments in support of society and to the amount of financial help they now require. The amount of aid must not be equal for everyone. Here in Montreal, at present, I get an old-age pension amounting to three hundred and ninety-two dollars a month through the Federal and Provincial Governments, just as any other Canadian of my age; yet many others have no additional source of income. Though it is not really needed, I accept my pension without guilt feelings, because it is derived from the taxes I pay. But, in comparison to what the government hands out for old-age pensions against my will, without regard to need or merit, it is actually a very small portion of my taxes that is being returned to me.

I have even more serious doubts about the management of unemployment insurance. Certainly, if someone has worked very hard and always tried to do his best only to lose his employment for reasons beyond his control, he deserves the security of unemployment insurance until he can find another source of income. However, in practice, at least here in Canada, unemployment insurance has become a normal mode of life for the least desirable members of our society. In fact, I know of people who have become experts at taking jobs from which they purposely get themselves fired at the end of the minimum period required by law in order to become eligible for renewed unemployment insurance. They make no effort to obtain another position, or to do any private work on their own initiative, as long as the unemployment checks come in. Others are somewhat more motivated and try to get remuneration for various temporary services which may pay even more than their regular jobs would but, being self-employed in the legal sense, they can cheat the system by not declaring their income to the government.

There is no doubt in my mind that some form of health insurance, such as the Canadian "Medicare" system, is highly desirable, as today's expensive medical care is becoming a terrible burden for the large majority of the population. Here again we must be fully aware that such systems can work only through altruistic egoism. People must be willing to pay taxes to cover the costs of medical care, whether or not they will directly benefit, and this requires altruism. But the beneficiaries must avoid abusing these services, and this can be done only by suppressing reckless egoism, which would spoil the whole system.

Whenever medical aid is free, numerous hypochondriacs will take up the doctors' time with any insignificant disorder, and invariably there are lonely people who consult physicians about their problems only to while away the time. Likewise, there will inevitably be a few unconscientious physicians who will arrange for innumerable brief consultations to get more income from the government. As they do not have to pay for their treatment personally, patients are generally eager to accept such "devoted" care. These unfair practices on the part of doctors and patients alike greatly inflate the costs of medical insurance. However, if we can accept altruistic egoism as an economically valid attitude, perhaps we might be able to diminish or even prevent the occurrence of such abuse.

Malpractice insurance is another sore point in the present medical system. A patient should rightfully receive compensation for damage resulting from incompetent treatment; but too often a jury will favor the patient, as he obviously needs the money, while the insurance company "can afford it." This kind of attitude virtually destroys medical practice in some parts of the world. The more often patients are rewarded for imaginary or insignificant errors of judgment on the part of the doctor, the higher the insurance rates will rise. Finally, the physician is forced to raise his fees so that he can pay the inflated malpractice insurance rates demanded to finance such a system. Even if his fees were covered by socialized medicine, the physician would have to price himself beyond the "Medicare" range to meet his insurance premiums.

All these types of insurance, and especially the ease with which they can be abused, only weaken motivation for those constructive guidelines of society which base rewards on merit. In other words, all forms of social insurance are practical only if they can count on altruistic egoism and if they are not sabotaged by reckless egoism.

On sexual freedom
In opposition to predominant contemporary views, I do not believe that the great sexual permissiveness, so fashionable today, is a desirable social development. I consider it to be bad, not so much because of moral reasons, but on the basis of biological and psychological considerations. Promiscuity tends to deprive sexual relations of the intense satisfaction of intimacy achieved between two people who do not make it a commonplace event. Little is to be gained, apart from immediate carnal satisfaction, from a succession of "love affairs" with different partners. The experience becomes cheap and routine.

A healthy young person develops a desire for making love and, as soon as puberty is reached, it is possible to launch into a series of sexual adventures. However, unrestricted immediate gratification of every sensual desire can have disastrous long-term effects mainly with regard to the psychological attitudes of the two sexes.

The uncompromising proponents of chastity before marriage and the advocates of countless physical relations with no need for marriage or any lasting associations are perhaps equally extreme. I am not particularly well-prepared to defend either religious or hedonistic views in this connection. All I can say as a physician is that the human body is so constructed that for complete self-realization all its parts should be used. If you do not use your muscles they undergo atrophy. I feel that to enjoy life completely you must explore all the possibilities that your body can offer. This does not mean that ascetic religious people who believe in perpetual chastity, or even martyrs who wish to suffer for their beliefs and will derive satisfaction from self-sacrifice, cannot lead a happy life. Some people completely renounce sexual satisfaction and retire into the solitude of the desert to meditate. If this mode of life makes them happy, why not? Everybody seeks pleasure in his own way. Yet as a biologist I believe that, in most cases, such privations lead to frustrations with repercussions in many domains.   Eventually, people tend to revolt in secret or even openly against the code which they initially imposed upon themselves.   It is illogical to blindly obey such self-imposed principles, justifying their maintenance with the belief that to embrace chastity as a penalty will expiate all sins, while at the same time experiencing a continuous state of hunger.   It is a fact well known to physicians that repressing Nature can lead to pathological complications.

Abortion, contraception and euthanasia
Most people, including myself, no longer consider contraception to be a problem of great practical importance.   The vast majority of women (married or unmarried) who do not wish to have babies practice some form of birth control.   Personally, I do not regard contraceptives as any more objectionable morally than any other techniques currently practiced to avoid pregnancy.   If there is no fear of unwanted pregnancy, two people who love and desire each other are free to enjoy the greatest degree of intimacy.

When birth control methods fail or premature termination of a pregnancy is desirable, the question of abortion comes into play.   Various countries have enacted laws making abortion either "legal" or "illegal."   We often hear emotional disputes about the morality of a mother deciding whether or not to end her pregnancy.   At the risk of being criticized by extremist proponents or opponents of abortion, I think that there is no solution to the problem that would be uniformly applicable.   The public likes to look for generalized answers, but the issue of abortion is far too complex to be settled by a rule to be followed in every case.   Just as we cannot formulate a code of behavior to be obeyed blindly, we cannot decide for or against the principle of abortion without specially appraising each case.

We must consider the girl who becomes pregnant following rape, the woman for whom pregnancy would present severe physical or psychological damage, the mother who already has several children and is quite unable to look after more.   How could we find a solution applicable to these cases, as well as to women who are perfectly capable socially, economically and psychologically to bear children, but who desire the freedom of a childless existence?

Still, we must put certain laws on paper; there is no way to write a civil or criminal code without stating what is legal and what is not. But in doing so, we must acknowledge that what is generally accepted as moral can, under certain circumstances, be highly immoral. Imagine the dilemma of the mother whose child is about to die of extreme hunger. She happens to be alone in the kitchen of a very wealthy family, where she could easily take all the food she needs without being discovered and without really hurting anyone. If she strictly obeys the law of her country or the commandment of God, she is forbidden to "steal." But is this really a crime, in such an extreme case? I think that the respect for the law which we generally regard as moral would be immoral in such a situation. Yet all countries and religions condemn theft, and in most instances we would agree with them.

Perhaps this extreme example exaggerates the principle, but the point is that no code can be applied to every person and every situation. It would be futile to develop our code of altruistic egoism to such an extent, trying to foresee every eventuality, leaving no decision to the individual. Instead, our goal should be to accept the responsibility and challenge of making our own decisions and directing our own lives as we see fit.

A mother who has taken thalidomide throughout her pregnancy is virtually certain to give birth to a child with monstrous deformities. In most countries the law is quite lenient about abortion in such cases, even if many theologians are not. A deformed child will undoubtedly be condemned to a life of suffering and will become a burden to itself and its parents. On the other hand, a life guided by altruistic egoism could make it worthwhile for such a tragically handicapped person to survive. With great love, understanding and wisdom, even children born with nothing but stumps for arms and legs can find a way to experience and give happiness.

The same principles apply to people suffering from seemingly hopeless diseases. I have boundless admiration for the eminent German-American bacteriologist, Hans Zinsser, who, knowing that he would die of an incurable cancer, still managed to get a great deal of satisfaction and give extremely wise lessons to many people (including myself), by writing his famous biography, *As I Remember Him.* Zinsser felt that even his desperate condition could be used to an advantage, because only a man who knows he will soon die can speak with real detachment, without wishing to influence anyone or obtain any benefits for himself. Those of us who knew him were full of admiration for his wise adaptability to an apparently hopeless situation. His motivation helped him to keep the inevitable out of his mind and, at the same time, this great scientist earned the gratitude of innumerable people, up to the very moment of his death. I know that his writings helped me immensely during my own periods of pain and trouble.

To avoid an appearance of trying to make a hero of himself, Zinsser did not reveal the identity of the man whose life and thoughts he recalled. I believe that the book would have accomplished even more good had he decided against anonymity and revealed that this was his autobiography. In this way he could have shown by example that, with the proper code of behavior and the will power to obey it, man can benefit even from insurmountable difficulty.

A case like Zinsser's serves as a strong argument against suicide or euthanasia. Far from being ready to be put to death peacefully, he was still able to make a lasting contribution as he lay dying. But anyone can appreciate the other side of the issue, once he has seen people who are dead by every criterion that we can appreciate, although their heart still beats because respiration is maintained by a machine. I cannot help being convinced that euthanasia is justifiable when I see people who obviously cannot think or feel and have no chance of recovery because the electrical activity of their brain has stopped. This is no longer a matter of depriving the patient of "life," as he is medically dead already. What is the point of keeping a human being in a type of suspended animation? We can maintain experimental animals, even after complete removal of the brain, by artificial respiration, reducing life to the level of cells kept in a test tube under suitable conditions. To submit anyone to such cruelty is senseless, both for the patient and for the loved ones who are condemned to view the torture permitted by the sustaining powers of medical progress.

Aside from the immense emotional ramifications of such an ordeal, the family, friends or state are subjected to an enormous financial burden in maintaining the extraordinary lifesaving measures. The alternative, euthanasia, is an awesome responsibility which is difficult to assume, for who is to decide when a life is no longer useful? The solution is even more evasive in cases of illness such as incurable cancer, when to end a life would be much less obviously a "mercy killing." Both physician and patient may wish to terminate life, but there is less evidence to assert with certainty that the situation is totally hopeless.

Such life-or-death questions are far more complex than the vociferous proponents of generalized laws believe them to be. Even a code like alturistic egoism which can be applied to most situations and individuals, cannot supply guidelines for every condition.

Is true loyalty possible?
My awareness of a lack of loyalty by me toward others and by others toward me has been a recurring cause of distress throughout my life. I have always felt that absolute loyalty, like absolute altruism, is incompatible with natural laws. In any event, with the possible exception of a few unusual people who blindly follow a prefabricated code of behavior without criticism, no one around me has ever been capable of obeying such guidelines of behavior without questioning or faltering.

It is undoubtedly a very comforting feeling that certain persons are loyal friends on whom you can count, whatever happens in life. Traditionally, we prescribe an oath of eternal loyalty to spouses, rulers and even members of certain social organizations. But how often are these really respected over a long and eventful lifespan? Sometimes such promises are rigidly kept because of a sense of duty; but this behavior is merely obedience to a self-imposed command, not an act of love. They lose their original purpose of providing warmth and friendship in human relations, for we cannot fulfill this aim if loyalty is based only on a feeling of obligation. So why must we formalize faithfulness by a solemn promise or oath?

In 1904, Sir Winston Churchill left the Conservative party and joined the Liberals. The story is told that, upon hearing her husband criticized as a "turncoat," Lady Churchill remarked, "I prefer my husband to be loyal to his ideals and not to a party that is no longer loyal to them."

To my mind, you can decide to be loyal to a god; to the laws of Nature, which are eternal and of which you form a part; or to an ideal under all circumstances, whatever the future may have in store for you, but you cannot make this promise to a person. Gods and ideals are or should be permanent; people change. Just as you cannot love on command, you cannot be loyal on command without exposing yourself to the distress of following a code of behavior in which you no longer believe. If you try to do it, you either develop inferiority complexes because of your failures or you become miserable by acting in a manner which does not suit your nature. The same is true for loyalty to king, country and even the everchanging identity of a particular religious denomination.

The longest friendship that I maintained on this continent is with Dr. John S. L. Browne, to my knowledge the only other person still alive who knew my parents and saw my father's clinic. He spent his postdoctoral years with me studying under Professor J. B. Collip and we made a trip together to visit my parents for an entire summer. John subsequently became chief of medicine at one of Canada's largest university clinics, the Royal Victoria Hospital. He was best man at my first wedding and, as our interests in research were very similar, we saw a great deal of each other during the following years. Later, I took real pleasure in introducing him for an honorary doctorate at the University of Montreal. I do not feel that we were ever disloyal to each other; however, eventually our friendship just faded away because our interests developed in different directions. I deeply regret not having been able to keep up closer contact with him; but it must be admitted that very few persons remain exactly as they were initially, and eventually even the closest ties loosen. This is a fact of life that we must all accept; after all, nothing much can be done about it.

I believe in loyalty and friendship; at least I have always appreciated it, knowing that I badly needed its support to enjoy the security and warmth of a happy life. It is the idea that loyalty should be absolute and unchanging that I consider to be unnatural. In fact, really great rulers who eventually became powerless advocates of a lost cause often formally relieved their subjects, and particularly their soldiers, of their oaths of loyalty, to spare them unnecessary guilt complexes and suffering. The same is true of the wise spouse who does not object to separation or divorce when the relationship becomes manifestly untenable. It is better to amputate a badly infected dying limb than to hang on to it until it kills you, merely because it is yours. I think that just as you have to perpetually earn your neighbor's love throughout life, you must continuously deserve the loyalty of your friends and associates; you have no right to demand it merely because of past agreements.

I have managed to be loyal to certain scientific and philosophical ideals throughout my life. Frankly, I could not devote the same faithfulness to many persons, because sooner or later they ceased to be the characters to whom I had decided to be loyal. Similarly, very few people have remained loyal to me throughout my life and I consider this to be my fault, for it is an indication of my inability to continue to earn their loyalty.

Perhaps my skepticism about pledges of undying devotion can be traced to my background. I was brought up to believe that you should be unquestioningly true to certain institutions— Catholicism, Hungary, marriage — but I have seen so many of these values destroyed that I learned how little it means to put your faith in so-called permanent institutions. So today I can be jaded enough to imagine a society where we no longer swear fidelity even to "God, apple pie and motherhood."

My first great love was my cousin Annemarie. I was nine and she was five when we made the irrevocable decision to get married as soon as possible. She subsequently took her doctorate in education and became *Regierungsrat* (Counsel to the Government) in charge of elementary schools throughout Austria. Actually, she never married me or anyone else, but she still makes a great case of bragging about her family of some 27,000 children for whom she cares each year. I still like Annemarie best of all my blood relations, and we try to spend a day or two together every time I go to Europe.   It's pleasant to see someone you have known all your life and with whom you can discuss even the most intimate problems.   Her altruism appears to contradict my belief that altruistic egoism is the only natural and possible way of surviving (although the proportions of altruism and egoism may vary according to individuals).   Fortunately, on rare occasions, I do detect moments when she thinks of her own good.

It's true that Annemarie and I took our "marriage vows" at an unusually early age, but it seems to me that couples are scarcely more equipped to judge their eternal compatibility even at age twenty or thirty.   So, in the end, my cousin and I were unfaithful to our promise; but how could kindergarten or elementary school children know anything about future problems of marriage, about which even adults know so little!

CHAPTER FOURTEEN

My Long-term Projects for the Future

I am rarely asked about my plans for the future. Many people think that at the age of seventy-one this is no longer an important issue. But as far as I am concerned, there are still many things I would like to accomplish. For me, the past and the future are a continuum.

It is generally recognized that medicine has made tremendous progress during the last three decades; this shows itself clearly in the statistically demonstrable great increase in life expectancy. A recent census indicated that there are about fifty million people in the United States above the age of sixty-five. This means that the problems of the elderly assume ever greater importance.

The more medicine progresses, the more we will find an increase in the proportion of older people in the general population. It is naturally invaluable to prolong life; yet I heartily agree with the masthead of the *Journal of Gerontology* (a medical publication devoted to the study of old age), which describes its objectives as: "To add life to years, not just years to life."

A very old man may be unhappy, bitter and a burden to those close to him because of his constant complaints, or he may always be radiating optimism and anxious to be useful to his relatives and friends by sharing with them the fruits of his long experience. You must keep in mind that biological age and chronological age are two entirely different things. Of course, this is equally true of women. Chronological age is easy to understand and determine in quantitative terms. It merely represents the number of years that we have spent in this world. Biological age is a less precise but much more important concept. There are many people who, at age forty-five, have the mentality and motivation customarily associated with advanced age; they would prefer to and should retire from their jobs, provided they have the means to do so. Others still adore life at eighty and are perfectly able to act in a manner which makes them useful to themselves and to society. Thomas Mann, for example, wrote *Doctor Faustus* when he was over seventy and his masterpiece *Félix Krull* when he was nearly eighty. Remember the accomplishments in old age of Michelangelo, Picasso, Toscanini, Arthur Rubinstein, Bertrand Russell and so many other greats!

I often think of my advancing age but I really have no fear of it. It seems to me that each period in a man's life has its advantages if he follows his own philosophy of life. Of course, as a rule, an adult will not get as much pleasure as a child from collecting colored pebbles on the beach or from playing with tin soldiers and dolls, but he will have other pleasures inaccessible to the child.

As we get older, we lose some of our adaptability to new conditions, along with the capacity for rapid recovery from disease and general resistance to hardship; on the other hand, we gather a great deal of experience. I feel happy about this state of affairs. If I regret certain losses, I console myself with the knowledge that Nature has endowed us with numerous compensatory mechanisms; when one channel is blocked, we learn to develop another.

Our aim should not be to arrive at absolute perfection in every respect but to attain the highest goal that we are able to achieve. If you can accept this view, you will not regret the inevitability of aging.

Few people like to think about death, and the prolongation of life is one of the most ancient ambitions of man. Yet to really love life is to accept death, as the latter is the natural endpoint of the former. In the words of Montaigne, *Le continuel ouvrage de notre vie, c'est de bâtir la mort.* (The ceaseless labor of man's whole life is to build the house of death.)

I was once asked how I would like to die if I could choose. My answer was spontaneous, although perhaps not very conventional: "I should like to be shot down like a mad dog by the jealous husband of a lovable woman . . . caught in *flagrante delicto* at the age of ninety-five."

Death is inevitable, but it is quite possible not to worry about it all the time. Having faced death before, I am fully determined to go on working as long as my health permits, and I constantly make plans that could not possibly be accomplished in less than ten, twenty or more years. Of course I know that I shall never finish these projects, but it gives me great satisfaction to think of myself dying suddenly in the middle of an enterprise for which I feel great enthusiasm and which has been developed to the point where it can be carried further by my successors.

More than half a century has passed between the time when I first conceived the notion of stress and the present day. These were really years of intense effort. Still, I do not consider my work on stress to be finished — far from it! I know very well that I shall never see the end of this study, for we are constantly faced with new ways of looking at almost every biological problem. I think I can safely say, without exaggerating the vitality of this work, that it will go on forever, as long as biology and medicine exist, just like the study of metabolism, heredity or growth.

I am not being falsely modest when I say that I do not consider myself important. I sincerely do not; but I believe my *work* is very valuable. I feel like a mother who has accomplished little in life besides raising a brilliant son. She recognized his talent very early and, though widowed and poor, worked exclusively to send him to the best schools. He eventually developed into a great writer who now brings culture and joy to the public. The mother is proud of her creation and believes unashamedly that she deserves all the honors and respect she receives for having produced such a fine man, but she knows that — except in relation to her son — she is a thoroughly unimportant and uninteresting person.

The concepts of stress and nonspecificity occurred to me without any voluntary planning, just as the mother conceived the genes of genius in her child. I am proud to be the father of the stress theory, but I feel that my personal significance ends there.

It has always been my hope that perhaps one of my students would take over where I leave off. This is why I dedicated *From Dream to Discovery* to an imaginary young scientist, "John" (the English word for Hans), in the following note:

DEAR JOHN,

Since you say you would like to continue my kind of research, I am sending you this bunch of loose Notes that I have jotted down in the course of the past thirty-five years about my impressions of science and scientists. They are rather intimate, personal reflections, "glimpses behind the scenes," none of which can be gathered from my technical papers and books. Yet I feel that what they reveal has played the decisive role in directing, not only my work, but my whole way of life. Of course, I do not want to force my views on you; you have to live your own life. All I ask is that you leaf through these Notes in moments of leisure, to see whether you might not profit a little from my experience, accepting the good, rejecting the bad. In a sense, this would splice our lives together, and you could start with what took me so long to acquire.

If I had known at the start what I know now, I would certainly have done things better; it takes time to polish the rough spots. The style of the first paper on "A Syndrome Produced by Diverse Nocuous Agents" (written at the age of twenty-eight) was nothing to be proud of. Indeed, if I had known then what I know now, I'm sure I could have formulated the stress syndrome with half the lab work and on a tenth of the paper. I think I could also have avoided much of the antagonism aroused by incidental speculations that did not mean much to me anyway. I certainly would have known better than to be bothered so much by whatever criticism is unavoidably leveled at any new concept.

If I had known how to handle my chiefs when I was an assistant and my assistants when I became chief! If I had known then how to get money and staff for research; how to organize sooner this big library of ours so one might really find what one is looking for; how to construct a set of labs to make them functional . . . by Jove, John, if I had known then what I know now, I might even have found you a couple of decades earlier — perhaps several of you — and think of what we could have done together!

I can already hear you say (or at least respectfully suggest in your inimitable way) that I have no statistical evidence of having made any progress since the beginning. But you must admit that I did not have nearly as much trouble with my later projects, such as the cardiac necroses or calciphylaxis. And the atmosphere in the lab is undoubtedly more congenial now than it was at the outset.

Perhaps the most important thing I have learned is self-confidence; nowadays I no longer waste so much time in justifying my ways to others and to myself. It is difficult for an objective young man to have self-confidence when he still lacks the evidence to prove that he is on the right track.

Take, for example, my great preference for the simplest possible methods. I like to hold a rat in the palm of my hand and just watch it. I like to look at its organs with a loupe or at histological sections stained with the simplest methods. Despite my Ph.D. in chemistry, I have never used complex chemical procedures. I have never employed isotope techniques, the electron microscope, X-ray diffraction or any of the more sophisticated new tools — not because I fail to appreciate their worth, but merely because I am more interested in the general picture than in details. Somehow I feel much closer to Mother Nature when I can observe her directly with the sense organs she herself gave me than when there are instruments between us that so often distort her picture. Easily recognized, manifest changes in shape or behavior are not only less subject to "instrument-error" but, because of their simplicity, they lend themselves better to the large-scale experimentation needed for the broad integration and correlation of many vital reactions.

For a while I was afraid that I was becoming obsolete in my passion for simplicity and the panoramic approach. The tendency in science today is all in the opposite direction. They are building ever more complex tools to dig ever deeper at one selected point. Of course, this must also be done, but not by all of us, John. Not by all of us! The specialist loses perspective, and by now I am sure that there will always be a need for integrators, for naturalists who keep trying to survey the broad fields. I am no longer worried about missing some of the details. There must remain a few of us who train men and perfect tools to scan the horizons rather than to look ever closer at the infinitely small. We must train men who can lead large teams to survey an extensive area, even though only with simple methods. We must construct huge documentation systems to keep us well informed on many things. Some of these problems are not yet yours at this stage, but I hope with a little time you will look into them. In any event, I could use your support to help me with what I am trying to do along these lines.

But I had another, much more personal and selfish reason for taking the time to edit these Notes for you. Up to now, there was really no one with whom I could share the world in which I live, the things that really interest me, the ideals that I consider worth living for. Most people consider me quite self-sufficient, but I do need the intimacy of sharing as much as anybody else does; probably more, because where my mind likes to be, there are no genial crowds. In fact, as far as I can see, there is no one really close by with whom I could talk things over properly, to whom I could feel bound by the kind of natural kinship that makes all defense and pretense unnecessary, and thereby offers a chance for mutually checking our bearings in the journey through life.

As regards the usual everyday problems, such intimate, warm relationships usually develop between members of the same family or clan, but the motives that most decisively direct my course are not the usual ones. I like the warmth of family life; I need the feeling of security that comes from doing something for others. But the satisfactions and contributions that are most characteristically mine stem from a kind of resonance with the general laws of Nature. These are too grandiose to stimulate any feeling but admiration unless their appreciation can be fully shared with others. This sharing is no easy matter for us. The farther you advance into the unknown, the fewer fellow travelers remain with you. In the forefront of your advance, if it is really beyond the point that anyone else has reached, you are finally alone. To me, you, John, are the symbol of the one who stays the course. That is why I have been looking for you all my life.

When I was very young, I imagined you as a father or teacher, later as a brother or wife, and now as a son or pupil; I have been lucky in finding warm kinships of all these kinds, but the gifts they brought me were of another nature. I value my relationships with them all, but now I am well past fifty and still searching for your kind.

Perhaps there are many of you. Perhaps even you are only a figment of my need. Perhaps my mind has no real, close kin. But time is running out and, while I do not know whether you really exist, I do know that I need you. That is why I had to invent you. In research, we soon learn that abstractions are often just as, or even more, effective than tangible, individual facts. So I have created you, John, as my spiritual younger brother and successor, with whom I can talk things over.

For, who is my brother? The man of my blood, even if we have nothing else in common — or the man of my mind, to whom I am bound only by the warmth of mutual understanding and common ideals? I keep on hoping that somewhere, sometime, you will materialize. Perhaps, by publishing these Notes, I may actually bring you into existence, thereby assuring my succession in the way of life with Nature that has given me so much pleasure.

Hans Selye

Université de Montréal
February, 1964

I was happy that I decided to publish these very personal thoughts, because the response was most gratifying. I began to get letters and visits from many students, all claiming to be that "John" I was seeking and, in fact, some of them signed their letters "John," with their real names in brackets underneath.

I have always considered the applicability of my research as totally independent of any race, religion, nationality or social position.   As long as my work dealt only with physiological, histological and biochemical problems, this viewpoint was easy to maintain; but it is difficult to be objective and convincing about it when one deals with humanity.

I have no intention of changing my goal in life. I began my study with biochemical and histological methods and went on to clinical applications.   My main concern now is to acquire and maintain a general view of the field of stress research, to prepare myself for interpretation based on everbroader correlations.

As I think back over my many years of struggling to get the stress concept accepted, it gives me infinite pleasure to see that several points that were so violently attacked are now commonplace.   I still remember how many people objected when I introduced the terms and concepts of biological stress, stressors, nonspecificity, corticoids, and especially my subdivisions of glucocorticoids and mineralocorticoids.   Yet yesterday I stopped by a pharmacy to pick up a cream prescribed by my dermatologist under a trade name that I did not immediately recognize, and on the printed label was written: "containing one of the most active anti-inflammatory glucocorticoids."

I can now see the fruits of my labor in the dubious onslaught of "stress syrups," "stress tabs" and "stress pills" being advertised in virtually every medical journal (although in this case my satisfaction would be increased if I were as sure of their usefulness as I am of that of the corticoids).

The evidence continues to mount, proving that my early struggle was worth the effort after all. A couple of years ago, I received this announcement in the mail:

Saint Joseph's Hospital   Tampa, Florida
Development   *Council*
3001 WEST BUFFALO AVENUE — TELEPHONE 871-5496 OR 871-5151
1976/77 HEALTH SERIES

STRESS
WITHOUT DISTRESS

THE 1975/76 "CYCLE OF LIFE" HEALTH SERIES HAS BEEN VERY SUCCESSFUL.
MEMBERS OF THE COMMUNITY ARE ASKING FOR MORE OF THESE TYPES OF EDUCATION
PROGRAMS.

THE DEVELOPMENT COUNCIL WILL CONTINUE THE HEALTH SERIES NEXT YEAR.
THE THEME FOR THE 1976/77 SERIES WILL BE "STRESS WITHOUT DISTRESS."
SPEAKERS WILL DISCUSS METHODS OF COPING WITH THE STRAIN OF MODERN LIVING
AND COVER TOPICS SUCH AS:

TEENAGERS	SEPTEMBER
MIDDLE AGE	NOVEMBER
AGING PARENTS	FEBRUARY
ILLNESS	APRIL
EXECUTIVE STRESS	MAY

No one can blame me if I take great pride in the fact that by
now the title of one of my most popular books has also been used
for innumerable other stress courses and articles on stress throughout the world, including special numbers published by the World
Health Organization and UNESCO.

At the present time, I attach the greatest importance to an
ambitious project, that of creating an International Institute
of Stress. I hope that this will be a center for documentation and
research about all problems related to stress, a field which touches
virtually every aspect of modern society. As we have assembled
here in Montreal the largest collection of documents on every
facet of this general topic (medicine, surgery, psychology, sociology,
business, industry, etc.), I am determined to use all the means at
our disposal to keep it up-to-date and accessible to the world.
Although we also have premises at the University of Montreal

(the school at which most of the stress concept was developed) and an additional beautiful mansion with a heated swimming pool and a tennis court in Pointe Claire, an elegant suburb of Montreal, we nevertheless needed a Downtown Center in the business district.   I therefore transformed my private house opposite McGill University into such a center, and installed in it all the equipment necessary for our documentation service and for smaller conferences.   The center acts as the heart of our world-wide reticulum concerned with stress, and I must say that I look with great pride upon the bronze plaque bearing the name "International Institute of Stress" every time I go home, since it is still my home, having retained at least one room for Louise and myself.

For decades, people have written to us or visited the institute, seeking access to the entire world literature on some particular stress-related subject.   In doing so, they have also had the advantage of consulting members of my staff who have had some personal experience in a particular field of study.

A large part of my daily work is to read, or at least skim through, everything that has recently been written about stress.   This permits me to maintain a good overview of such a complex subject and to direct the updating of my library and documentation service, my most important tool for the coordination of the very diverse data in this vast field.

My documentation service orginated in 1931 when I purchased the library of endocrinology of my teacher, Professor Arthur Biedl, from his widow for $1,000 plus packing costs (a formidable sum to accumulate at that time).   I did so using the modest means I had at my disposal as a graduate student.   I also brought it over from Europe at considerable expense.   The stress concept was not yet known but this represented the largest collection of endocrine literature in existence.   Biedl had amassed it to write the first encyclopedic treatise on endocrinology, published in 1913.   For many years I paid all maintenance costs from my own Rockefeller scholarship.   Later, as the literature on endocrinology assumed gigantic proportions, I also added what was to me an even more important collection, the beginnings of a stress library. Eventually, my means became manifestly insufficient and I had to seek additional assistance from various governmental and philanthropic organizations.

My library was virtually destroyed by fire in 1962; but as it was already well known throughout the world, we received contributions for its restoration from many countries and often from very odd outside sources. I can still clearly remember the profound personal satisfaction I experienced when I realized how many people wanted to participate in the reconstruction of this scientific monument.

Immediately after the fire, my assistants and I held an emergency meeting in my office. This was in midwinter and, with the central heating system out of action, the windows broken by fire and the outside temperature well below zero, we were very cold. We sat in our winter coats, shivering and feeling miserable as I brought up the question of whether or not it would be worthwhile to undertake the gigantic task of reconstruction. It might be just as well, I suggested (hoping they would not agree) to abandon the effort and destroy the remnants; half of the index had burned down and the incomplete residue was of no use. After a short discussion the group voted unanimously to fight for a rebuilt library, because the aim appeared worthwhile and attainable, despite all difficulties.

After the worst debris had been cleaned up, the graduates, librarians, laboratory and office staff went to work as a team, separating the irretrievable from the usable documents. Many of the latter had to be carefully dried; the fire hoses caused nearly as much damage as the fire itself. We then employed a temporary staff of about thirty people to search through all the medical indexes for literature on endocrinology and stress, to establish what we still had and what had been lost.

Finally, I wrote letters to the editors of five major medical journals explaining that I wished to obtain the assistance of my colleagues all over the world in the form of donations of journals, reprints and books, as well as the financial assistance of public agencies and private philanthropists to cover the cost of reconstructing my collection, which had been only partially insured.

The response was extraordinary! It was perhaps one of the greatest satisfactions of my career to see how many people wanted to help us. We received reprints, books and entire sets of medical journals from universities and scientists of almost every country.

Furthermore, we obtained enough financial help to cover the salaries of the large additional staff required to look after this enterprise.

I shall never forget one day when my morning mail contained two letters. The first, written in pencil on cheap paper by a farmer's wife from Northern Quebec, read:

Dear Sir,

We are very poor people but, after reading about your tragedy in our local paper, we decided that it wouldn't make much difference whether we had meat for supper tonight or not. So you will find one dollar enclosed, which we could save by doing without this luxury. It's not much, but we wanted to do our part for science and hope that many others will feel the same.

Respectfully yours,
A.M.

I was deeply touched; and although the next letter contained a $75,000 check given for the same purpose by a governmental institution, that hard-earned dollar in cash was even more effective in raising our morale. Like Banting's $500 grant when my stress research was just beginning, this money came at a time when I was about to give up. These gifts were of even greater help in strengthening my determination to go on than the approximately $750,000 that was needed annually to run the institute in later years. So you can see that in a way I do have a private life and very private sentimental pleasures, although they all seem to be mixed up with my research.

I do not know yet exactly what will happen to my unique collection of stress documents because nobody seems to have the funds necessary for its extremely expensive permanent maintenance. Still, with my incurable optimism, I continue to look for and am virtually sure to get assistance somewhere. Meanwhile I go on as if success were certain. We accumulated more than one million reprints and books on endocrinology in my original library but we do not have the means to continue that. However, I still hope we will find somebody who can maintain this unique collection; in any event, the 150,000 reprints and books concerning stress have all been transferred to our Downtown Center. I managed to raise enough funds to maintain about fifteen key personnel to look after the documentation service, and this assures us that we are a world center for information in this field.

As the concept of stress was originally formulated in Montreal, it is to our group that people turn most frequently for expertise in this domain. It would be a terrible shame if we allowed all this effort to disintegrate simply because we cannot find the means of maintaining the continuity of our work. I offered my collection of documents as a gift to the University of Montreal, to share its tremendous potential with colleagues throughout the world, but the school does not have the necessary funds to maintain it without outside help. I am certainly not going to make the purely symbolic gesture of a donation which is doomed to become nothing more than an historical curiosity. Eventually, I fear, it would all be stacked away in some inaccessible cellar or garret, gathering dust, because a scientific documentation service becomes totally useless within a few years if it is not kept up-to-date.

It is not only the library and documentation service I wish to keep functional. Within the frame of the International Institute of Stress, I want to maintain the necessary laboratory space to go on doing animal experimentation and training successors, not only for basic research on stress but also for making its fruits available to clinical medicine and sociology as well as for the correlation of all the research that goes on in this field throughout the world.

The institute is legally incorporated, but unfortunately at this moment the funds in our bank account consist almost exclusively of my honoraria for lectures and royalties on books, which I donate as "seed money" for this center of stress research and the teaching of specialist physicians, nurses and sociologists.

I hope that our own federal and provincial governments will decide to give us some substantial assistance, and possibly I shall also be aided by the international institutions (UNESCO, WHO, etc.) who have already published reports on our activities in their journals, which made the concept known throughout the world. With the means left to me I am beginning to find candidates who could staff this center and keep it useful indefinitely.

Despite my age, I continue to study new things and build for the distant future. Even if I never attain my final goal, I get great pleasure from doing my best as I see it.

Whatever the future of the institute, it gives me much personal satisfaction to be able to say that, beginning with my first publication at the age of twenty, until today at seventy-one — that is, for half a century — I have done all that I possibly could in my chosen field. I intend to continue with this work until I die, an event which I do not consider sufficiently imminent to justify planning for it.

Yet the older I get the more I have the feeling that my lectures are well received, not for their content but because of the audience's deference to my position as "founding father" of the stress concept. It's as if they said to themselves, "Well, the old guy's been at it for so long, and he wants to earn his neighbor's love so badly, let's give him what he wants." This almost invariably ends in a long standing ovation. I hope to be lecturing twenty years from now, but I want to be appraised for my continuing contribution and not merely because I'm still around after so many years.

I began to think about this back in 1964 and even included a few thoughts on the subject in *From Dream to Discovery*. I worried that as the popularity of the stress concept grew, I would become a mere symbol of it and would be condemned to supporting every cause and organization that came along, spending endless hours on podiums with no other purpose than "lending my distinguished presence." Thus, I reasoned, "fame kills the real person by petrifying the man into a monument to his own past accomplishments, but it may take as much energy to fight the consequences of fame as it took to do the work that made him famous." This was not the sort of future I looked forward to.

What was then a matter of curiosity has become a reality, but I refuse to let myself slip into fossilization — at least not without a fight. If I am the indisputable contemporary authority on stress some have tried to make me, my concepts may last no longer than I do. I like the idea of having been useful, and even necessary, in laying the groundwork for stress research and its application to a general philosophy of life, and I hope my code will survive long after I am gone.

I have managed to stay in the saddle with a full professorship six years past the obligatory age of retirement, and I cannot help noticing that very capable younger people are now eyeing the space I occupy at this University with justified impatience. I would hate to feel that I held them back, but at the same time I know there is still an important job to be done and I want to do it.

Having stuck with the stress concept since its birth, and having outlived many of those who entered the field afterwards, I find myself in a unique position today. I witnessed all the growing pains and the battles that raged around the weak points of my theory, so that when these are reactivated from time to time I know exactly how to handle the situation. We are still far from understanding stress in all its forms, but my preparation helps me act as a catalyst and coordinator of work done in the field of "stressology."

Even so, I am aware that I cannot do everything alone; I am only one man. When I have to quit, it will be up to others to carry on where I left off and to continue research on the concept of stress. My work has been more than a simple intellectual exercise; it is rather an effort to develop an everlasting system giving guidance in medicine and human behavior. The human condition does not change, even if time moves on.

I think that with the information now available through my own work, and that of innumerable scientists throughout the world who have become interested in this topic, the stress concept has been sufficiently clarified to reach the "critical mass" necessary for its continued growth.

The idea of the *vis medicatrix naturae,* the healing power of Nature, is extremely old. Man knew, long before the work of Walter Cannon and Claude Bernard, that there is a built-in mechanism in all living beings designed to help them right themselves, to restore their integrity when they become wounded or damaged in any way. The principle of the stability of the *milieu intérieur* has been known for centuries; and along with it stress has long been considered as some kind of tension, fatigue or suffering. But it took many carefully conducted and often tedious experiments and observations, all of which had to be critically evaluated, before we could arrive at the stress concept in its present form, including its implications upon behavior.

The meaning of my life has been to convey, not just to my colleagues in medical science but to the general public, what I have learned through my research — how we can live with stress and make it work for us.

It is this code that has served me so well throughout my life, and it is this code that I want to convey to others. I bring to this effort the scientific experience of a long career as well as the undiminished, youthful enthusiasm of a man who loves life and looks forward to entering his eighth decade. It gives me great satisfaction to know that so many others who followed my precepts have reached a similar stage of contentment at an advanced age, and I have every possible intention to go on perfecting my code of behavior for as long as I live.

I have managed to be happy, and I hope productive, throughout my life, although there were always many difficulties to overcome. But now, at seventy-one, I do not feel at all that I am approaching the sunset of my life. Now, the sun is rising! I have finally reached the peak of the mountain, and the horizons I see from here are wonderful. After many unsuccessful efforts (largely because I am so difficult to live with), I have found Louise!

Most of my readers are much younger than I am and will think that it is impossible for a man of my age to be deeply in love with his wife, but Louise is just my girl. As far as I'm concerned, she is my most valuable possession and also the greatest source of strength for my future scientific accomplishments. Louise doesn't know a thing about science, but she knows all about me, and she has been able to put up with my extremely strong and monomaniacal scientific personality for nineteen years. Obviously, ours is not a marriage on the rebound.

No longer do I make my breakfast alone. Louise gets up whenever I get up, even at four o'clock in the morning. She starts dancing around and is very cheerful, although at my age I am increasingly grumpy at such early hours.

With my two artificial hips, I sometimes have difficulty driving in snow, so Louise, who is an excellent driver, brings me to the university. Then she drives to the Downtown Center, where she acts as motherly coordinator of the entire library staff, looking after all their personal problems as well as those of the organization. She also acts as chauffeur, personal adviser, purchasing agent, and errand girl, and as a receptionist for the many visitors who come to see our Documentation Center.

In the evening, she comes to take me home, because by that time I'm usually too tired to drive myself. (She never complains if I have to complete some urgent matter and cannot leave immediately.) Then we go to the part of the Downtown Center that is now our home — a real, warm home to which I return with great anticipation rather than fear of quarrel. We have dinner together in the kitchen. Louise has become accustomed to eating the odd things that I like, such as Hungarian goulash made with the strongest red pepper you can buy in Montreal, almost-raw horsemeat, and marmot shot by a friend of her brother-in-law.

Having invented a modification of Oriental batik art, which is painted on Japanese or Chinese silk, Louise insists on living on her own income, which she earns by selling her now quite recognized "neobatik" at art shows. Acting the role of the great lady at official receptions, she always wears formal batik dresses that she made herself, and I am invariably proud to enter a scientific or diplomatic gathering with my Mrs. Selye on my arm.

I may have messed up two marriages, but I still feel that I won in the end. Louise, without any special training and with her feminine good sense, has created our private life as well as helped me to build a structure that can diffuse the fruits of my scientific work throughout the world. And Louise will keep me happy until the end, I am sure, because if I should lose her, that would be the end. She understands that I want to be her old racehorse, Frank, racing toward a useful goal, carrying his little pigtailed Louise on his back.

My goal has always been science, and although the blond pigtails are turning to gray and "Frank's" mane is white, the spirit has not changed.